Reading Theory

WITHDRAWN
FROM STOCK

For Albert and Edward

Reading Theory

An Introduction to Lacan, Derrida, and Kristeva

Michael Payne

BLACKWELL
Oxford UK & Cambridge USA

The right of Michael Payne to be identified as author of this work has been
asserted in accordance with the Copyright, Designs and Patents Act 1988.

First published 1993

Reprinted 1993

First published in USA 1993

Blackwell Publishers
238 Main Street
Cambridge, Massachusetts 02142
USA

108 Cowley Road
Oxford OX4 1JF
UK

Library of Congress Cataloging-in-Publication Data

Library of Congress CIP data has been applied for

ISBN 0–631–18288–8; 0–631–18289–6 (pbk.)

British Library Cataloguing in Publication Data
A CIP catalogue record for this book is available from the British Library.

Typeset in 10.5 on 12pt Garamond
by Graphicraft Typesetters Ltd, Hong Kong
Printed in Great Britain
by TJ Press (Padstow) Ltd., Cornwall

This book is printed on acid-free paper

Contents

List of Plates   vi

Preface   vii

Acknowledgments   xi

List of Abbreviations   xii

1   Theoretical Beginnings: Introductions to Lacan, Derrida, and Kristeva   1

2   *Écrits: A Selection*   26

3   *Of Grammatology*   110

4   *Revolution in Poetic Language*   162

5   Reading Paintings   212

    Appendix I: Lacan's Use of Freud's German Terms   234

    Appendix II: Abbreviations used in *Of Grammatology*   237

    Appendix III: Some Kristevan Terms   239

Index   242

List of Plates

Plate 1:   Hans Holbein the Younger, *Double Portrait of Jean de Dinteville and Georges de Selve (The Ambassadors)*. 1533, oil on wood, 207 × 209.5 cms. Reproduced by courtesy of The Trustees of The National Gallery, London.   215

Plate 2:   Hans Holbein the Younger, *The Body of the Dead Christ in the Tomb*. Reproduced by permission of Kunstmuseum, Bale. Photograph: Giraudon, Paris.   218

Plate 3:   Vincent Van Gogh, *Oude Schoenen (Old Shoes)*. Reproduced by permission of the Vincent Van Gogh Foundation, Vincent Van Gogh Museum, Amsterdam.   221

Preface

The two modest aims of this book are suggested in the ambiguity of its title: to provide a reading of major texts by Lacan, Derrida, and Kristeva and to trace the outlines of the reading theories they propose. Although several introductions to the thought of these writers are available, none so far proceeds by closely examining the rhetorical strategies of their principal texts. Such a procedure seems simply to follow from the examples provided by the readings of other texts that appear in the writings of these theorists. Lacan heralds a return to the writings of Freud in order to hear in his texts the voice of the unconscious; Derrida proposes to examine so carefully the structures of the texts he reads as to discover the deconstructive openings in those texts to structures of thought that are outside or beyond them; Kristeva extends the methods of semanalysis, a psycho-analytically enhanced semiotics, to an examination of the speaking subject and the signifying structures of social practice. It is not surprising, therefore, to find that these texts, which advocate such careful and extraordinarily reflective reading processes, are themselves highly wrought and meticulously structured.

The readings that follow are arranged in five groupings. Chapter 1 examines three short papers that conveniently serve as Lacan's, Derrida's, and Kristeva's own introductions to their work. Chapter 2 offers a detailed examination of seven of the papers that Lacan selected for the English edition of *Écrits*. Chapter 3 looks closely at Derrida's *Of Grammatology*, which is not only a classic statement of and about deconstruction but also Derrida's most influential book. Chapter 4 considers the uses of allusion, argument by metaphor, and other textual strategies in Kristeva's *Revolution in Poetic Language*, only the first third of which has so far been translated. Chapter 5 brings the three theorists together again in the same chapter, as each experiments with ways of reading and writing about paintings: Lacan on Holbein's *The Ambassadors*, Kristeva on Holbein's *The Body of the*

Dead Christ in the Tomb, and Derrida on Van Gogh's *Old Shoes*. Although I assume that most of my readers will be consulting the English translations of these texts, I often cite the French editions either to support an observation about a particular stylistic practice or to suggest that there may be reasons for questioning the translation of a specific passage. The amount of space I devote to portions of these texts reflects my sense of the difficulties readers are likely to encounter with them, rather than my judgment of the relative importance of those parts.

The present book can only claim to be a work of theory in the limited sense that it attempts to look closely at what is happening in the theoretical texts it reads, while being as self-reflective as possible. Indeed, it may be more appropriate to consider this a study in theoretical criticism, in which the methods used and the textual processes considered – for example, argument by metaphor and the rhetoric of allusion – are all familiar to literary criticism. Here, however, the texts that are critically examined position themselves primarily in the disciplines of psychoanalysis, philosophy, and linguistics, rather than in what has come to be narrowly thought of as "literature." Readers accustomed to the writing and reading conventions in those disciplines may be less well acquainted with the signifying possibilities of metaphor and allusion in contexts that are not obviously literary. For those who have become suspicious either of recent impositions of what seem to be literary categories or of the invasion of literature by cognitive disciplines, it may be useful to recall that in his *Dictionary* (1755) Samuel Johnson defined "literature" with the single word "learning." Many recent developments in literary theory offer some hope that such an ecumenical understanding of literature (and of criticism) as Johnson's may be reasserting itself.

I have undertaken this project for two reasons. First, I find the texts considered here extraordinarily stimulating in the vitality of their thought, in the art of their prose, and in the rewarding difficulty of their arguments. If what Lacan writes about the human subject, what Derrida writes about language, and what Kristeva writes about the social practices of the speaking subject are true, then massive reassessments not only of the humanities and human sciences but also of human understanding itself are urgently needed. The claims of these texts are far-reaching and powerful; and the experience of reading them is sufficiently disruptive as to make human beings, language, thought, and social practice seem suddenly unfamiliar and perhaps alienating – or, in my view, radically new and engaging. Second, I find it something of a scandal in contemporary writing about theory that many accounts of theoretical work, not only in the mass media, but also in scholarly publications, manage to epitomize, to denounce, or to acclaim – but recently most often to denounce – such work as a whole with often no attempt to discriminate among theorists or to refer with any specificity to their texts. I have cited such polemical practices when it becomes relevant to reading the particular texts I discuss.

For Lacan, Derrida, and Kristeva, writing and reading are activities of immense importance, since they are means of representing the unconscious, of challenging and reassessing the history of thought, and of understanding the signifying processes of the human subject. Such a high estimation of activities that usually seem rather private and ordinary is not unique to contemporary theoretical discourse, as the three theorists examined here readily acknowledge. Augustine, for example, in *The Confessions*, charted the stages of his life by recalling the impact of specific books on his mind; Dante's vision of God in the *Paradisô*, likewise, was textually focused –

> In that abyss I saw how love held bound
> Into one volume all the leaves whose flight
> Is scattered through the universe around;

and Phillis Wheatley, one of the first African-American writers, discovered in her reading of Terence and Milton the means of breaking the bonds of slavery and of giving birth to an African-American literary tradition that transmutes her classical heritage. Although they do not cite these examples, Lacan, Derrida, and Kristeva share with them, it seems to me, the conviction that acts of reading have the power to transform and to liberate human beings, who are necessarily subjects only in the sense that they are born into structures of signification that they have the power to disrupt, just as those structures have the power to undermine any sense of static identity or individuality.

I am pleased to acknowledge that my thinking about these texts has been stimulated by seminars and discussions held under the auspices of the Centre for Freudian Analysis and Research (London), the Institute for Romance Studies (University of London), the Department of Philosophy, Keynes College (University of Kent, Canterbury), and the Andrew W. Mellon Seminars in Literary Theory (Bucknell University). On these and other occasions I have greatly benefited from the personal and professional generosity of Malcolm Bowie, Peter Brooks, Terry Eagleton, Richard Fleming, Pauline Fletcher, Rafey Habib, James Heath, Barbara Johnson, Frank Kermode, John Kirkland, J. Hillis Miller, Toril Moi, John Murphy, Christopher Norris, Kathleen Page, Jacqueline Rose, Demetrius Teigas, and especially Harold Schweizer. I wish to thank the many librarians who have helped me with my work at the British Library, the Senate House Library (London), the library of the Warburg Institute (London), the Dr Williams Library, and the Bertrand Library (Bucknell). To them I am no less grateful for not knowing them by name; Tom Mattern at Bucknell and Paul Taylor at the Warburg Institute will have to stand for them all. Along with her loving companionship, Laura Payne has been the best of readers and has given me her honest criticism and tolerant understanding. As always, Stephan Chambers, Philip Carpenter, Andrew McNeillie, Jack Messenger, Brian Goodale, and their associates at Blackwell Publishers have been unfailing in their professional advice and friendship. I am also grateful to the undergraduate and graduate students in my Bucknell seminars in literary theory, who helped me to puzzle over the texts discussed here and, I hope, to read them better.

Acknowledgments

I am grateful to the following publishers for permission to quote from these texts:

Écrits: A Selection by Jacques Lacan, trans. Alan Sheridan (London: Tavistock/Routledge Publications; New York: W. W. Norton, 1977), quoted by permission of the publishers.
Of Grammatology by Jacques Derrida, trans. Gayatri Chakravorty Spivak (Baltimore: The Johns Hopkins University Press, 1976), quoted by permission of the publisher.
Revolution in Poetic Language by Julia Kristeva, trans. Margaret Waller (New York: Columbia University Press, 1978), quoted by permission of the publisher.
The Standard Edition of the Complete Psychological Works of Sigmund Freud, trans. James Strachey (London: The Hogarth Press and The Institute of Psycho-Analysis, 1974), 24 vols. Quotation is by permission of Sigmund Freud Copyrights, The Institute of Psycho-Analysis, The Hogarth Press, Harper/Collins Publishers, and W. W. Norton.

List of Abbreviations

É   *Écrits* by Jacques Lacan (Paris: Éditions du Seuil, 1966).

ED   *L'Écriture et la différence* by Jacques Derrida (Paris: Éditions du Seuil, 1967).

G   *De la grammatologie* by Jacques Derrida (Paris: Les Éditions de Minuit, 1967).

R   *La Révolution du langage poétique* by Julia Kristeva (Paris: Éditions du Seuil, 1974).

SE   *The Standard Edition of the Complete Psychological Works of Sigmund Freud*, trans. James Strachey (London: The Hogarth Press and The Institute of Psycho-Analysis, 1974), 24 vols.

1

Theoretical Beginnings:
Introductions to Lacan, Derrida, and Kristeva

Although Jacques Lacan, Jacques Derrida, and Julia Kristeva have been extraordinarily well served by their translators and commentators, direct access to their writings continues to be difficult because of the sheer bulk of their publications and because of the proliferation of misleading popular accounts of their theories.[1] Fortunately, however, each of these theorists has written a brief and strategically accessible paper that serves well as an introduction to their work. These papers offer a way in to their richly complex thinking about spoken and written language, about the importance of language for an understanding of the unconscious and the politics of culture, and about interrelationships among literature, philosophy, linguistics, and psychoanalysis. Despite the difficulty and complexity of their texts, Lacan, Derrida, and Kristeva are not gratuitously obscure writers. They obviously want to be understood, and they often anticipate – and caution their readers against – misreadings or misappropriations that are unproductive. Nevertheless, they are also suspicious of uncritical, docile discipleship. Thus the introductions they offer are not epitomes or essentialistic formulations of their thinking but rather places to begin reading. Although there is an intricate network of influences that links these writers, there is also as much difference and opposition among them as there is unanimity. They are, however, all three opponents of simplistic reductiveness, even though their writing manifests the need to step back occasionally from difficult theorizing in order to provide readers with rhetorical signposts – introductions, summaries, aphorisms – especially when the textual terrain gets particularly rough or dense.

The introductions that I am referring to are these. Lacan's "Seminar on 'The Purloined Letter'," which was written in 1956 on the basis of a seminar conducted in the previous year, is the first text in the French edition of *Écrits*. An English translation was published in *Yale French Studies* in 1972, five years before the appearance of

Écrits: A Selection. Derrida delivered "Structure, Sign, and Play in the Discourse of the Human Sciences" at the Johns Hopkins University in 1966, marking his entrance into American intellectual life. It was subsequently published in *Writing and Difference* in 1967, Derrida's remarkable year in which *Of Grammatology* and *Speech and Phenomena* were also published. Kristeva's "The System and the Speaking Subject" appeared in *The Times Literary Supplement* in 1973 and has been often reprinted. This essay serves both as a critical survey of semiotics for British and American readers and as a summary of Kristeva's most ambitious linguistic text, *Revolution in Poetic Language*, which appeared a year later. Even in these three essays it is possible to anticipate the intellectual conflict that will develop between Derrida and Lacan, as well as Kristeva's critically selective but generous appropriation of their work.[2]

"Seminar on 'The Purloined Letter'"

Lacan's "Seminar on 'The Purloined Letter'" is one of his most sustained examinations of a single text, but it requires a readjustment of what were in 1956 – and perhaps in some ways still are today – common assumptions about literary interpretation. Lacan reads the Poe story as an imaginative theoretical text in which literature and psychoanalysis interrogate each other without either being assumed to have a privileged status over the other. This procedure is doubly controversial. The meticulous seriousness with which Lacan reads the story and his readiness to interpret it as an allegory of psychoanalysis will disappoint those who wish to advance the scientific and medical rigor of psychoanalysis.[3] On the other hand, Lacan's reading through and beyond "The Purloined Letter" in order to continue his investigation of Freud's *Beyond the Pleasure Principle*, which was the subject of his seminars in 1955, will disturb those who want from psychoanalysis only a method for literary exegesis. Lacan would seem to have anticipated both kinds of discomforted responses, for which he offers an epigraph from part one of Goethe's *Faust*:

> And if we score hits
> And everything fits,
> It's thoughts that we feel.[4]

Indeed, Lacan's brilliant interweaving of careful analysis of Poe and Freud with his own oracular theorizing does create the sensation that thoughts are being felt, as though what is being said or written is coming from within the reader's own mind.

Although Lacan writes in such a way as to retain the sense of his original oral presentation, the seminar is, nevertheless, carefully structured in a seven-part argumentative sequence.[5] Part I announces the texts of Freud and Poe to be considered. Freud's discussion of "repetition automatism" [*Wiederholungszwang*] in *Beyond the Pleasure Principle* (1920) provides Lacan's point of departure. In that text Freud proclaims an important turn in the development of psychoanalysis. For the previous twenty-five years psychoanalysis had been "an art of interpreting" and uncovering the resistances of the patient, with the aim "that what was unconscious should become conscious." It has now become clear, Freud declares, that such an aim cannot be completely achieved because the patient may never be able to remember what is most necessary in order to cooperate with the physician in assigning such repressed material to the past. Instead, the patient "is obliged to *repeat* the repressed material as a contemporary experience" (SE, XVIII: 18). During treatment the patient continually relives painful situations and emotions. Furthermore, Freud observes, such compulsion to repeat what is unpleasurable is not unique to neurotics:

> Thus we have come across people all of whose human relationships have the same outcome: such as the benefactor who is abandoned in anger after a time by each of his protégés, however much they may otherwise differ from one another, and who thus seems doomed to taste all the bitterness of ingratitude; of the man whose friendships all end in betrayal by his friend; or the man who time after time in the course of his life raises someone else into a position of great private or public authority and then, after a certain interval, himself upsets that authority and replaces him by a new one; or, again, the lover each of whose love affairs with a woman passes through the same phases and reaches the same conclusion. (SE, XVIII: 22)

This "repetition automatism," as Lacan calls it, requires Freud to move beyond the pleasure principle, to modify the early vision of psychoanalytic aim, and to accept a darker and less hopeful understanding of human life. Is such a move toward the tragic necessary, however? Lacan argues that it is not.

Building on Freud's fundamental insight, Lacan locates the basis of repetition automatism, as he does other unconscious processes, in language. The "insistence of the signifying chain" and the capacity of the symbolic dimension to capture "the most intimate recesses" of the human being provide ways of understanding repetition automatism that are both continuous with Freud's discovery and also beyond it. But Freud's own insistence on going beyond his own previous theory based on pleasure warrants in advance Lacan's going beyond the argument of *Beyond the Pleasure Principle* itself. Already on the first page of the seminar, two of Lacan's recurring strategies for reading Freud have been put into operation. Lacan is true to Freud by not being bound to him, and his way of being true without being bound is to supply linguistic underpinnings for Freudian theory. In his second paragraph Lacan anticipates the lesson of the seminar that has only just begun. Such "imaginary incidences" as repetition automatism do not in fact represent "the essence of our experience," as Freud pessimistically claims, unless "they are related to the symbolic chain which binds and orients them" (39). Here Lacan proposes to save Freudian theory before 1920 as well as Freud's departure from it in *Beyond the Pleasure Principle*. This he proposes to do by affirming the reality of symbolically manifest compulsion but not its universal necessity. In the opening two paragraphs of the seminar Freud's new theory is situated within Lacan's own theory of the imaginary and symbolic orders. The imaginary, which Lacan carefully explores in his paper on "The mirror stage," is epitomized by the tendency of the child to constitute its ego by reference to a being similar to itself and, in turn, to mistake itself for such an image. The symbolic, on the other hand, is a term Lacan borrows from Freud and radically redefines. Whereas Freud's *die Symbolik* refers to a network of symbols with constant meaning united to them by processes of unconscious association, Lacan's *symbolique* is structured as language.[6] For Lacan, unlike Freud, the symbol is characterized precisely by its not being united to what it represents. Because the structure of the symbolic system is primary and available for investigation and because its relation to what it represents is secondary and unstable, the symbolic is not reducible to the imaginary even though it carries traces of the imaginary stage. To reduce the symbolic automatically to what it represents is to remain bound by the imaginary. Lacan insists that he does not wish to diminish the importance of such "imaginary impregnations" as repetition automatism, but these are like images stamped on coins [*Prägung*]. They are "partializations of the symbolic alternative" (40), whereas the symbolic chain is governed by "the specific law" of displacement, which is manifest in such forms as foreclosure, repression, and denial. Indeed, so powerful is the displacement of the signifier from the signified (the symbol from what it represents) that imaginary factors are only "shadows and reflections" in the symbolic process. It is specifically in order to illustrate these characteristics of the symbolic order and the manner in which the symbolic constitutes the human subject that Lacan has chosen Poe's "The Purloined Letter". Although Lacan, with obvious irony, claims that the choice of the story is arbitrary, still it is the discontinuous character of the symbolic – the arbitrary relation of signifier and signified – that "makes the very existence of fiction possible" (40).

Lacan first considers the structure of Poe's tale. Although the reader may be tempted to distinguish the story's drama from its narration, the commentary and point of view provided by the narrative are of critical importance for understanding the drama and its dialogues. The story has two scenes, a primal scene followed by its repetition, in the sense noted by Freud in his theory of repetition automatism. The primal scene takes place in the Queen's boudoir. At the arrival of the Minister, the Queen places a compromising letter on the table with its face down and address visible. The Minister notices the letter and the Queen's distress. He takes a letter of similar appearance from his pocket, pretends to read it, and places it next to the first letter on the table. After conversing with the Queen and King, he takes up the Queen's letter and leaves. Just as the Minister had thoroughly observed the Queen's behavior with the letter, so she has seen what the Minister has purposefully done; but she can say nothing without attracting the suspicion of the King. She then rolls the Minister's abandoned letter into a ball. The second scene of the story takes place in the Minister's office at his hotel some months later. The Prefect of Police has in the meantime been informed of the theft, and the police have exhaustively searched the Minister's office and the surrounding area for eighteen months but have found nothing. Yet it is obvious that the Minister has the letter within reach. Having been brought into the case as a consultant by the Prefect, the detective Dupin now calls on the Minister. "When his glance catches a rather crumpled piece of paper – apparently thrust carelessly in a division of an ugly pasteboard card-rack, hanging gaudily from the middle of the mantelpiece – he already knows that he's found what he's looking for" (42). Dupin leaves his snuff-box on the table as a pretext for returning the next day with a facsimile of the letter. This he does, substituting the copy for the original while the Minister is distracted by an incident in the street outside his window. Although he does not know it, the Minister no longer has the Queen's letter. In its place is Dupin's facsimile with a quotation written in Dupin's unmistakable handwriting: "So infamous a scheme, / If not worthy of Atreus, is worthy of Thyestes." Lacan concludes the first part of the seminar by outlining the repetitive structure of the tale, which consists of "three moments, structuring three glances, borne by three subjects, incarnated each time by different characters" (44). The glance of the King and the police sees nothing; that of the Queen and Minister sees that the first sees nothing, but they delude themselves that they have hidden their secret; that of the Minister and Dupin sees that the first two glances have left exposed, so that it might be seized, what should be hidden. The purloined letter is "a pure signifier" that is displaced, Lacan says, and in its displacement it assumes the status of repetition automatism.

Having delineated the story's structure in part I of the seminar, Lacan next proceeds to comment on its disruptions and dissonances. It is doubtful that the tale is simply a police mystery because all of the conventions of the mystery are eliminated as each episode begins, as though in anticipation of the reader's generic expectation. If there is mystery here, it may be found in the "dissonance" between Dupin's remarks on his method and his actual manner of investigation. Here again the relationship of the dramatic to the narrative structure is important. The two dramatic scenes, Lacan observes, are narrated in separated dialogues. The elaborate narrative complexity of the first dialogue between the Prefect and Dupin highlights the problem of language in the tale and the fictional character of truth. Here Dupin's friend narrates the meeting between Dupin and the Prefect during which the Prefect reveals to Dupin the report he has received from the Queen concerning the Minister's substitution of his own and theft of her letter. The second dialogue moves from the exactitude of mutually enclosed frames of address to the intersubjectivity of truth. Here Poe's tale, like Heidegger's references to the play of truth [*aletheia*], insists that it is in hiding that truth "offers herself . . . *most truly.*"[7] In contrast to the reductive attention of the police to the possibility of spatial concealment, the narrative stresses the obscurity of what is simple and the concealment of what is in the open. The most important revelation of the search for the letter is that it cannot be located anywhere. The material stability of the signifying letter is odd, *singulière*. The letter is nowhere; it is unaffected by being cut into pieces; it is the symbol of an absence. What is hidden is what is missing from its place. Whereas the real "is always in its place" (55), the symbolic refuses to remain localized or to be held in place. As realists, the police believe that what is written remains [*scripta manent*], whereas the tale is an exemplary illustration of the truth that the letter is purloined.

"To whom does the letter belong?" Lacan asks in part III. The sender of the letter and its contents are never revealed in Poe's story. Although it is clear that the Queen must keep "her lord and master" from knowing about the letter, neither she nor anyone else who has the letter can be rightly said to possess it. Even Baudelaire's translation of the story's title – "The Stolen Letter" ["*La Lettre volée*"] – is misleading. Lacan traces the etymology of *purloin* in order to show that the title indicates that the letter has been "diverted from its path," its course "prolonged," its delivery held up (59). Although the letter is required "to leave its place," it will return "to it by a circular path" (60). In part IV Lacan replays these characteristics of the letter in terms of Freud's theory of repetition automatism in order to recover the shock of Freud's discovery: "The displacement of the signifier determines the subjects in their acts, in their destiny, in their refusals, in their blindnesses, in their end and in their fate, their innate gifts and social acquisitions notwithstanding, without regard for character or sex, and . . . willingly or not, everything that might be considered the stuff of psychology, kit and caboodle, will follow the path of the signifier" (60). Although the Minister was so well able to see the symbolic situation of the Queen – that she is literally caught in the letter's signifying chain – he is unable to see that he becomes similarly caught. Indeed, in the story's second scene the Minister reenacts the Queen's role.

Part V is the most difficult and most fascinating section of the seminar. Here Lacan offers his reader a textual equivalent of Poe's letter and clearly marks it as such. Not least of the difficulties posed by this section is that Lacan has already identified three suspect ways of dealing with texts: the Queen's futile attempt to keep the letter out of circulation; the Minister's appropriation of the letter, followed by his concealment of it by leaving it in the open; and Dupin's repetition of the Minister's strategy of substitution and appropriation in order to return the letter to the Queen. The temptation that Lacan's reader faces in part V is now to purloin his text – to divert or prolong it – in order to deprive it of its strange, shocking mystery. Without citing it, Lacan recalls Freud's paper on "The 'Uncanny'," which was written a year before *Beyond the Pleasure Principle* and which already begins to anticipate his theory of repetition automatism. After several pages devoted to the etymology of the words *canny* [*heimlich*] and *uncanny* [*unheimlich*], Freud writes,

> What interests us most in this long extract is to find that among its different shades of meaning the word "*heimlich*" exhibits one which is identical with its opposite, "*unheimlich*." What is *heimlich* thus comes to be *unheimlich* . . . In general we are reminded that the word "*heimlich*" is not unambiguous, but belongs to two sets of ideas, which, without being contradictory, are yet very different: on the one hand it means what is familiar and agreeable, and on the other, what is concealed and kept out of sight. (SE, XVII: 224–5)

Poe's story is as useful for Lacan in its ambiguous power to be both simple and complex, mechanical and mysterious, as in its pliant allegorical manifestation of the waywardness of the signifier. Lacan repeatedly celebrates Freud's uncanniness, which he works to recover from texts that may have become too familiar or read too easily. Freud himself observes that he turns to works of art – especially to literature – for that purpose also, to recover uncanniness (SE, XVII: 219). Thus, in turning to Poe in order to read Freud, Lacan is following Freud's example. But rather than simply reporting what he finds in such an apparent detour, Lacan re-creates in his own text the encounter with the uncanny. Like Poe and Freud before him, he transforms the ordinary into the mysterious by its repetition. What is commonplace and close at hand becomes suddenly odd, *unheimlich*, *singulière*.

Part V of the seminar replays in Lacan's symbolic register the moment in Poe's story when Dupin sees the letter in the Minister's office:

> At length my eyes, in going the circuit of the room, fall upon a trumpery fillagree card-rack of pasteboard, that hung dangling by a dirty blue ribbon from a little brass knob just beneath the middle of the mantel-piece. In this rack, which had three or four compartments, were five or six visiting cards and a solitary letter.[8]

Lacan argues that at this moment the Minister repeats the Queen's role: he attempts to conceal the letter by leaving it in the open; he believes himself undetected but becomes just as vulnerable to being seen as she had been; he appropriates the letter by readdressing it in "an extremely delicate feminine script" (65); and he stamps it with his own seal. Here is Lacan's description of the story's climactic moment:

> Just so does the purloined letter, like an immense female body, stretch out across the Minister's office when Dupin enters. But just so does he already expect to find it, and has only, with his eyes veiled by green lenses, to undress that huge body.
>
> And that is why without needing any more than being able to listen in at the door of Professor Freud, he will go straight to the spot in which lies and lives what that body is designed to hide, in a gorgeous center caught in a glimpse, nay, to the very place seducers name Sant' Angelo's Castle in their innocent illusion of controlling the City from within it. Look! between the cheeks of the fireplace [*les jambages de la cheminée* (É 36)], there's the object already in reach of a hand the ravisher has but to extend ... The question of deciding whether he seizes it above the mantelpiece as Baudelaire translates, or beneath it, as in the original text, may be abandoned without harm to the inferences of those whose profession is grilling. (67)

Here reading is an act of ravishing, which simultaneously is Dupin's going straight to the letter in the Minister's office, Lacan's going through Freud's door to the center of the text of *Beyond the Pleasure Principle*, the analyst's getting to the center of the analysand's language, and Lacan's ultimate theoretical ambition of getting to the unconscious by way of language. Lacan has devilishly extended this sequence by involving his reader in the same process. One cannot help but read his seminar and find here in this metaphorical and metonymic passage the center of the argument.[9]

Lacan first tempts his reader in part V to purloin his text by repeating one of the three strategies for dealing with letters exemplified by Poe's story. Then in part VI he argues that Dupin himself has been unable to resist the compulsion to repeat the Minister's role as soon as the letter comes into his hands: Dupin, thus, receives his remuneration from the Prefect, reinstates the power of the police, and makes the letter "re-enter the order of the Law" (69). This part of the seminar interprets the last episode in "The Purloined Letter" as an allegory of the analyst's responsibility during transference. One of Freud's major topics in *Beyond the Pleasure Principle* is a reassessment of "the dynamics of transference."[10] His earlier view had been that the therapeutic encounter consisted in uncovering the patient's resistances as quickly as possible, pointing them out, and inducing the patient by suggestion to abandon them (SE, XVIII: 18). As early as 1910, Freud had acknowledged, however, that the patient's influence on the unconscious of the analyst – what he called "counter-transference" – limited the possibilities of treatment: "no psycho-analyst goes further than his own complexes and internal resistances permit," he warned (SE, XI: 145). Repetition automatism – "the compulsion to repeat . . . from the past experiences which include no possibility of pleasure" (SE, XVIII: 20) – greatly complicates for both patient and analyst the processes of transference and counter-transference. The clear goal of making conscious what were formerly unconscious resistances so that the patient might abandon them has been lost in Freud's new theory of a psychoanalysis not confined to the pleasure principle. Part VI of Lacan's seminar takes on the burden of Freud's need to rethink the profession of "grilling." Lacan begins this section by offering a new description of psychoanalysts as those "who become the emissaries of all the purloined letters which at least for a time remain in sufferance with us in the transference" (68). He then describes in terms of Poe's story two ways in which the analyst's professional responsibility becomes compromised. Money, the remuneration received for professional services by Dupin or Lacan, threatens to neutralize the detective's or analyst's responsibility to be an emissary of purloined letters. To whom does the analyst finally deliver the letter "in sufferance"? Here is the second opportunity for professional irresponsibility. Dupin turns the letter over to the police, who had hired him in the first place. In Lacan's allegorization of Poe, psychoanalysis becomes an extension of "the order of the Law" (69), which Lacan had witnessed himself during his year at the Infirmary for the Insane of the Police Prefecture.[11]

Part VII of the seminar has been read in radically different ways, as one would expect of such an ironic text. One possible reading is that Dupin as analyst is fated to repeat the ways of the Minister, sapping the signifier of its signifying powers and turning toward the reader "the medusoid face of the signifier nothing but whose obverse anyone except the Queen has been able to read" (71). According to this reading, the story is an exact replication of Freud's shocking discovery of the inescapable force of repetition automatism. A second possible reading, darker yet, sees the perversities of psychoanalysis in Dupin's succumbing to the temptations of money, his working for the police, and his using his advantage over the Minister for the pleasures of revenge. According to this view, the Minister remains a strangely admirable if "unprincipled man of genius" (71). As gambler, poet, and mathematician, he alone knows the unstable signifying ways of dice, mathematical symbols, and purloined letters. A third reading, however, would see both the Minister and Dupin as negative or irresponsible models of psychoanalysis, the first acting outside the law and engaging in ludic manipulation of signs, the other acting as an agent of the police and prostituting his interpretative skills. Unlike the Queen, however, neither of them is able to read the letter that comes into his hands. In contrast to their ways with texts there is the promising assurance of the seminar's conclusion:

> The sender, we tell you, receives from the receiver his own message in reverse form. Thus it is that what the "purloined letter," nay, the "letter in sufferance" means is that a letter always arrives at its destination. (72)

In this model of transference the patient receives his own message back from the analyst but not in the form it was sent. Even though the letter, in such a therapeutic encounter, arrives at its destination, the ability to read it presupposes an ambitious theory of language, the unconscious, and the human subject that Lacan proceeds to develop in the rest of *Ecrits*. This reading would credit the seminar with outlining Lacan's theoretical ambition – to read Freud in full acknowledgment of his development as a theorist, to follow his example in the use of works of art as imaginative complements of his theories, and to be willing to be propelled by Freud's own example beyond what Freud wrote in the interest, especially, of providing linguistic underpinnings for his theoretical work – but it would also credit the seminar with being able to forecast the tasks to follow in the volume of Lacan's writings: to distinguish the imaginary and the symbolic more fully, to demonstrate the link between the structure of language and that of the unconscious, and to provide a comprehensive account of the human subject. Such high theoretical ambitions Lacan was eager to fulfill.

"Structure, Sign, and Play"

In 1965, the year before Derrida delivered his paper "Structure, Sign and Play in the Discourse of the Human Sciences" at the Johns Hopkins University International Colloquium on Critical Languages and the Sciences of Man, he had published an abbreviated version of *Grammatology* in the journal *Critique*. Both papers are brilliant condensations of the argument of that book. Lacan also participated in the Colloquium, which had been organized by René Girard as an American celebration of French structuralism.[12] At that time Lacan was 66, and his theoretical project was largely complete. Derrida, twenty years younger than Lacan, was just beginning to achieve international recognition. The character and extent of their influence on each other continues to be difficult to determine. Even in this paper, although Derrida never mentions Lacan, it is possible to forecast the widening gap that continued to develop between them from their first meeting at Johns Hopkins. In his later critique of Lacan, Derrida concentrated specifically on the "Seminar on 'The Purloined Letter'" as the text that epitomizes their differences.[13]

Derrida begins "Structure, Sign and Play" by announcing an important "event" that has taken place in the concept of structure. Acknowledging that it may seem strange to use the word *event* in relation to structure, he nevertheless proceeds to show that a "rupture" has occurred in this concept and in its history. "Structure" as word and concept is as old as Western science and philosophy. Indeed, it is so much a part of the root network of ordinary language and thought that it is easy to forget its metaphorical character. In this forgetfulness bred of excessive familiarity, "the structurality of structure" (278) has been neutralized; and it has been allowed to assume a center, point of presence, and fixed origin in language and thought. This has been done to limit the play [*le jeu*] of structure. *Le jeu*, like the English word *play*, conveys the sense of movement as well as amusement. Structure, especially the center of a structure, keeps play within limits, however.[14]

The center operates as a metaphor within the metaphor of structure. It "closes off play" (279) and does not allow for substitution, permutation, or transformation. It is that "which is by definition unique" in a structure. Although center governs structure, it is not structured in turn. The center is a still presence from which the attempt may be made to conceive of structure itself as "a full presence which is beyond play." The entire history of the concept of structure, however, manifests the substitutions of one center for another or the assignment of different forms or names to the center. Here Derrida claims, in a sentence that replays such substitutions, that "the history of metaphysics, like the history of the West, is the history of these metaphors and metonymies" (279). One may wish to step back at this point to consider how such a sentence might be read. In its manifestation of the substituting power of structural centrality, is this sentence blind to (or immune from) its own critical claim? So far Derrida has taken his reader from structure to center to presence to the history of metaphysics to the history of the West, all of which are centered on or structured by metaphor and metonymy. Derrida soon assures his reader, however, that to step back in this way, to reflect on the structure of structure, to question the language of centrality and presence is precisely to effect the disruption or rupture that he began by announcing. Strangely, such disruption is a matter of repetition. To think through the structurality of structure and to recognize center and presence as metaphors is not to do initial violence to the structure of language, say, or the structure of a given text. On the contrary, it is to be aware of what structure is and has been; it is to reflect on "a central presence which has never been itself, has always already [*toujours déjà*] been exiled from itself into its own substitute" (280). At such moments of critical reflection as this, language ceases to be a transparent medium of reflection or the undifferentiated substance of thought; it now becomes part of "the universal problematic." Furthermore, at such moments everything becomes discourse in the sense of "a system in which the central signified, the original or transcendental signified, is never absolutely present outside a system of differences" (280). This is to retain such words and concepts as essence, existence, substance, subject, transcendentality, consciousness, God, man, but to acknowledge that they are unthinkable without rupture, disruption, absence, difference. Such a move simultaneously conserves and disrupts by recovering the necessary play of metaphor and metonymy in thought. This is not to say, however, that these topics are nothing but metaphors or metonymies, for that would simply substitute (or rename) one center for (or with) another, thereby promoting rhetoric to a theological office of transcendental signification. Derrida's aim is rather to extend "the domain and play of signification infinitely" by subjecting the medium of thought and signification to scrutiny.

Derrida is quick to acknowledge that the critique of structurality, centrality, and presence also has a history and that the rupture or redoubling of structure is not suddenly taking place "now." Before settling on the word "deconstruction" (282) to mark this scrutiny of the language and concept of structure, Derrida employs as approximate synonyms the words *disruption* and *destruction*. (Although silent here, his debt to Heidegger for his interpretative language is fully cited in *Grammatology*.[15]) Disruption would seem to occur *in* a structure when it is subjected to close examination and its discourse carefully examined for metaphorical displacements, whereas destruction is what is purposefully done *to* structures when they are subjected to critical interpretation by such thinkers as Nietzsche, Freud, or Heidegger. It would be a mistake, however (or so Derrida implies), to hold these thinkers responsible – or to give them credit – for the disruption of structure. Deconstructive processes are "always already" occurring in discourse, although these processes have waited for Nietzsche, Freud, Heidegger, and their intellectual descendants to theorize rupture. The move of these thinkers beyond structure, like Freud's move beyond the pleasure principle, is not a rejection of structurality (which is "unthinkable" (279)); rather, it is a development in the theory of structure that supplements what was previously thought. Even to think or write about what Derrida carefully avoids calling "poststructuralism" requires the implementation of the language and concepts of structure: "we can pronounce not a single destructive proposition which has not already had to slip into the form, the logic, and the implicit postulations of precisely what it seeks to contest" (280–1).

As an example of being held in the grip of what one wishes to contest, Derrida turns to the concept of sign. Although up to this point in his paper he has worked to demonstrate that "there is no transcendental or privileged signifier" and that the "play of signification" has no limit, it is not possible to reject the concept and word *sign*. The word *sign*, Derrida recalls, has always been understood as a signifier referring to a signified different from itself. A sign refers to something else. Even though, by metaphysical slight of hand, attempts have been made to claim that meaning is *in* signs or that certain signs make truth present, the concept of the sign as a signifier that is different from the signified requires the magical fiction of presence in order to think of such presence as deferred: "we cannot do without the concept of the sign, for we cannot give up the metaphysical complicity without also giving up the critique we are directing against this complicity, or without the risk of erasing difference in the self-identity of a signified, reducing its signifier into itself" (281). Indeed, this paradox of the sign – that its reduction needs the opposition it reduces or the presence it finds absent – is exemplary in the discourse of structure. Not only did Nietzsche, Freud, and Heidegger work within this tradition of metaphysics in order to write critiques of it, each of them takes on in turn the thought of a predecessor, as Nietzsche does with Plato or Heidegger with Nietzsche, in order to work their way beyond their inheritance.

In the first part of his paper Derrida demonstrates his own necessary complicity with the deconstructive history he has just described by offering a brief critical reading of Lévi-Strauss, who for him is no less strategic a choice than Lacan's selection of Poe. This section simultaneously develops the theory of deconstruction already begun and applies it to Lévi-Strauss. The human science of ethnology, which Lévi-Strauss's work has done so much to advance, is historically and systematically contemporaneous with the European critiques of ethnocentrism and metaphysics. Derrida finds in ethnology the implementation of traditional concepts that it also struggles against. Indeed, "the ethnologist accepts into his discourse the premises of ethnocentrism at the moment when he denounces them" (282). This observation provides the context for Derrida's first use of the word *deconstruction* in this paper: "It is a question of explicitly and systematically posing the problem of the status of a discourse which borrows from a heritage the resources necessary for the deconstruction [*déconstruction* (*ED*, 414)] of that heritage itself" (282). The sequence of Derrida's argument is important for understanding its economy and strategy. He begins in the historical mode by tracing an event in the history of structurality (the rupture of its continuity as a consequence of its being critically examined). He then proceeds to reflect on the discourse of structure, considering structure as a metaphor and anatomizing its constituent metaphors (center, presence, play). In the concept of *sign* he finds a disruption taking place (between signifier and signified) even before the event of structurality's disruption, by the critique of its discourse unleashed by Nietzsche, Freud, and Heidegger. Then, in the discourse of the human sciences, he observes the simultaneity of the rise of the science of ethnology, the critique of discourse and metaphysics, and the critique of European ethnocentrism, all of which are manifestations of "decentering." The shift of attention and value from what was once thought central – one's own language, literature, or culture, for example – necessarily reflects back on the concept of centrality and its "central presence" in all concepts of structurality. The violence and purposeful instability of Derrida's language – as in the important sequence *rupture, disruption, destruction, deconstruction, de-constitution* – highlight the momentousness of the intellectual events they chronicle.

Like Lacan in his readings of Poe and Freud, Derrida in his reading of Lévi-Strauss prefers to find in the texts he examines prior recognition of the thought he wants to advance. "In a *more or less explicit manner*" the work of Lévi-Strauss declares a certain doctrinal choice in its invocation of the opposition between nature and culture. This opposition is part of a chain of concepts even older than Plato that sets nature over against law, education, art, technics, liberty, the arbitrary, history, society, mind. Although he uses this opposition in his work, Lévi-Strauss also finds it impossible to accept as truth. He begins *The Elementary Structures of Kinship* (1949) by defining *nature* as that which is universal, spontaneous, and not dependent on a particular culture or norm; and *culture* as that which is dependent on a system of socially regulating norms and which varies from one social structure to another. Having set up this definitional opposition, however, Lévi-Strauss proceeds to announce a conceptual "scandal." The incest prohibition, on the one hand, is universal and therefore natural, but on the other hand is normative and therefore cultural. It is exemplary, then, of "a scandalous fact, a nucleus of opacity within a network of transparent significations" (283) framed by the opposition of nature and culture. This example is important for Derrida because it shows that "language bears within itself the necessity of its own critique" (284). Lévi-Strauss recognizes this as well. Instead of undertaking an historical examination of the concepts of nature and culture, however, he is able to continue to use them as old tools that no longer have any truth value. In this way "their relative efficacy is exploited, and they are employed to destroy the old machinery to which they belong and of which they themselves are pieces" (284). This method of using the means at hand Lévi-Strauss calls *bricolage*. Derrida affirms this method but proceeds to raise it to a higher power: "If one calls *bricolage* the necessity of borrowing one's concepts from the text of a heritage which is more or less coherent or ruined, it must be said that every discourse is *bricoleur*" (285).

Here Derrida reads Lévi-Strauss by fully entering into the structure of his text, which in this example involves not only the structural opposition of nature and culture but also the confession of discontent with that opposition in light of incest prohibition. The patient investigation of the whole of Lévi-Strauss's argument uncovers the self-critical resources of that argument, which make possible a move beyond it. Indeed, Lévi-Strauss's text points to the way beyond itself. What most fascinates Derrida is Lévi-Strauss's heroic search for a new kind of discourse that bravely abandons, by calling into question, its own centrality. When he allows his discourse to reflect on itself and to call into question the structural categories it uses, Lévi-Strauss enables his readers to "rediscover the mythopoetical virtue of *bricolage*" (286). Thus, in *The Raw and the Cooked* (1964), he confesses that his study of myths "is itself a kind of myth" (287). Here his own discourse takes on the character of the mythopoeic, which it sets out to examine.

Derrida at this point is quick to anticipate an unproductive misreading of his own method. By advocating the self-critical examination of philosophical texts to the extent of highlighting the resources within texts for questioning the adequacy of their own formulations, Derrida is not abandoning philosophy. Rather, he is "continuing to read philosophers *in a certain way*" (288). Far from being antiphilosophical, he is attending with great care to the textuality of philosophy. In what, then, does "the passage beyond philosophy" [*le passage au-delà de la philosophie (ED,* 421)] consist? There is no suggestion here that it consists in reading philosophy as literature, any more than the reading of Lévi-Strauss was an attempt to read ethnology as rhetoric. Attempting to escape from philosophy by "turning the page of philosophy" (288) is simply to do philosophy badly or naïvely. "The passage beyond philosophy" no more leaves philosophy behind than Lévi-Strauss's *bricolage* leaves ethnology behind or Freud's move beyond the pleasure principle leaves psychoanalysis behind. Elisabeth Roudinesco points out that the term *poststructuralism* was coined in English to designate what emerged from the Johns Hopkins Colloquium in 1966.[16] Nevertheless, Derrida's method as formulated in this paper and in his subsequent writings is not an abandonment of either structuralism or philosophy. *Poststructuralism* would seem to mix temporal and spatial metaphors in a way that Derrida finds suspicious in the first sentence of "Structure, Sign and Play." What is *post* comes after and thus abandons or leaves something else behind. In contrast, "the passage beyond philosophy" is the way philosophy gives birth to new philosophical thought. It follows a path that philosophy has already marked.

The final sentences of "Structure, Sign and Play" provide a metaphorical grounding for *le passage au-delà de la philosophie* by identifying *le passage* with the birth canal. In these apocalyptic final sentences the event of the deconstruction of structurality, which has been the theme of this paper, is imagined in terms of "the operations of childbearing." Conception, formation, gestation, labor are here the critical stages in deconstruction's critique of structurality and its passage beyond philosophy. Derrida arrests his metaphor at the stage at which the child cannot be named or even identified as a distinguishable human form: "the as yet unnameable which is proclaiming itself . . . as is necessary whenever a birth is in the offing" (293) [*qu'une naissance est à l'oeuvre*

(*ED*, 428)]. Here Derrida's concern, however, is less with the new-born than with the response of those who "turn their eyes away" when faced with what to them is a "terrifying form of monstrosity," which is what the nativity of the new often appears to be.[17] Derrida carefully notes that he does not exclude himself from such a society, which awaits but cannot quite watch the birth of new forms out of the self-critical structures of the old. In contrast to the image of reading as textual violation in part V of Lacan's "Seminar on 'The Purloined Letter,'" Derrida's metaphor thus links reading with being a witness to childbearing.[18] This image envisages the text in advanced stages of labor with the new and as yet unnamed life just ready to be born. Like the birth of the revolutionary Orc in Blake's prophetic poems, the birth of the new is here greeted, even in this text from the 1960s, with great anxiety. The "formless, mute, infant, and terrifying form of monstrosity" (293) is already asserting, even before its first cry, its irreducible difference [*différance*] from its structural mother. In preparation for this powerful conclusion to his paper, Derrida contrasts Rousseauistic with Nietzschean responses to the origin of new structure. Rousseauistic reception, based on the model of catastrophe (a model shared with Lévi-Strauss), longs for what it knows to be the "impossible presence of the absent origin." Its mood is sadly negative and nostalgically guilty, in contrast to the Nietzschean affirmation of a playful "world of signs without fault, without truth, and without origin" (292). Although attempts have been made to read Derrida as a strictly Nietzschean advocate of *le jeu*,[19] he is careful here, as in *Grammatology*, to trace his intellectual lineage back to both Rousseau and Nietzsche. As the title of his paper suggests, *sign* mediates between the concepts of structure and play without ending the dream of presence or the continual disruptions of *différance*.

"The System and the Speaking Subject"

Whereas much of the engaging complexity of Lacan's "Seminar on 'The Purloined Letter'" arises from the way it reads Freud's *Beyond the Pleasure Principle* by looking through Poe's short story, Derrida's "Structure, Sign and Play" successfully disguises its introduction of an alternative lexicon for interpreting structure — *play, center, presence, deconstruction, bricolage, différance, monstrosity* — by enveloping these terms in a conceptual history that moves from the rupture of structurality to the metaphorical birth of unnameable new structure. Kristeva's "The System and the Speaking Subject," while relying less on narrative and metaphor than these other two papers, generates its intellectual power by argumentative synthesis and condensation. In the space of twenty-four paragraphs this paper outlines the field of semiotics, details its history, responds to its critics, summarizes its limitations, celebrates its achievements, positions its discourse in relation to linguistics and psychoanalysis, and announces its potential for contributing to the development of critical theory.

As a result of its study of ideologies as sign systems, semiotics has discovered that all social practices are also signs and that they are, therefore, "articulated *like* a language" (25). This means that every social practice, whatever else it may be, is also subject to the rules of signification, bound by the difference between signifier and signified, and therefore split between the referent and the symbolic. Semiotics has, then, discovered the social law that "the symbolic dimension which is given in language" governs every social practice. The immediate consequence of this discovery is to refuse the rival claims of idealism and "sociologism" by resisting the polarities of absolute internal and external determination. Neither a human essence detached from social phenomena nor a mechanistic capitulation to ideology provides an adequate foundation for semiotic causality. Even while it passes through the gulf that threatens to separate completely the humanities and the social sciences, semiotics also challenges two competing positions within linguistic science. By accepting the claim that language is a form of social communication that is determined by social practices, linguistics confines itself to being able to speak only of those practices. If, however, linguistics focuses its attention primarily on "the privileged areas" where language is "put to non-utilitarian use" (26) – such as art, ritual, and myth – it risks abandoning all other social contacts but play, pleasure, and desire. While resisting the extremes of these competing positions, semiotics must also, according to Kristeva, not allow itself to be simply "a mere application to signifying practices of the linguistic model." Rather, its principal task is to identify "the systematic constraint within each signifying practice," which will also enable it to determine the specific constraints of discrete practices.

That task was largely completed by the first phase of semiology that began with Saussure and Peirce. A legitimate critique of their "semiology of systems," in Kristeva's view, must begin with a theory of meaning "which must necessarily be a theory of the speaking

subject" (27). Generative grammar has begun this project by supplementing structuralism's view of language as a system with the
revival of "the Cartesian conception of language as an *act* carried out
by a *subject*."[20] The danger here, however, is that the "speaking
subject" may be equated with a transcendental ego. At this point
Kristeva reaches out to Freud, not only to provide a check against
this equation, but also to enlist for semiotics the power of "the
Freudian revolution," which has "achieved the definitive displacement of the Western épistémé from its presumed centrality" (28).
Here Kristeva is obviously reflecting on the same "event" in the
history of structurality that Derrida refers to in the opening sentence
of "Structure, Sign and Play." Her immediate concern at this point,
however, is with establishing a necessary link between linguistics
and psychoanalysis. In the absence of such a link, linguistics must
work with an impoverished conception of the human subject and
psychoanalysis with an inadequate understanding of language.
Kristeva accordingly cites Lacan for having "superbly and author-
itatively" worked out "the effects" of the Freudian revolution. At the
time she is writing (1973) Lacan's theoretical ambitions were largely
fulfilled,[21] even though semantics ("the theory of meaning") finds
itself immobilized at a crossroad. In one direction lies the formalistic
claim of an increasingly sophisticated logico-mathematical model for
linguistics that threatens to cut off the speaking subject from its body,
its unconscious, and its history. In the other direction lies the theory
of the divided subject, split by the rival claims of the conscious and
unconscious, driven by bio-physiological processes that are part of
signifying processes, and subject to social and economic constraints.
In choosing the second path, Kristeva suggests, semiology might best
be renamed *semanalysis*, which would announce its structuralist
inheritance, its support of the Freudian revolution, and its resistance
to the temptation of a specialist linguistic abstraction that would
separate an already divided subject from its body and the world.

   The project of semanalysis is to give a comprehensive account of
the primary linguistic-psychoanalytic processes (displacement and condensation, or metonymy and metaphor), the compulsion to repetition
(which was Lacan's principal concern in his "Seminar"), and the
acceptance and transgression of symbolic law in the interest of its
renovation as play (which was Derrida's concern in "Structure, Sign
and Play"). In carrying out this project, however, semiotics or
semanalysis must deal with its own condition as a metalanguage. As
soon as it begins to speak about the heterogeneity of language, it

begins to homogenize it by linking it to a theory or system. Indeed, it loses its subject as soon as it grasps it. The best check on this besetting reductiveness of its own theory is for it to maintain a renewing correspondence with "the signifying practices which set off the heterogeneity at issue" (30). These practices include music, dance, painting, but above all for Kristeva, poetic language when it is "making free with the language code." The continuing challenge for semiotics is to "apprehend the heterogeneity of the signifying process other than by reducing it to a systematicity." To meet this challenge semiotics must turn its attention to its own theoretical language, which is also a signifying process; and in doing so, it is compelled to stress candidly its own limited capacities. The ambiguities of sem-analysis pervade its activities. Its work to demystify transcendental reduction necessitates the systematic study of discrete signifying practices; although a successor of Hegelian dialectic, it is committed to dealing with that materiality that Hegel neglected but without being reduced to the "merely economic externality" (31) of mechanistic Marxism; by its efforts to recover the heterogeneity of signifying practice, it restores the play of practice as "an agent of social cohesion."

Kristeva concludes her manifesto for semiotics by arguing that this work has become historically necessary. Current mutations within capitalism, along with the political and economic "reawakening" of such countries as China and India, have discredited both the Western subject as an adequate model for the transcendental subject and exposed the inadequacy of Marxist theory for its inability to provide a theory of meaning or of the speaking subject. Semiotics is therefore ready to fill the gap between dialectical materialism and psychoanalytic transference. In this capacity semiotics is a mode of *bricolage* that refuses to follow the dominant discourses of the established disciplines and sciences into the self-chosen exile that Mallarmé called *indicible qui ment*. Refusing to be intimidated by its heterogeneous task or to remain silent about the limitations of its own theory, semiotics "is ready to give a hearing to any or all of those efforts which, ever since the elaboration of a new position for the speaking subject, have been renewing and reshaping the status of meaning within social exchanges to a point where the very order of language is being renewed" (32). Unlike Lacan, who sought to renew psychoanalysis by returning to the disruptive power of Freud's theoretically imaginative texts, or Derrida, who finds in written language deconstructive processes always already at work, Kristeva constructs an eclectic, self-reflexive theory to account for the heterogeneity of the speaking subject's symbolic practices. Although the intellectual legacies of Hegel, Nietzsche, Freud, and Heidegger are no less important for her than they are for Lacan and Derrida, Kristeva is more immediately concerned than they with the social realities of the speaking subject. In part this reflects her resistance to the reduction of the subject to a transcendental ego, which she finds as untenable in Cartesian linguistics as Lacan and Derrida found it in post-Freudian psychology.

These papers by Lacan, Derrida, and Kristeva provide some important clues to their orientation as theorists of reading. A master stylist himself, Lacan prizes literature for what it can teach the psychoanalyst. In this respect, as in so much else, he follows Freud's lead. Both in his own writing and in his interpretation of other texts, Lacan emphasizes metaphor, metonymy, allegory, narrative, and dialogue not for their aesthetic value but for their capacity to reflect the elusive and uncanny ways of the unconscious. Literary language is not in this respect a mode of discourse distinct from other forms of language. If literature has a particular utility for the psychoanalyst it is in its calling attention to its own processes of signification and fictionality. Spoken language above all has the power for Lacan to make accessible the totality of the unconscious. Like the purloined letter in the card-box above the fireplace in the Minister's room, texts, truth, and the unconscious have a center hidden somewhere in the open, waiting to be found. Derrida's texts are no less stylistically self-conscious than Lacan's in their ability to reenact the processes of thought and language that they set out to explore. Derrida, however, is less sanguine than Lacan about finding truth's undisplaced center. Speech – Lacan's privileged medium – too often, in Derrida's view, conceals the fictionality of its claim to make truth present. The most valued places in written language for Derrida are not initially focal points or centers but margins and partly concealed cracks or openings. When truth finds an opening in an otherwise self-contained discursive structure, then occurs the exciting but terrifying moment of conceptual birth. At such times the entire structure of language is challenged by the as yet unnamed, and theory takes its greatest imaginative risks. For Kristeva there is a danger in both Lacan and Derrida of not adequately respecting the heterogeneity of the human subject and the social dimension of language. Although she is no less suspicious of sociologism than she is of idealism, her eclectic theories manifest the complex mesh of linguistics, psychoanalysis, philosophy, politics, literature, and social theory she thinks necessary for understanding human beings and their signifying practices. No one discipline, much less a single theory, can contain the multiple structures and uses of language. All signifying practices are highly charged space fields in which many signifying systems are at work. In *Revolution in Poetic Language* Kristeva will use the term *intertextuality* to refer to the intertransposition of systems of signs, where all vie for centrality and for critical attention.[22] This intertextual network, which is an index of the heterogeneity of the human subject, is in turn reflected in Kristeva's polylogic theoretical texts. As important as these three papers are as introductions to Lacan, Derrida, and Kristeva, they can, however, provide little more than a map of these theorists' complex textual topographies. They invite their readers to explore more carefully their distinctive theoretical terrains.

NOTES

1 Peter Brooks has written a useful assessment of recent hostile responses to theory in "Western Civ at bay," *TLS* (January 25, 1991), 5–6. See also subsequent correspondence in the *TLS* published under the running title "Tenured Radicals." The most reliable of the general studies of these theorists are Malcolm Bowie, *Lacan* (London: Fontana Press, 1991); Christopher Norris, *Derrida* (London: Fontana Press, 1987); and Toril Moi, *Sexual/Textual Politics* (London: Methuen, 1985), esp. 150–73.

2 Citations in the following discussion refer to "Seminar on 'The Purloined Letter,'" trans. Jeffrey Mehlman, *Yale French Studies*, 48 (1972), 39–71; "Structure, Sign and Play in the Discourse of the Human Sciences," in *Writing and Difference*, trans. Alan Bass (Chicago: University of Chicago Press, 1978), 278–93; and "The System and the Speaking Subject" in *The Kristeva Reader*, ed. Toril Moi (Oxford: Basil Blackwell, 1986), 25–33. I have adopted a few of Mehlman's corrections from the reprint of his translation in *The Purloined Poe: Lacan, Derrida, and Psychoanalytic Reading*, ed. John P. Muller and William J. Richardson (Baltimore: Johns Hopkins University Press, 1988).

3 For excellent accounts of the literary and medical receptions of psychoanalysis in France, see Elisabeth Roudinesco, *Jacques Lacan & Co.*, trans. Jeffrey Mehlman (London: Free Association Books, 1990), esp. chs 1 and 3, and David Macey, *Lacan in Contexts* (London: Verso, 1988), ch. 2.

4 J. W. von Goethe, *Faust*, trans. Walter Kaufmann (New York: Doubleday, 1963), 245. I am indebted to John P. Muller and William J. Richardson's excellent notes on Lacan's seminar in *The Purloined Poe*.

5   The French text clearly marks the unnumbered divisions in the argu-
     ment, which correspond to the following pages and line numbers in the
     Yale French Studies translation: I, p. 39 to p. 45 line 10; II, p. 45 line 11
     to p. 56; III, p. 57 to p. 60 line 2; IV, p. 60 line 3 to p. 61 line 19;
     V, p. 61 line 20 to p. 67 line 5; VI, p. 67 line 6 to p. 70
     line 27; VII, p. 70 line 28 to p. 72.

6   Jean Laplanche and J.-B. Pontalis, *The Language of Psycho-analysis*
     (*Vocabulaire de la psychoanalyse*, 1967), trans. Donald Nicholson-Smith
     (London: Hogarth Press and Institute of Psycho-Analysis, 1973), is
     indispensable, particularly for comparative study of Freud's and Lacan's
     technical vocabulary.

7   See, for example, the chapter on *aletheia* in Heidegger, *Early Greek
     Thinking*, trans. David Krell and Frank A. Capuzzi (New York: Harper
     and Row, 1975 (1954)), esp. 113. Heidegger's return to Heraclitus can
     be read as a swerve away from the legacies of Plato and Aristotle, for
     whom *aletheia* is usually the genuine or non-deceptive.

8   "The Purloined Letter," in *The Purloined Poe*, 21.

9   So Derrida has done in his paper, "The Purveyor of Truth," in *The
     Purloined Poe*, 187. Muller and Richardson have been strangely reticent,
     however, in their commentary on this section; see 94–5. Jane Gallop
     offers some helpful comments on the problem of where to begin read-
     ing Lacan, but she maintains her distance from the text of Lacan's
     "Seminar" by reading it through Derrida's critique: *Reading Lacan*
     (Ithaca: Cornell University Press, 1985), 55–73. Barbara Johnson's "The
     Frame of Reference: Poe, Lacan, Derrida," *Yale French Studies*, 55–6
     (1977), 457–505 is a brilliant essay on what she calls the "vertiginously
     insecure position" of the reader of the Poe-Lacan-Derrida triptych.

10   Cf. Freud's paper by that title in SE, XII: 97–108, which presents his
     earlier theory of transference.

11   For an account of this period in Lacan's training and his work with
     Clérambault, see Roudinesco, 105–9. She describes Lacan's later view
     of the relation between psychiatry and criminology this way: "He sent
     packing, back to back, the adepts of both responsibility and irrespons-
     ibility. For him to explain a crime was neither to forgive nor condemn
     it, neither to punish nor accept it. It was, on the contrary, to 'derealize'
     it, that is, to restore to it its imaginary, then symbolic dimension" (127).

12   Lacan, in what may have been a tactical mistake, gave his remarks in
     English. He had the heroic assistance of Anthony Wilden as translator,
     however. His paper, "Of Structure as an Inmixing of an Otherness
     Prerequisite to Any Subject Whatever," is reprinted in *The Structuralist
     Controversy*, ed. Richard Macksey and Eugenio Donato (Baltimore:
     Johns Hopkins University Press, 1970), 186–200.

13   See *Positions* trans. Alan Bass (Chicago: University of Chicago Press,
     1981), 106–13; "The Purveyor of Truth," reprinted as part of *La Carte*

postale de Socrate á Freud et au-delà (Paris: Aubier-Flammarion, 1980); and the important discussion of Lacan and Derrida in Philippe Lacoue-Labarthe and Jean-Luc Nancy, *Le Titre de la lettre: une lecture de Lacan* (Paris: Éditions Galilée, 1973), 142–8. Lacan refers to the Lacoue-Labarthe and Nancy critique in *Le Séminair XX: Encore* (Paris: Éditions du Seuil, 1975), 68, claiming that he is not read as carefully by his disciples as by those who attack him.

14 This may explain in part the common mixed metaphor in English, "centered *around*," instead of "centered on."

15 For an enlightening discussion of the terms *Abbau*, *Destruktion*, and *deconstruction*, see Rodolphe Gasché, *The Tain of the Mirror: Derrida and the Philosophy of Reflection* (Cambridge, MA: Harvard University Press, 1986), 109–20.

16 Roudinesco, 411.

17 Derrida is here alluding in part to Saussure's image of writing as "a genuine orthographic monstrosity": Ferdinand de Saussure, *Course in General Linguistics*, trans. Roy Harris (La Salle, IL: Open Court, 1983), 31.

18 There may be a subtle allusion here also to Mallarmé, who draws a parallel in "Don du poéme" between the poet–poem relationship and that of the mother and child. See Barbara Johnson, "Mallarmé as Mother," in *A World of Difference* (Baltimore: Johns Hopkins University Press, 1987), 141. Cf. Derrida on Socrates as midwife in *Dissemination*, trans. Barbara Johnson (Chicago: University of Chicago Press, 1981), 153–4.

19 By Richard Rorty, for example, in *Contingency, Irony, and Solidarity* (Cambridge: Cambridge University Press, 1990), esp. 125–9.

20 There appears to be at least one printing error at this point in Kristeva's text: the phrase "*national* language" (27, line 34) should perhaps be "*natural* language." The "*systematic* aspect" referred to also on 27 would appear to be a reference to *syntactic* structure in contrast to the reference to semantics earlier in the paragraph. The allusion here to the work of Noam Chomsky is made explicit in Kristeva's fuller discussion in *Revolution in Poetic Language*, trans. Margaret Waller (New York: Columbia University Press, 1984), 21–4. Kristeva is by no means confining herself to Chomskyan syntactic theory, however.

21 Although Derrida seems to be pushed aside at this point, it may be helpful to recall that an interview between Kristeva and Derrida entitled "Semiology and Grammatology" had been published on June 3, 1968 in *Information sur les sciences sociales* and reprinted in *Positions* in 1972. See also *Revolution in Poetic Language*, 40–2.

22 *Revolution in Poetic Language*, 59–60.

2

Écrits: A Selection

Before the appearance of Écrits in 1966, Lacan had published a series of professional articles on medicine and psychiatry, his doctoral thesis on paranoia (*De la psychose paranoïaque dans ses rapports avec la personnalité*, 1932), and a long essay of considerable importance on the family ("La Famille") for the *Encyclopédie française* (1938).[1] Despite its now notorious difficulty, Écrits was an immediate bestseller in France. Although the title of the book is not *Les Écrits*, it can, nevertheless, be read as either a monolithic volume of Lacan's *oeuvre* or a collection of discrete papers.[2] This 900-page text collects material published between 1936 and 1966. Many of the individual papers have a complex bibliographical history, reflecting the evolution and ambition of Lacan's theorizing, the problems of transition from the spoken to the written word, and difficulties in translation. The organization of the book is not chronological but strategically argumentative. Like a vast novel or narrative poem, Écrits manifests a continuing tension between the temporal and the spatial as Lacan rewrites his past in the interests of constructing a monumental theoretical text.[3] When Lacan selected nine papers for Alan Sheridan's English translation, he managed to achieve a more exact chronological sequence, while retaining on a smaller scale the architectural shape of the French edition. Both books are carefully wrought constructs of the theoretical imagination.

I

"The Mirror Stage"

The English text opens with "The mirror stage as formative of the function of the I," which is Lacan's most famous piece of writing.

Nevertheless, in his first sentence Lacan already involves his reader in intricate problems of sequence and priority. He reminds his audience, assembled in Zurich for the International Congress of Psychoanalysis in 1949, that he had introduced the concept of the mirror stage at the previous conference held thirteen years earlier in Marienbad. That 1936 version, despite its listing as the first item in the chronological bibliography in the French edition of *Écrits*, was in fact never published.[4] The published text of the paper is, therefore, "a much revised later version" of a superseded and, apparently, lost original. In addition to this curious textual history, there is also Lacan's repeated claim that he originated the conception of the mirror stage. Nowhere in his paper does he explicitly refer to the work of Henri Wallon, who edited the volume of the *Encyclopédie française* in which Lacan's essay on the family appeared in 1938. In fact Lacan's "The mirror stage" is in part a reading of Wallon's original mirror experiments with animals and children, which he had published in 1931 and 1934.[5] Lacan's appropriation of Wallon's work appears in his several references to the behavior of chimpanzees, monkeys, pigeons, and locusts in contrast to the behavior of children before a mirror. Far from being a lapse in bibliographical etiquette, however, Lacan's silence about Wallon's contribution to the mirror stage conception is but one indication of how radically different his theory is from Wallon's. Whereas Wallon is concerned with physiological and conscious processes in animals and children, Lacan interprets the mirror experience from the perspective of the unconscious. In so doing, he "radically transformed a psychological experiment into a theory of the imaginary organization of the human subject."[6]

Lacan's theoretical escalation of the mirror concept is announced in his first paragraph. He is returning again to speak of the mirror stage, he says, precisely because of its importance for seeing how psychoanalysis has come to understand the formation of the "I" and because this understanding also clarifies the opposition of psychoanalysis to any philosophy – such as Sartre's existential psychoanalysis – that would grant priority to consciousness with the consequence of the virtual extinction of the unconscious. The mirror conception, on which so much depends, originates in an apparently commonplace feature of human behavior that has been illuminated by work in comparative psychology: "The child, at an age when he is for a time, however short, outdone by the chimpanzee in instrumental intelligence, can nevertheless already recognize as such his own image in a mirror" (1). The sign of his recognition during this "aha experience"

[*Aha-Erlebnis*] is the child's "illuminative mimicry." Unlike the monkey who masters and then becomes indifferent to the experience, "the child in a series of gestures . . . experiences in play the relation between the movements assumed in the image and the reflected environment, and between this virtual complex and the reality it reduplicates – the child's own body, and the persons and things, around him." Whereas Wallon's monkeys, ducks, and dogs are interested in the image only so long as it appears to be another monkey, duck, or dog, the child becomes even more fascinated when he recognizes that the image he gazes upon is the image of the child's own self. The meaning Lacan gives to this behavior is that the mirror stage is "an identification" in the technical sense of "the transformation that takes place in the subject when he assumes an image . . . indicated by the use, in analytic theory, of the ancient term *imago*" (2).

Freud seems to have used the term *imago* for the first time in "The Dynamics of Transference" (SE, XII: 100). Although he does not often use the word, it does appear with some consistency when he writes about the "ever-increasing detachment" of the child from the parents when their significance for the child's superego development recedes. During such periods, when the ego is becoming more self-sufficient, the imago the parents have left behind in the child becomes linked with the influences of other, more impersonal figures of authority (SE, XIX: 168). Furthermore, by the age of puberty, Freud writes, the child has adjusted its "affectionate fixations" on its parents in light of the barriers against incest and has passed on "from the objects which are unsuitable in reality" to find "a way as soon as possible to other, extraneous objects with which a real sexual life may be carried on." The choice of these new objects, he concludes, will be made on the model [*imago*] of the infantile ones and will consequently attract the affection that had been tied to the earlier objects (SE, XI: 181). In these passages Freud uses the term *imago* to refer to the child's internalized image of its parents' authority and affection, which enables the child to retain its past without being bound to it during the process of normal development.

Before Lacan invokes the term *imago*, however, he warns his reader that a passage through the Surrealist realm of Salvador Dali is about to take place by saying that the meaning he has given to the mirror experience accords with his reflections on "paranoic knowledge" (2). Lacan requested a meeting with Dali after having read his text "The rotten donkey" ("L'âne pourri" 1930), where Dali describes his working through a paranoid process in order to create in his paintings a double image that simultaneously represents two objects, neither of which is itself distorted, deformed, or abnormal. The process is paranoid in that the meticulous (or classical) representation of the physical world serves to promote by its doubling an obsession that becomes valid for the viewer's perception as well as the artist's.[7] Dali's serious interest in Freud is reflected both in his writing and in his three drawings of Freud, who was in turn so impressed by Dali that he modified his initially negative assessment of Surrealism.[8] Dali greatly admired Lacan's 1932 doctoral thesis on paranoia, which was most probably influenced by Dali's "paranoia criticism," even though Lacan does not cite his work.[9] In his thesis, as well as here in "The mirror stage," Lacan prefers to allude covertly to Dali under the phrase "paranoic knowledge" [*connaissance paranoïaque*].[10] An important ingredient in Lacan's theory of the mirror stage is his reading of Wallon's psychological experimentation through the refracting lenses of Freud's *imago* and Dali's paranoic-criticism. What the child sees in the mirror, which appears to be the source of such playful delight, is a Surrealistic image that will model or form the "I" in ways that later give rise to irreparable division and alienation. It is not surprising, therefore, that Lacan develops his theory in this paper through a succession of images. His understanding of what the child sees is presented in a matrix of metaphors that also captures and interprets the theories of Wallon, Freud, and Dali.

Although the child is "jubilant" in front of the mirror, he is in fact captivated by his own "specular image" before he has developed any facility with language or experience in dealing with others. Thus, the "I" in its "primordial form" is "precipitated" too early, just as his birth occurs before he is anatomically complete (4). The child's ego is, then, situated, formed, determined by a fiction that both anticipates and warps what it will become. The fiction, which is "a mirage" of maturation (2), is that the "I" is single, unified, and exterior. The child sees himself as a unity in the world. This image (fiction, imago, mirage) is anticipatory in two senses. On the one hand, it looks forward to the ego's unachievable goal of unified identity that would be the foundation for its power in the world. On the other hand, this *Gestalt* is "pregnant" with the ego's alienating future. Only in the world of its own making [*fabrication* (*É*, 95)] will the "I" be homogeneous. If, however, one is guided by the surrealistic "imago of one's own body" (3) as it appears in dreams, then the double or heterogeneous structure of the subject begins to manifest itself. Just as Lacan is about to move at this point in his argument from the conscious fiction of ego unity to the unconscious truth of the subject's heterogeneity, he takes a detour through a catalogue of examples of psychological experiments, such as Wallon conducted, illustrating the effects of mirror experiences on the physiological development of animals. The point of these experiments for Lacan – especially when they are supplemented by Roger Caillois's theory of mimicry as "an obsession with space" and Lacan's surrealistic concept of paranoic knowledge – is that it is "the organic insufficiency" (4) of children that makes them susceptible to the mirror's "spatial captation."[11] The child, born as he is too early, is captivated, seized, or lured by the decoy [*leurre* (*É* , 97)] of his reflection into adopting a spatial or static image of himself. The mirror stage is then a particular case that illustrates how the *imago* functions in establishing a relation between the mental world [*Innenwelt*] and the environment [*Umwelt*].

The natural world is important for Lacan's theory of the formation of the ego precisely because of the inadequacy of natural or specifically biological processes as a foundation for understanding the mental world. In order to be useful at all for this purpose, nature has to undergo a metaphorical metamorphosis. As a storehouse of images, biology has a certain utility for psychoanalysis. Here again, Lacan follows the trajectory of Freud's own theorizing but reaches a conclusion beyond Freud. In his *Project for a Scientific Psychology* (1895), Freud struggles to define the ego in biological terms:

> [The ego] can easily be depicted if we consider that the regularly repeated reception of endogenous [intercellular quantities] in certain neurones [ultimate units of the nervous system] . . . and the facilitating effect proceeding thence will produce a group of neurones which is constantly cathected and thus corresponds to the *vehicle of the store* required by the secondary function. Thus the ego is to be defined as the totality of the [cathected system of impermeable neurones], at a given time, in which a permanent component is distinguished from a changing one. (SE, I: 323)[12]

Freud is here already wrestling with the problem of theorizing the structure and temporality of the human subject. In contrast to his early confidence in the biological basis for such a theory, however, Freud announces in the preface to the third edition of *Three Essays on Sexuality* (1914) that his work "is characterized not only by being completely based upon psychoanalytic research, but also by being

deliberately independent of the findings of biology" (SE, VII: 131).
One index of the evolution of Freud's theory of the ego is his gradual
abandonment of biological language for describing its structure and
function. In *The Ego and the Id* (1923), the ego is no longer a pulsating
mass of nerves but rather "a constitutional monarch, without whose
sanction no law can be passed but who hesitates long before imposing
his veto on any measure put forward by Parliament" (SE, XIX: 35).
As in his reading of Freud in the "Seminar on 'The Purloined Letter,'"
Lacan works to preserve Freud's earlier theory – in this case both his
biologism of 1895 and his 1914 emancipation of psychoanalytic
research – in the interest of accounting for the permanent and changing components of the "I." This he does by stripping biology of its
explanatory power while exploiting its metaphorical resources. In so
doing, he reads biology as a text.

Dehiscence, the most striking of Lacan's biological metaphors, is
called upon to account for nothing less than the intersection of the
mental and the natural worlds. Dehiscence lies "at the heart of the
organism," and it accordingly has mythical proportions. As a manifestation of "primordial Discord," its eruptive force is "betrayed by
the signs of uneasiness and motor unco-ordination of the neo-natal
months" (4). In a single sentence Lacan first brings his metaphor
into play, then mythically inflates it by linking it to the Heraclitean
notion of Discord, and finally brings it to bear upon the anatomical
incompleteness of the new-born child. Dehiscence, the spontaneous
opening of the structure of a ripe plant, has for Lacan none of the
lush vitality of Heidegger's metaphors for the natural order. The
Heideggerian *physis* is characterized by "self-blossoming emergence"
or "inward-jutting-beyond-itself" [*in-sich-aus-sich-hinausstehen*].[13] Lacan,
however, employs the image of dehiscence for its sense of explosive
development, as in time-lapse photographs of the bursting open of
seed pods. Just as the fruit, anther, or sporangium splits open its sides
as it ripens, so the once unified fiction of the child's ego is destined to
become fragmented and alienated. Rather than being cast free by this
process, the child is destined to retain the remnants of its early unde-
veloped state as a kind of "fetalization," or persistence of its imma-
turity, into its later life. The lure or mirage of future integrity will
persist even in the face of a continuous present in which wholeness
has not been achieved.

As though to mimic in his style the biological and mental processes
he has been describing, Lacan offers this brilliantly baroque condensation of the mirror stage concept:

The *mirror stage* is a drama whose internal thrust precipitated from insufficiency to anticipation – and which manufactures [*machine* (É, 97)] for the subject, caught up in the lure of spatial identification, the succession of phantasies that extends from a fragmented body-image to a form of its totality that I shall call orthopaedic – and, lastly, to the assumption of the armour of an alienating identity, which will mark with its rigid structure the subject's entire mental development. (4)

The scene of the child before the mirror is part of the drama of the individual's development in which he thrusts himself into the world as a leap from anatomical prematurity to the anticipation of later power. While he is caught up in the spatial lure of this image of his assumed future, the child witnesses a pageant or parade of carefully machined phantasies of what he might become. This succession includes the nightmare of a fragmented or dismembered body, the "orthopedic" image of the body's restored totality, and the armor-plated rigidity of terminal alienation. This dramatic sequence is also an elaborate network of puns and metaphors. Already the mirror *stage* [*le stade du miroir*] is losing its biological dynamism as one of a series of developmental steps and is being transformed into a stilted theatrical event before becoming a fortress or stadium [*stade*] (5). A similar sense of vulnerable rigidity in the child's ego is conveyed by Lacan's play on the etymology of *orthopedic* [*ortho* + *pais*], meaning "straight child." Lacan is quick, however, to supplement his tragic drama of the ego's brittle future with an alternative but carefully ambiguous image that suggests Leonardo's Vitruvian man. If dehiscence is a breaking out of the circle of the *Innenwelt* into the *Umwelt*, then it "generates the inexhaustible quadrature of the ego's verifications" (4). Here the emphasis on generation and inexhaustibility restores a sense of the child's capacity for dynamic growth. If, however, the "breaking out" is simply a move from a constrictive mental circle into the squared boundaries of nature, then the ego's anticipation of what is possible for the individual must always be restrictive and partial. For the moment, the drama of the mirror stage only allows one to look back on the nightmare of the fragmented body [*corps morcelé*] or forward to the ego's unending quadrature.

Lacan proceeds to ground the metaphors he has been developing by turning to works of art. He alludes to Bosch's paintings of disjointed limbs, exoscopic organs, and anatomical fragments that grow wings and arms in fantastic visual metonymies. In his triptychs of the *Last Judgment* and *The Garden of Earthly Delights*, Bosch would seem to have arrived, centuries before Dali and Lacan, at the concept of paranoic knowledge. The clarity and precision of detail amidst the confusion of sensual and horrific fantasy, the simultaneous impression of total fragmentation and obsessive order, and the double vision of hell's frenzy and heaven's calm add visual specificity to Lacan's theoretical language. Even when he seems to have moved away from painting to describe dream symbolism, Lacan could just as well be commenting on Renaissance allegorical poetry. Spenser's House of Alma, for example, gives architectural shape to the human body such that its frame seems "partly circulare" and "part triangulare," while between these two structures "a quadrate was the base" (*The Faerie Queene*, II. 9. 22). Lacan steps back from his brief investigation of the Renaissance topos of the body's castle to offer his own allegorical commentary:

> Similarly, on the mental plane, we find realized the structure of fortified works, the metaphor of which arises spontaneously, as if issuing from the symptoms themselves, to designate the mechanisms of obsessional neurosis – inversion, isolation, reduplication, cancellation and displacement. (5)

Had he attempted to deal directly with "these subjective givens alone," Lacan insists, his theoretical work would be vulnerable to the charge that it attempted to project itself "into the unthinkable of an absolute subject." That is why his interpretation of the mirror stage, while being grounded in "objective data," has been a search for "a method of symbolic reduction." His theory draws its imaginative energy from the same symbolic resources as the mirror experience itself.

The mirror stage comes to an end when the child becomes increasingly engaged in "socially elaborated situations." With the advent of "the desire of the other" all of human knowledge and culture takes on the role of mediation in that it offers an "abstract equivalence" of what the subject desires. Culture becomes in effect the metaphor for desire. As its "equivalent" or "mediatization," culture moves the desiring subject beyond his primary narcissism by which he had been joyfully transfixed before the mirror. That first experience of himself as other and the anticipation of a future that will never be now, nevertheless, make possible his entry into the symbolic order. Here Lacan fulfills the promise of his first paragraph by showing how his interpretation of the mirror stage leads to the opposition of "any philosophy directly issuing from the *Cogito*" (1). Sartre's existential psychoanalysis denies the child the entry into the symbolic. In its determination to grasp negativity by self-sufficient consciousness, existential psychoanalysis has over-invested in the ego. Indeed, Lacan implies, it knows little else than primary narcissism, as Sartre's repeated use of the mirror as a metaphor for language suggests.[14] In direct opposition to existentialism, Lacan argues that the ego "in all its structures" is constituted by its misconstructions [*méconnaissances*], failures to know, and illusions of autonomy. This is precisely why the "captation" (7) of the subject is so powerfully illuminated by the mirror stage. That experience provides "the most general formula" not only for certifiable madness but also for the madness that universally "deafens" the world. The willingness of psychoanalysis to learn from madness threatens societies where the passions are dead. As important as the task of psychoanalysis is, Lacan warns, it must self-critically reflect on its limitations. While he can accompany the patient to his oxymoronic "ecstatic limit," the analyst cannot bring him to "that point where the real journey begins."

II

"Aggressivity in Psychoanalysis"

"Aggressivity in psychoanalysis" begins with a clear announcement of its theoretical ambition. Here Lacan proposes to develop a concept that will transform the variability of clinical experience of aggression and will, thus, be "capable of scientific use" (8). In direct rebuttal to the charge that psychoanalysis is dogmatic, Lacan stresses its readiness to evolve and its receptivity to new ideas. Like the human subject it studies, psychoanalysis retains "the living mark of the different stages of its elaboration." It is, therefore, an open system, always ready to accept the challenge and to recognize the need for theoretical development. Openness implies gaps. Indeed, Freud in his heroic intellectual journey found himself at such a gap, or unpassable pass [*aporia*], when he encountered the death instinct, which confronted him like the figure of the Sphinx. Lacan repeatedly uses the word *aporia* here to capture for psychoanalysis its traditional importance in philosophy. For example, Aristotle in the *Nicomachean Ethics* (1145b 2) argues that it is one of the principal tasks of philosophy to confront the difficulty posed by *aporiai* that arise from

irreconcilable but equally plausible beliefs. If the Sphinx is the metaphor for such moments in theoretical development, perhaps it is
Freud's cherished artifact that Lacan is asking his reader to remember.
That small figure, which recalls the monumental source of Oedipus's
riddle, is both beast and woman, winged yet solidly earth-bound.
Even the term *death instinct* [*Todestrieb*] manifests this sense of an
aporia that is more than a riddle. Here *death* suddenly appears on the
"register of biology" and threatens to break what Freud called the
"Darwinian line" of his thought (SE, I: 303). In the famous sentence
in his autobiography (1925) where he describes his decision to
become a medical student, Freud balances the theories of Darwin
with a reference to an essay on nature by Goethe, which also figures
prominently in one of Freud's dreams. Strachey notes, however, that
the "Fragment über die Natur" to which Freud refers was not actually written by Goethe (SE, XX: 8). One way of reading this passage
is to allow it to claim that there never was a purely scientific or
biological phase in Freud's work, that Darwin was from the start
overshadowed by Goethe (or pseudo-Goethe). The brief autobiography was, however, written four years after *Beyond the Pleasure Principle*
(1920) and may be a strategic reshaping of Freud's intellectual history.
As in his "Seminar on 'The Purloined Letter' " and "The mirror
stage," Lacan here wants to save the biological Freud by turning that
side of him into metaphor and myth, which may indeed follow
Freud's own example. The theoretical advance requires an imaginative rereading of what comes before.

Language, Lacan emphasizes, is fundamental to psychoanalysis.
The "dialectical grasp of meaning" in psychoanalytic experience
presupposes "a subject who manifests himself . . . to the intention of
another" (9). In this paper Lacan is particularly concerned with the
other's intentions. When analysis succeeds, a subject has offered
"himself as being capable of being understood," and the analyst has
sustained "the role of ideal impersonality." Like all human activities,
however, psychoanalysis cannot avoid the possibility of error. Far
from simply coming to the analyst to recount aggressive behavior
outside the consulting room, the analysand transmits aggressivity "by
recurrence" during therapy. He relives his past as he communicates it
and thus involves the analyst in its symbolic reenactment in the present. Aggression, then, is inseparably a part of the "bipolar structure
of all subjectivity" (10). What concerns Lacan here is aggression
in the analyst no less than in the analysand. The psychoanalytic dialogue is charged at both poles by aggressivity. Lacan uses the term

l'aggressivité to signify a particular set of aggressive characteristics that manifest themselves in psychoanalysis. Aggressivity is constitutive of the human subject; it is an intentional form of aggression; it determines the form and technique of analysis; it is a correlative of narcissism and thus provides an index of the ego's structure; its prevalence offers the occasion for an understanding of modern neurosis and the perennial discontent with civilization. From the first page of his paper Lacan creates a powerful rhetorical tension between his theoretical project to account for the crucial role of aggressivity in psychoanalysis – including Freud's aporia of the death instinct – and his warning to practicing therapists that their role in the psychoanalytic encounter must be one of "ideal impersonality" in which they offer the analysand "the pure mirror of an unruffled surface" (15). Here theoretical expansiveness is balanced by strict therapeutic control.

On both sides of the analytical dialogue Lacan tightens the tension. Symbolic intention pervades the analytic experience (10). The discourse of the subject – even in his hesitations, silences, slips, inaccuracies, late arrivals, absences – is entirely purposive. It is also deliberately debilitating, no less for the analyst than for the analysand's dependants. Here too aggressivity works both ways. Just as the subject undermines and disintegrates those who are dependent on him, so too his parents may be intimidating to him by their very presence. Because aggressivity is a symbolic process, however, the absent parent is no less powerful. The inescapable, internalized images (imagos) have a "formative function" (11) on the subject. Especially powerful are the imagos of the fragmented body, which were also of critical importance in Lacan's account of "the mirror stage." To illustrate this dimension of aggressivity, Lacan ranges from the mimetic depiction of children, between the ages of two and five, disemboweling a doll to the works of Bosch, which have the power to "torment mankind." Here Lacan's theoretical language presents his translator with impossible difficulties. The task is made increasingly demanding by Lacan's assumption of a thorough understanding of Bosch's symbolic language in *The Garden of Earthly Delights*, of the possible relationships of that triptych to the *Last Judgment*,[15] of Lacan's use of both as a visual allegory of aggressivity, and of all these together as an emblem of the unsettling discoveries of psychoanalysis. At this point in Lacan's text, every reader may be entitled to offer his or her own speculative translation. My collateral (but by no means substitute) translation would be, "The prevalence among [the aggressive images in Bosch's work] of images of a primitive autoscopy of oral organs and cloacal derivatives has engendered the forms of demons" ["La prévalence parmi elles découverte par l'analyse, des images d'une autoscopie primitive des organes oraux et dérivés du cloaque, a ici engendré les formes des démons" (*É*, 105)]. Lacan then points to "the ogee of the *angustiae* of birth" (11), the double "S" shapes and birth "straits" in the painting.[16]

The central panel of the triptych is filled with visual equivalents of Lacan's image of "a vital dehiscence that is constitutive of man" (21). Exploding seed pods give birth to human forms, which in turn feed on berries and other fruits, along with Bosch's ubiquitous birds. Aquatic plants produce transparent spheres that are both pleasure domes and veined embryos. Openings in these structures, which are usually embellished with ogees, are simultaneously oral, anal, and vaginal. The right wing of the triptych, which depicts demons in hell, is no less filled with images of destruction than the central panel is packed with scenes of eroticism. Here Bosch's synaesthesia becomes horrifyingly violent. The senses of touch and sight in the left wing become mixed with taste in the central panel. In the right wing musical instruments are turned into implements of crucifixion and anal torture. A jagged knife protrudes from between two ears in place of the brain and other sensory organs. A gigantic bladder has been turned into a bagpipe. And a demonic bird of prey devours the bodies of the damned and defecates their recycled remains into a hell-hole. In so far as the three panels form a sequence, this right wing takes the viewer beyond the pleasure principle and reveals the protean aggressivity at the source of art and music. Although Freud does not allude to Bosch, it is perhaps more fitting to his and Lacan's purposes to think of the hinged wings of the triptych as closed over the central panel, which would bring Eden and Hell into proximity with the Garden of Earthly Delights, thus intermingling the images of pleasure and destruction and combining the sensual experiences of the separate panels.

Perhaps because he wishes to stress the openness of psychoanalysis to theoretical revision, Lacan portrays Freud as transfixed before the aporia of the death instinct and as failing "to recognize the existence of everything that the ego neglects" (22). Indeed, Freud would seem to mythologize the ego as an embattled warrior which is forced to fight on two fronts because of its mediating position between the internal and external worlds: "it has to defend its existence against an external world which threatens it with annihilation as well as against

an internal world that makes excessive demands" (SE, XXIII: 200).
In *Civilization and Its Discontents* (1930), however, Freud's theory of
the ego had developed to a position much closer to Lacan's:

> Normally, there is nothing of which we are more certain than the feel-
> ing of our self, of our own ego. This ego appears to us as something
> autonomous and unitary, marked off distinctly from everything else.
> That such an appearance is deceptive, and that on the contrary the ego
> is continued inwards, without any sharp delimitation, into an uncon-
> scious mental entity which we designate as the id and for which it
> serves as a kind of façade – this was a discovery first made by psycho-
> analytic research.

After citing the experience of being in love as a common instance
of the blurring of the line of demarcation between the ego and "the
outside," Freud continues,

> Pathology has made us acquainted with a great number of states in
> which the boundary lines between the ego and the external world
> become uncertain or in which they are actually drawn incorrectly.
> There are cases in which parts of a person's own body, even portions
> of his own mental life – his perceptions, thoughts, and feelings –
> appear alien to him and as not belonging to his ego; there are other
> cases in which he ascribes to the external world things that clearly
> originate in his own ego and that ought to be acknowledged by it.
> (SE, XXI: 65–6)

Here Freud's developing theory of the ego rests neither on the early
biologism of 1895–1914 nor on the heroic mythology of 1938, which
suited both the war years during which *An Outline of Psychoanalysis*
was written and its public purpose of summarizing the findings of the
crusading science with which Freud's name had become synonymous.[17] Rather, in *Civilization and Its Discontents*, Freud imagines the
mercurial and destabilized ego in a theory that anticipates Lacan's
reflections on the nightmare of the fragmented body and his repeated
allusions to Bosch in the first two papers of *Écrits: A Selection*. The
development of Freud's thinking about the ego seemed to require the
fruitful misconstruction [*méconnaissance*] of those earlier theories.

Although Lacan explicitly refers to *Civilization and Its Discontents* in
the final section of his paper (28), he gives much greater attention at
this point to a passage in *The Ego and the Id* on "negative therapeutic
reaction." In that text Freud tries out a number of images to account

for the analyst's role in therapy, alternating between metaphors of overt and subdued aggression. The analyst is engaged in a difficult "battle" with the patient's unconscious sense of guilt. Unable to overcome such an obstacle directly, the analyst adopts the gradual procedure of "unmasking" its unconscious roots. What is needed is a "similar order of strength" in the treatment to the intensity of the sense of guilt in the analysand. Such strength can only come from the personality of the analyst if he is able to allow "the patient's putting him in the place of his ego ideal." But if this happens, the analyst faces his greatest temptation, which is "to play the part of prophet, saviour and redeemer to the patient," which would deprive the patient of the freedom to come to terms with his own pathological reactions (SE, XIX: 50n.). In order to be an effective force for treatment, the analyst's aggressivity – the strength and power of his personality – must be kept in check, on the model of Christ, Socrates, or Prospero. Socrates, in Lacan's view, is "the precursor of psychoanalysis" (323), and Socratic self-effacement is a model for the necessary impersonality of the analyst.[18] By cultivating deprivation of facial expression, concealment, depersonalization, and impassibility (13), the analyst checks that tendency of self-love [*amour-propre*] which La Rochefoucauld saw as the secret motivation in all human action. Lacan credits La Rochefoucauld as having had an early insight into the divided character of the ego.[19] On the one hand, the analyst must resist the patient's attempt to involve the analyst in his illness; and on the other hand, he must resist his own temptation to adopt the role of prophet. Instead, the analyst, like Socrates, is an intellectual midwife or "maieutic" (15), who assists the patient in giving birth in a state of consciousness to what were previously latent conceptions.

The penultimate section of Lacan's paper reaches a crescendo of allusion. The studies in child development carried out by Melanie Klein, Charlotte Bühler, and Elsa Köhler; Pierre Janet's work on paranoia; Henri Wallon's mirror experiments (fully cited this time); and the anticipation of psychoanalytic discoveries by Heraclitus, St Augustine, and La Rochefoucauld are all introduced to advance the argument that "aggressivity . . . determines the formal structure of man's ego" (16). Far from being a solid fortress of defense, the ego engages in a continuous series of offensive acts, running "the whole gamut of belligerent forms;" and including "the cold war of interpretative demonstrations" (16). The ego's aggression is not only directed into its *Umwelt*. Encompassing a network of "bad internal objects" [*kakon*], the ego also has a seemingly unlimited capacity to

account for the subject's "alienation from all living contact" (20).[20]
Lacan summarizes at this point his mirror stage concept in order
to stress how much the child is deceived by its reflected image and
falsely projected future. The deception makes him get everything
wrong: both his place in the world and the solidity of his ego are not
as he expects them to be. In place of empathy and sympathetic understanding [*Einfühlung* (19)] there is only the mirror's "captation." The
failure of psychoanalysis, then, to understand the aggressivity and
alienation of the ego is in one sense perfectly understandable. It is
indeed commonplace, Lacan says, to resort to metaphors of military
fortification to describe the workings of the ego, which carefully
hides its methods of disguise, displacement, denial, and division (14).
Thus, Freud's *méconnaissance* in failing to recognize everything that the
ego "ignores, exhausts, and binds in the significations that it receives
from language" (22) might be seen as in fact providing a crucial
insight into the *méconnaissances* of the ego itself. Furthermore, "the
antidialectical attitude" of our culture works to reduce all subjectivity
to the ego precisely in order to allow "objectifying ends" to dominate
(23). To understand aggressivity as an intentional coordinate of the
ego has far-ranging implications that extend from the history of
psychoanalytic theory to the ideology of culture.

Lacan concludes his paper by exploring these implications, and
in the process he considerably escalates the rhetorical power of his
theory of aggressivity. Here Lacan's principal allusion is to Hegel's
famous section in *Phenomenology of Spirit* on the master and the slave
(B. IV. A. paras. 178–96). Lacan reads Hegel through the teaching of
Alexandre Kojève, who is not mentioned anywhere by name in *Écrits*,
however. From 1933 to 1939 Kojève conducted a series of seminars
on Hegel's *Phenomenology* at the École pratique des hautes-études,
which Lacan regularly attended. According to Kojève's reading of
Hegel, the dialectic of master and slave is of crucial importance in the
formation of consciousness. Although Hegel had been introduced
into France during his lifetime by Victor Cousin, his thought was
heavily gallicized in the process. A century after Cousin, Kojève
initiated a return to Hegel's text by concentrating on particular
chapters of the *Phenomenology* in his seminars. Like Kojève, Lacan was
to conduct a series of famous seminars in the interest of recovering
the work of an earlier master. Kojève and Lacan, who were the same
age, were both charismatic teachers; both became theorists of desire
[*Begierde*]; both were oral performers who left problematic textual
records of their thought.[21] As Elisabeth Roudinesco observes, "Lacan

was to Freud what Kojève was to Hegel; he was the interpreter of a text, but . . . Lacan identified with the 'role' of Kojève in order to re-vive . . . a subversive and initiatic vision of the Viennese discovery."[22] An important feature of Kojève's reading is that he sees Marx already anticipated in Hegel's writing, perhaps nowhere more inescap-ably than in Hegel's use of the term *self-consciousness* [*Selbstbewusstsein*], which carries the connotation of self-confidence in German, in sharp contrast to its sense of embarrassment in English. At first it may seem that the master enjoys the ultimate privilege of self-consciousness in his power over things and over the slave. But in fact what the master "does to the other he also does to himself." The only adequate recog-nition of the master's power can come from an independent consciousness, but all the slave can offer is servility. Hegel continues, "Just as lordship showed that its essential nature is the reverse of what it wants to be, so too servitude in its consummation will really turn into the opposite of what it immediately is; as a consciousness forced back into itself, it will withdraw into itself and be transformed into a truly independent consciousness." Desire seeks not an object but another's reciprocal desire. Instead of such desiring recognition, the master has engendered the slave's total alienation [*Entfremdung*]:

> Its whole being has been seized with dread; for it has experienced the fear of death, the absolute Lord. In that experience it has been quite unmanned, has trembled in every fibre of its being, and everything solid and stable has been shaken to its foundations.[23]

This passage is the seedbed from which develop Marx's concept of alienated labor and Lacan's concluding reflections on aggressivity.[24]

Aggressivity is commonly misunderstood, Lacan argues, as normal and virtuous strength, which is regarded as a natural part of the development of the ego and as indispensable in the functioning of society. Lacan audaciously suggests that such pervasive social Darwinism was already in Darwin himself, who "projected the predations of Victorian society . . . and . . . justified its predations by the image of a *laissez-faire* of the strongest predators in competition for their natural prey" (26). According to this reading, Darwin's anthropomorphic metaphors unmistakably mark the ideological foun-dation of his theory. Lacan's earlier turn to biology for his own theor-etical metaphors and his simultaneous discrediting of any sense of a literal biologism in Freud have anticipated this reading of Darwin. "The barbarism of the Darwinian century" (26) in which we live had, however, been explained even before Darwin in Hegel's master–slave conflict, which enabled him to deduce "the entire subjective and objective progress of our history." In place of the Socratic or psychoanalytic maieutic, war has come to be "the inevitable and necessary midwife of all progress" (27). Tragically, the modern promotion of the ego and its accompanying utilitarian conception of human life have made feeling seem undesirable. The machine of the modern state demands neutral subjects. Therefore, the task of psychoanalysis, before which each analyst cannot help but feel inadequate, is to confront aggressivity in the ego, to recognize the death instinct that halted even Freud, and to open up for the patient "the way of his meaning" in a world that offers the stark choice of "a discreet fraternity" or "the most formidable social hell."

III

"The Function and Field of Speech"

"The function and field of speech and language in psychoanalysis" (or the "Rome Discourse" as it is often called) is a carefully revised and expanded version of the report Lacan delivered to the Congrès des psychanalystes de langue française, which was held at the University of Rome in 1953. As he explains in the preface to the paper, Lacan is addressing the effects of a secession in the French group that led to the founding of the Société française de psychanalyse.[25] The immediate occasion of institutional politics and the effort by some analysts to stifle the speech and dissent of other members is brilliantly seized by Lacan as an opportunity to assert the fundamental importance for psychoanalysis of speech and language. If psychoanalysis is the "talking cure" (SE, XI: 13), what future can it have if analysts cease to listen to each other or neglect the language of their patients and the textuality of Freud's theories? Rome is the perfect setting for Lacan's manifesto, not only because it has traditionally been the "Universal City" (31), but also because it provided Freud with one of his most elaborately developed archaeological images for the mind in *Civilization and Its Discontents* (SE, XXI: 69–71). A major concern of Lacan's in this paper is to focus attention on "the poetics of the Freudian corpus" (102), which Freud emphasized himself in his

Roman metaphor. Rome is also symbolically suited to Lacan's purpose because of the etymological association of Mons Vaticanus with the origins of speech, according to Aulus Gellius's *Attic Nights*.[26] In order to recover the foundations of psychoanalysis in speech and language, Lacan adopts an ironic style that retains a fictional sense of oral delivery. Several times he explicitly refers to his text as a speech (55, 93) and reflects on the situation of his listeners' attempt to understand his words. Yet he also carefully indicates in his footnotes where he has amended his original text in preparing a written version for publication. Perhaps the most unusual feature of his discourse, however, is his extensive use of T. S. Eliot's *The Waste Land* as a structural analogue. Not only does he quote Eliot several times (71, 77, 106–7), he also follows Eliot's example in using his footnotes ironically. Like the notes to *The Waste Land* (or Virginia Woolf's to *Three Guineas*), Lacan's both provide his reader with the means for turning directly to neglected psychoanalytic and poetic texts and also bear witness to the fragmented condition of modern culture. In the manner of Aulus Gellius, Lacan ranges over a heterogeneous assortment of material. Citations from Rimbaud, Boileau, Mallarmé, Pascal, Molière, Valéry, and Ponge are interspersed with references to Lévi-Strauss, Malinowski, Plato, Hegel, Heidegger, and of course Freud.

There is a serious epistemological purpose in this polymathic display. In the final section of "Aggressivity in psychoanalysis" Lacan touched lightly on the place of psychoanalysis in relation to the other human sciences (26). In the "Rome Discourse" he gives this topic his sustained attention even though he avoids offering the kind of schematic account available, for example, in Michel Foucault's *The Order of Things* (*Les Mots et les choses: une archéologie des sciences humaines*, 1966). Foucault argues that from the beginning of the nineteenth century, biology, economics, and philosophy offered alternative and in some ways competing models for understanding human beings. Biology centered on the concept of function, economics on conflict, and philology on the sign. As psychology, sociology, and literary studies later emerged as distinct disciplines, each had an affinity for one of these concepts. The most creative and revolutionary work in these sciences, however, occurs, Foucault argues, when a hybridization of these concepts takes place.[27] Such cross-fertilization is particularly evident in Freud, who, in Foucault's words, "brought the knowledge of man closer to its philological and linguistic model."[28] Lacan sees an intimate relationship between the neglect of Freudian philology – particularly in the training of psychoanalysts – the increasing authoritarianism of psychoanalytic institutions, and the abandonment of creative innovation in psychoanalytic theory and practice. In no other field than psychoanalysis does the practitioner so regularly expose the capacity (or incapacity) of his judgment or so constantly need "the dialectical testing of contradictory views" (32). Neither divergence nor innovation for its own sake is of particular value, however. Rather, Lacan concludes,

> it is to be an urgent task to disengage from concepts that are being deadened by routine use the meaning that they regain both from a re-examination of their history and from a reflexion on their subjective functions. That, no doubt, is the teacher's prime function . . . If this function is neglected, meaning is obscured in an action whose effects are entirely dependent on meaning, and the rules of psychoanalytic technique, by being reduced to mere recipes, rob the analytic experience of any status as knowledge and even any criterion of reality. (33)

In order for psychoanalysis to recover its health and find a way out of "its own opacity" (34), it must become theoretically self-reflective by turning its own analytical methods back upon itself, which Lacan began to do in his reflections on the aggressivity of the analyst in his previous chapter. Now his task is to reexamine some of Freud's key theoretical concepts – without breaking "with the tradition of their terminology" (32) – by establishing their "equivalence" to certain terms and concepts in contemporary anthropology and philosophy. Here again Lacan proposes to follow Freud's example of cross-fertilizing biology and philology, but in this instance he will introduce theoretically revitalizing strains from anthropology and philosophy. Although he claims to be carrying out this ambitious project in haste – perhaps even deriving certain benefits from the urgency of his task – this is largely a rhetorical exaggeration that is consistent with his carefully crafted impression of oral immediacy and dynamic spontaneity. Lacan's language works to restore vital energy and intellectual fertility to psychoanalytic theory and practice stultified by authority, routine, professional complacency, and the neglect of Freud's vital texts.

In his brief paper on "The Acquisition of Fire" (SE, XXII: 187–93), Freud develops his allusion to Prometheus in *Civilization and Its Discontents* (SE, XXI: 90n.) by considering Prometheus as a culture hero. Lacan not only turns this language back on Freud himself by referring to his discovery of the unconscious as "truly Promethean"

(34) but also insists that such heroic discovery recurs in the daily psychoanalytic experience of the ordinary practitioner.[29] But the fire of psychoanalytic discovery is simultaneously a source of attraction and fear: "Such is the fright that seizes man when he unveils the face of his power that he turns away from it even in the very act of laying its features bare" (34). There are several controlled ambiguities in this image of Moses's veiled face that emphasize the inescapable opportunity for self-discovery by the analyst in the encounter with the analysand. After Lacan's careful attention to the negative therapeutic encounter (13), it is hardly possible to read this simply as the unveiling of the face of the analysand by the analyst. The analyst is uncovering the face of his own power [*la figure de son pouvoir* (É, 242)]. Lacan's quotation from Browning – "Flesh composed of suns" – helps to close the gap between the Promethean fire of Freud's discovery and the power of the individual analyst. Lacan's concern is with the neglect or diminishment of that power as a result of the decline in interest on the part of analysts in language and speech. As he reviews the current literature of psychoanalysis, Lacan detects a shift in emphasis away from the symbolic and toward the function of the imaginary, the concept of libidinal object relations, and the importance of counter-transference in the training of the analyst. All three of these recent emphases tempt the analyst to abandon the foundation of speech on which psychoanalysis rests. Thus, the analyst turns his back on the Promethean fire, rather than seizing it from the gods, and comes to resemble the modern anti-hero "famous for his vain exploits" (36). Cheerlessness, terror, and empty ceremonial formalism are now the distinguishing features of psychoanalysis, which has come to resemble obsessional neurosis in its mechanistic, ritual practices. By applying the psychoanalytic method to the profession of psychoanalysis, much of what passes for professional rigor is seen as an elaborate structure of defense against the power of language, against the exposure of the analyst in the therapeutic encounter, and against the misconceptions [*méconnaissances*] that mark critical moments in the history of psychoanalytic theory. When confronted, for example, with Freud's two- and three-term models (conscious-unconscious, id-ego-superego) or with his sudden discovery of the death instinct and consequent move beyond the pleasure principle, analysts are tempted to adopt an ahistorical uniformity and to ignore the creative importance of these aporiai and *méconnaissances* for the advance of theory. Lacan particularly finds this defensive strategy actively at work in the United States, where

behaviorism, human engineering, and psychology are "at the antipodes of the psychoanalytic experience" (37–8).[30] Psychoanalytic technique cannot be understood or applied without the theoretical concepts on which it is based. This requires that Freud be read, since the Promethean power of his discovery cannot be recognized without reading what he wrote. Similarly the analyst's "veil" may either be seen as the veil of Moses (Exod. 34: 33–5), which purposefully masks the analyst's power as part of the negative therapeutic encounter, or as the veil of Paul (2 Cor. 3: 13–16), which keeps understanding from taking place.

Before proceeding to examine the three parts of Lacan's paper, it may be useful to consider what he calls his "ironical style" (31). The classical definition of irony, according to Quintilian, is a figure of speech or rhetorical trope in which what is understood is contrary to what is said (*Institutionis Oratoriae*, IX. xxii. 44). Lacan's irony is much broader and deeper than this formula allows. Early in part III Lacan brings together in a single paragraph Socrates, Plato, Hegel, and Kierkegaard in order to claim that in Socrates's desire can be experienced "the still-intact enigma of the psychoanalyst" (80–1). This passage not only picks up on the identification of the psychoanalytic vocation with that of Socrates, which appears in "Aggressivity in psychoanalysis"; it also provides an important key to Lacan's sense of irony. In *The Concept of Irony* Kierkegaard finds in Hegel the understanding of irony as "infinite absolute negativity."[31] Socrates, of course, is the ultimate example of such irony considered as a way of life. The best description of Socratic irony in this larger sense appears in Gregory Vlastos's recent book *Socrates: Ironist and Moral Philosopher*:

If you are young Alcibiades courted by Socrates you are left to your own devices to decide what to make of his riddling ironies. If you go wrong and he sees you have gone wrong, he may not lift a finger to dispel your error, far less feel the obligation to knock it out of your head. If this were happening over trivia no great harm would be done. But what if it concerned the most important matters – whether or not he loves you? He says he does in that riddling way which leaves you free to take it one way though you are meant to take it in another, and when he sees you have gone wrong he lets it go. What would you say? Not, surely, that he does not care that you should know the truth, but that he cares more for something else: that if you are to come to the truth, it must be by yourself for yourself.[32]

Irony in this sense is more than a matter of rhetoric or tone. It constitutes a particular manifestation of a subject, whose power lies precisely in how he restrains his power, and in his affirmation of his listener as one who shares the same dialectical plane with him. When Lacan begins the French text of *Écrits* with Buffon's "Style is the man himself" and then modifies that to "Style is the man to whom one speaks" (*É*, 9), he would seem to be preparing for this full manifestation of his Socratic irony.

This sense of irony as a style that implicates both the speaker and the auditor is brought centrally into the psychoanalytic experience in the first paragraphs of part I of Lacan's "Rome Discourse." Socratic irony is not just the mode of presentation that Lacan has selected for this particular paper. It is the medium of exchange in therapy as well:

> psychoanalysis has only one medium: the patient's speech; . . . there is no speech without a reply, even if it is met only with silence, provided that it has an auditor. (40)

Far from celebrating speech and language for their creative, expressive, or healing potential, Lacan instead focuses on their defects and excesses. The void of silence, the labor of free association, the subject's frustration with what he says, the worn out speech act – these are neglected but critically important linguistic functions for psychoanalysis. The void of silence offers an almost irresistibly seductive temptation for the patient, analyst, or teacher. Even when the temptation to fill the void with sound is resisted and the silence is maintained, it is too easy to misinterpret the silence as marking a moment of introspection. Similarly, the labor of free association or "working through" (SE, XII: 155) may become little more than another seductive performance (100) in which the labor carried out for the analyst is but an imaginary construct in which the subject's "fundamental alienation" (42) can be rediscovered as he plays Hegelian slave to his analyst's master. Lacan's language at this point again borrows images of alienated labor from Alexandre Kojève's reading of Hegel by way of Marx, and Lacan makes the Hegelian connection with "working through" [*durcharbeiten*] explicit later in his discourse (99–100). Although he soon makes it clear that he does not value Marx as a historian, nevertheless, his positive interest lies in Marx's role as an "ideal" and as another source of revitalizing language for psychoanalysis (51). Lacan, thus, reads Marx and Hegel much as he read Darwin in the paper on aggressivity, in order to make possible the intellectual cross-fertilization that Foucault was later to describe.[33] Lacan's present point, however, is that without sufficient theoretical reflection on the function of speech and language in psychoanalysis, the therapist runs the risk of misperception and destructive intervention, which can only serve to renew the subject's "static state" (43) of alienation. What the analyst may be most reluctant to face is that he might too easily betray his own anxiety in that "his patient's freedom may be dependent upon his own intervention." Again like Socrates, the analyst must keep the subject's "certainties" in suspension "until their last mirages have been consumed" (43).

Having emphasized so unsparingly the problematics of speech, Lacan turns to Mallarmé's image of common language as a coin that has become effaced by having been passed from hand to hand. Even when it is worn out, Lacan says, speech has a valuable function as a *tessera*. Here he seems eager to exceed Mallarmé's metaphor with a more powerful and more mysterious one of his own. In the image of speech as *tessera*, or the fitting together of two halves of a broken piece of pottery to form a mysterious password, there is the sense of two active participants, unlike Mallarmé's coin metaphor. Also, Lacan goes on to suggest, the analyst is accustomed to working like an archaeologist who pieces together the shards of the patient's speech. This may, however, give the analyst the illusion of some direct "contact" with the subject's reality when in fact all that is within the analyst's reach is "the imaginary relation that links him to the subject *qua* ego" (45).

Anamnesis lies at the opposite extreme from the several examples of empty speech that Lacan has so far given. With this term he alludes in part to Freud's reflections on the technique of simply asking the patient to give an account of his own symptoms. Freud was, however, quick to stress the unreliability of this method:

> When we set out to form an opinion about the causation of a pathological state such as hysteria, we begin by adopting the method of anamnestic investigation: we question the patient or those about him in order to find out to what harmful influences they themselves attribute his having fallen ill and developed these neurotic symptoms. What we discover in this way is, of course, falsified by all the factors which commonly hide the knowledge of his own state from a patient. (SE, III: 191)

Lacan, however, works to recapture an archaic sense of anamnesis, which may be implied already in Freud's unearthing of a concept that has even greater antiquity than Plato's theory that ideas recalled in life have their origin in the pre-existence of the soul (*Meno* 85d). Lacan turns to the transition from ancient epic to the beginnings of Greek tragedy for an adequate image of hypnotic recollection. The analysand in such a state "brings back into present time the origins of his own person" (47), much as the epic poet manifests in his oral performance the origins of his culture. But in neither case is the speech a mere replaying of what has already been. Rather, the subject is as much shaped by his narrative as by the past events he relates. Here Lacan cites Heidegger's discussion of "having been" [*gewesen*] in *Being and Time*, where he argues that authentic human existence arises from the anticipation of one's own death and the full understanding of one's past.[34] The present, Lacan suggests, interweaves anticipation with recollection, and "the existent marks the convergence of the having beens" (47). For this reason psychoanalytic anamnesis is a question of truth rather than reality, of a delicate historical balance of a conjectured past and a promised future. But again Lacan insists that for such truth to come to light, interlocution is necessary. The continuity of the subject cannot be restored without an intersubjective continuity between himself and the analyst. Although the unconscious is part of the discourse of the subject, he cannot on his own get access to it in the interest of reestablishing the discursive continuity of consciousness.[35] The interlocutor makes possible this intersubjective continuity. Homer's monumental performance, for example, presupposes auditors, and Greek tragedy is played out in the presence of a chorus and spectators (47).

Part I concludes with a lengthy meditation by Lacan on his own use of metaphor and includes a directive to his readers to return to the works of Freud with continuous attention to Freud's poetics. Lacan begins by playing variations on the image of the unconscious as a verbal text: it is a "censored chapter"; the hysterical symptom can be deciphered "like an inscription"; childhood memories are "archival documents"; the recovery of one's past is an "exegesis" of an "adulterated chapter" (50). The truth of the subject's history "is not all contained in his *script*, and yet the *place is marked* there by the painful shocks he feels from knowing only his own *lines*, and not simply there, but also in *pages* whose disorder gives him little comfort" (55, emphasis added). Although the analysand recounts his unconscious experience in language (the sole medium of the psychoanalytic encounter), Lacan is not arguing here that the sole medium of the unconscious is language. Indeed, one of the principal reasons for placing such emphasis on metaphor appears to be that speech and language are too often misperceived as either transparent to reality or totally opaque to it, as though ruling out metaphorical translucence. All of language may in fact constitute an elaborate metaphorical structure. In calling attention to the metaphoricality of the subject's speech and of Freud's texts, Lacan insists that he is being stubbornly unoriginal (57). But so few analysts read Freud, preferring instead to read someone else on Freud, that Lacan's reiteration of Freud's metaphors may seem novel.[36] It is tempting to see an indebtedness by Lacan to Jakobson surfacing in his extensive discussion of metaphor in this paper, but he may be simply reflecting on Freud's rhetoric of jokes that begins with condensation and ends with metaphor and allusion (SE, VIII: 41–2).[37]

The climax of this section is Lacan's observation that the rare student who reads Freud will see that all these metaphors (Freud's, Lacan's, the analysand's) "lose their metaphorical dimension, and he will recognize that this is so because he is operating in the proper domain of the metaphor, which is simply the synonym for the symbolic displacement brought into play in the symptom" (51). Metaphor is the key to understanding the language of the patient and the poetics of Freud. If we were to reverse Lacan's priorities in the interest of understanding the processes of metaphor, this passage would say that in the "proper domain of the metaphor" where, presumably, one passes beyond the conscious linguistic choices of rhetoric and style, metaphors and symbolic displacement become indistinguishable. *Displacement* as a term has a long history in Freudian theory. It has a biological origin (SE, I: 368–71) before it passes fully into language (SE, VIII: 50–6). Laplanche and Pontalis helpfully condense this history of the term in their compact definition of it as referring to "the fact that an idea's emphasis, interest or intensity is liable to be detached from it and to pass on to other ideas, which were originally of little intensity but which are related to the first idea by a chain of associations."[38] Displacement is a process already at work in the unconscious. When it manifests itself in language – whether the analysand's, Freud's, or Lacan's – it appears as metaphor. But the analyst's imperative is to retrace its path, back from metaphor to its dynamics as symptom. The direct contrary (or negation) of this process is analogy. To take the behavior of the threadworm, jellyfish, or shrimp as analogous to that of human beings is to forget the symbolic function entirely. "Analogy is not metaphor," Lacan declares; and he concludes this section by reflecting on the consequences of reading Freud selectively, which inevitably sacrifices Freud's emphasis on specific subjectivity, the unique history of the patient, and the metaphorical language that makes him accessible in analysis.

Part II begins with a fragment of John 8:25, which was spoken by Jesus to his disciples but is now appropriated by Lacan and addressed to his auditors: "Why indeed do I speak to you at all?" This anticipates Lacan's efforts in this section to bring his own language into the foreground for theoretical self-reflection. Language and speech are, then, topics of concern on four related levels: in the unconscious, where metaphor is a synonym for the symbolic displacement of symptom; in the language of the patient during analysis, which may alternate between the empty speech of alienation or silence and the full speech of anamnesis; in the language of Freud's theories, which is highly metaphorical and strategically allusive to other disciplines, including philology; and in the language of Lacan, which taps the neglected resources of Freud's texts in order better to understand the language of the patient, which provides the only analytically available means of access to his unconscious. John's theology of the incarnate word provides an apt allusion with which to suggest the mutual interdependence of these levels in Lacan's theoretical text. Lacan reminds his listeners that his injunction "to return to the work of Freud" (57) has as its purpose the rediscovery of the psychoanalytic experience itself.

When readers take up *The Interpretation of Dreams* [*Traumdeutung*], they immediately discover that a dream "has the structure of a form of writing" (57) and that dream interpretation is a "translation" or rhetorical analysis of what might be called "oneiric discourse" (58). What this analysis uncovers is that the dream is the expression of desire. The meaning of desire, however, is to be found in the desire of the other, in the longing to be recognized by another person. Although Lacan does not mention the work of Ferdinand de Saussure explicitly in this paper, he is, nevertheless, at this point in his argument introducing Saussurean linguistics under the name of Freud. Saussure observed that it is commonly assumed that language is a nomenclature or "list of terms corresponding to a list of things".[39] This assumption, however, rests on the presupposition that ideas exist independently of words and conceals in turn two components of a sign. The sign, he argues, consists of a concept (signification) and sound pattern (signal); and "the link between signal and signification is arbitrary." Saussure speculates that an understanding of linguistic signs, because they are "entirely arbitrary," provides the best model for the study of signs – whether linguistic or not – in all aspects of social life. Linguistics, then, was to become the basis for a new science. Semiology, the science of signs, he proposed, would assume an important place in psychology.

Like Lacan, Saussure developed his theories in a series of oral presentations. Despite his ambition to position semiology centrally within psychology, Saussure's *Course in General Linguistics* alternates between meticulous descriptive detail concerning phonology and grammar and tantalizing speculation about the future of linguistic and semiological theory. Although Freud and Saussure were exact contemporaries, they had no influence on each other. Indeed, when Saussure explains the arbitrariness of the link between signal and signification as implying "simply that the signal is *unmotivated*," he seems most in need of Freud's discovery of the unconscious. Lacan brings Freudian and Saussurean theory together in order to account for the discourse of dreams and to summarize Freud's investigations of language in the psychopathology of everyday life with the elegant aphorism, "every unsuccessful act is a successful . . . discourse" (58). Saussure enables Lacan to explain the linguistic processes of the patient from two complementary points of view. On the one hand, the patient's speech is a manifestation of a continuing and unconditional desire for recognition. On the other hand, especially once "analysis becomes engaged in the path of transference" (58), his dreams are shaped, as though in anticipation of their interpretation, by the discourse of the analytic experience. In the absence of fixed concepts and signals, the signified itself is arbitrary and subject to semiological feedback from the sign.[40]

A key Freudian text for Lacan's Saussurean argument that the word is "a presence made of absence" (65) is a brief passage in *Beyond the Pleasure Principle* describing a game Freud's infant grandson invented when he was just beginning to speak. Freud describes the game in language of charming simplicity:

> The child had a wooden reel with a piece of string tied round it . . . .
> What he did was to hold the reel by the string and very skilfully throw
> it over the edge of his curtained cot, so that it disappeared into it, at
> the same time uttering his expressive "o-o-o-o." He then pulled the
> reel out of the cot again by the string and hailed its reappearance with
> a joyful "*da*" [there]. This, then, was the complete game – disappear-
> ance and return. (SE, XVIII: 15–16)

Freud and the child's mother suspected that the "o-o-o-o" was the boy's way of saying *fort* [gone]. In an important footnote that relates this story to the mirror experience, Freud explains that one day when the child's mother had been away for several hours, the boy found a way of "making *himself* disappear" (15n.). This he did by playing in front of a mirror and crouching low enough to make his image vanish from the glass. When his mother returned, he greeted her by saying, "Baby o-o-o-o!" By turning the mother's absences into a game, the child was able, Freud argues, to turn what had been painful into a pleasurable experience over which he had active control. Although Freud suggests the connection between the child's use of language and the game of *Fort! Da!*, neither here nor in his other reference to the incident in *The Interpretation of Dreams* (SE, V: 461n.) does he work out the implications of that connection. By bringing Freud and Saussure together, however, Lacan brilliantly extends the thought of both:

> Through the word – already a presence made of absence–absence itself gives itself a name in that moment of origin whose perpetual recreation Freud's genius detected in the play of the child. And from this pair of sounds modulated on presence and absence . . . there is born the world of meaning of a particular language in which the world of things will come to be arranged . . . It is the world of words that creates the world of things. (65)[41]

Freud stops short of turning the child's game into a linguistic allegory. Lacan, however, reads Freud's account of the disappearing reel as a potential theory of the play of language, implying that the child's words – *Fort! Da!* – have given rise to the game. The symbolic substitution of the reel for either the disappearing mother or the vanishing baby captures not only the arbitrariness of the link between signal and signification but also the power the child discovers he has over his world because of his symbolic faculty. The symbol has made the child what he is, in Lacan's view. His infant sounds contain the seeds that will grow into "the world of meaning" within which "the world of things" will derive its arrangement.

Lacan concludes part II by turning to Lévi-Strauss, who will be transformed into a source of ethnological metaphors with which to enrich psychoanalytic theory, just as Darwin had been in Lacan's paper on aggressivity. In "The mirror stage" Lacan borrowed freely from Wallon but did not acknowledge his debt until he later summarized the mirror concept in "Aggressivity in psychoanalysis" (18).

Similarly Lacan introduces the richly speculative ideas of Saussure
in the "Rome Discourse" but does not pay tribute to him by name
until "The Freudian thing" (125). Lévi-Strauss is also subjected to
the delayed Lacanian citation. From Lévi-Strauss's *The Elementary
Structures of Kinship* (1949), Lacan derives an important metaphor for
his distinction between the socially operative forms of discourse –
such as kinship names – and the unconscious structure of language.
Like Freud, transfixed before the death instinct in *Beyond the Pleasure
Principle*, Lévi-Strauss confronts the aporia of the incest prohibition
that frustrates his distinction between nature and culture. In Lacan's
view this prohibition becomes "identical with an order of language"
(66) through the maintenance of kinship names. The paternal function, manifested in the "name of the father" (67), combines imaginary
with real relations, language with law, signifier with signified – all in
a social formalism that conceals a powerful unconscious arbitrariness
and structural instability. Having established this uncertainty about
paternal names, Lacan identifies Rabelais's "anticipation of the discoveries of the anthropologists" (68) before he actually names Lévi-
Strauss. Once he has gone out of his way to stress the uncertainties of
language, Lacan then proceeds to his key observation that the child is
born into language, which has a more certain grip upon him than his
paternity. Language shapes the child's destiny, preceding him to "the
very place where he *is* not yet" (68), and continues to shape what
he was after his death. When it functions fully, speech not only
articulates the desire of the subject to become what he is not yet; it
also encompasses "the discourse of the other" (69) whose recognition the subject longs for. The same instability, incompleteness, and
unconditional desire is, however, also there in the other's speech.
Both the subject and the other share the dream of full speech – a
desire for the pleroma of the Word – that is no less true for being
impossible of satisfaction.[42] The life of the ego in modern society,
with all its illusions of unity, stability, and self-sufficiency, both sustains the longing for authentic communication and makes impossible
the achievement of full speech. Lacan finds an "authentic" expression (71) of the shadow that falls between desire and its enactment
in T. S. Eliot's "The Hollow Men" and *The Waste Land*. Linguistics,
however, holds the greatest promise in Lacan's view of serving as a
model for the human sciences. Its position in "the vanguard of
contemporary anthropology" (73), its advocacy of a concept of
science in the tradition of Plato's *Theaetetus* – dismissing the equation
of sense perception with knowledge (72) – and its investigations of a

wide spectrum of symbolic forms from poetry to mathematics (74–5) suit it to this role.[43] If psychoanalysis makes proper use of this model in order to recover a sense of the importance of language in analysis, it can achieve "the recreation of human meaning in an arid period of scientism" (76).

Although it is not labelled as such, part III might be read as Lacan's manifesto for a Freudian poetics. Perhaps the most unusual feature of Lacan's argument, however, is his allusive turn to Indian aesthetics for the purpose of theoretically grounding his reading of Freud. One dimension of Lacan's text is associative, taking him from Freud's account of the *Fort! Da!* game to the repetition of "Da" in the final section of *The Waste Land* and on from there to the *Upanishads*. Lacan appropriates as an epigraph for part III Eliot's epigraph for the final section of his poem; both are, however, quoting from the Latin text of the *Satyricon* that includes a quotation in Greek from the Cumean Sibyll, whose words might be taken as a summation of Freud's *Beyond the Pleasure Principle*: "I wish to die." Lacan completes the Eliotic frame by ending his paper as Eliot does his poem with phrases quoted from the *Upanishads*. The text of the *Bridhadaranyaka Upanishad*, (5.1), which attracts them both, concerns the fullness of speech, its source, and its withdrawal.[44]

The key passage for Lacan, as for Eliot, is the dialogue between Prajapâti, who is the Lord of Creation, and his offspring:

1. The threefold offspring of Prajapâti – gods, men, and devils (*asura*) – dwelt with their father Prajapâti as students of sacred knowledge (*brahmacarya*).

Having lived the life of a student of sacred knowledge, the gods said: "Speak to us, sir." To them then he spoke this syllable, "*Da*." "Did you understand?" "We did understand," said they. "You said to us, 'Restrain yourselves (*damayata*).'" "Yes (Om)!" said he. "You did understand.'

2. So then the man said to him: "Speak to us, sir." To them then he spoke this syllable, "*Da*." "Did you understand?" "We did understand," said they. "You said to us "Give (*datta*).' " "Yes (*Om*)! said he. "You did understand.'

3. So then the devils said to him: "Speak to us, sir." To them then he spoke this syllable, "*Da*." "Did you understand?" "We did understand," said they. "You said to us, 'Be compassionate (*dayadhvam*).'" "Yes (*Om*)!" said he. "You did understand".

This same thing does the divine voice here, thunder, repeat: *Da! Da! Da!* that is, restrain yourselves, give, be compassionate. One should practice this same triad: self-restraint, giving, compassion.

Several of Lacan's themes in the "Rome Discourse" can be seen as anticipated here. The arbitrariness and instability of the link between Prajapâti's syllable and the meanings assigned to it by his three groups of auditors recall Lacan's theory of the reshaping of the sign by feedback from signification, his allusion to Freud's interpretation of his grandson's game of *Fort! Da!*, Lacan's Saussurean supplement to that interpretation in the interest of turning the game into a linguistic model, his persistent reflection on the dynamics of his own speech with its demand for active participation by his auditors, and his insistence that psychoanalysts revive theory and practice by a renewed attention to Freud's poetics and the speech of their patients.

Lacan cites Kanti Chandra Pandey's *Indian Aesthetics* as the source of his material on the Hindu tradition of *dhvani*, which provides a theoretical grounding for his concepts of full speech and Freudian poetics. Pandey's comprehensive study of Eastern and Western aesthetics is no less polymathic and multidisciplinary than the writings of Aulus Gellius, Freud, and Lacan himself. Like Roman Jakobson, whose work informs Lacan's "Agency of the letter in the unconscious", Pandey was convinced that poetics and linguistics are allied disciplines. Poetics, he argues, "is an embodiment of the discoveries of the ways and means of the linguistic expression of the ideal contents of a poetic vision, for which the conventional language is inadequate."[45] Lacan's note (110n.) indicates that Pandey's study of Abhinavagupta was what most interested him. Pandey describes Abhinavagupta (AD 950–1020) as a poet and philosopher, specializing in tantra and poetics, who developed a new aesthetic theory "from the phenomenological point of view" (85). Pandey sees important similarities between Abhinavagupta and Hegel, especially in the way both thinkers assign "definite places to other systems" (85) in their philosophical work. Abhinavagupta's thought is seen by Pandey as the culmination of a tradition of "suggested meaning" [*dhvani*]. In this tradition "inspired poetry is an expression of a basic mental state," such as grief, which requires an alliance among poetics, linguistics, philosophy, and psychology for an adequate understanding of the phenomenology of its reception. Pandey does not refer to T. S. Eliot, but his understanding of tradition is strikingly similar to Eliot's view in "Tradition and the Individual Talent":

> When a theory is formulated by a genius, who discovers certain facts unknown before and reveals them to others, who are less gifted than himself, he gets a following. Thus a tradition is formed and is followed

till a greater genius comes, finds out fresh facts and formulates a theory
which, though apparently different from those of his predecessors, is
yet simply an improvement upon theirs, inasmuch as it has to take
those facts also into consideration, on which the previous theories
were based. Thus every later writer is substantially helped by the
discoveries of the earlier workers in the same or similar fields of literary activity.

What is of particular use to Lacan here is the sense of a necessary
complementarity between the original poetic utterance and the theoretically grounded response to it. The words of Prajapâti are kept
alive in the differing ways his auditors respond to his suggested
meaning and the ways such responses have been theorized by those,
like Abhinavagupta, who have kept alive the tradition of *dhvani*.
Pandey keeps that tradition alive, too, as does Lacan, who appropriates it as a model for Freudian poetic theory.

Freud's texts, like Prajapâti's "Da," manifest the inexhaustibility
of the human subject in such a way that no interpretation has yet ex-
hausted them. The point of reading and interpreting Freud by giving
careful attention to his language is not to be able to imitate him but
rather to discover the principles that govern his discourse. Although
Freud draws on the resources of "the dialectic of the consciousness-
of-self" (79) that extends from Socrates to Hegel, he does so by
"decentring" (80) the subject and recognizing its fundamental
division.[46] The immediate consequence of this discovery is that such
words as *one, other*, and *individual* can no longer be used to signify
human beings except to identify their "mirages" (80). The word *individual*, for example, asserts an indivisibility that Freud overthrows
with his discovery of the unconscious. Although Lacan retraces the
trajectory of the psychoanalytic inheritance that arcs from Socrates
and Plato through Hegel and on to Kierkegaard, he is careful to
emphasize the difference between the situation of Socrates's interlocutors and the analyst's. This he does by returning to Hegel's master-
slave dialectic, which played an important part in the argument of
the paper on aggressivity. Whereas analysts have to deal "with slaves
who think they are masters," Socrates extracts from the discourse of
slaves what is necessary to give "authentic masters" the means to
shape their power into justice by giving them access to the "truth of
the master words of the city" (81). Analysands, in contrast, want to
rely on a "universal" language to maintain their servitude. Although
it is not possible to make analysands masters of the signified, the

goal of analysis is at least to restore in them a mastery over the
signifier. The symbolic language that is brought into the light by
analysis is language that "seizes desire at the very moment in which it
is humanized" and is, therefore, "absolutely particular to the subject"
(81). In order to understand language as the pulse of desire, Lacan
makes his dramatic swerve away from the work of such ego
psychologists as Ernst Kris, who relies on the mistaken notion that
language is a sign (83), and toward the Hindu tradition of *dhvani* that
culminates in the theories of Abinavagupta.

In contrast, for example, to the dance of the bee, language (in
Lacan's view) "defines subjectivity" by referring "to the discourse
of the other" in such a way as to invest "the person to whom it is
addressed with a new reality." Speech, therefore, "always subjectively
includes its own reply." This suggests an "antinomy" in the relationship of speech to language. As language becomes increasingly func-
tional, it ceases to be proper for speech, and as speech becomes
increasingly "particular to us," it ceases to function as language (85).
Language as speech is measured by the extent of its "intersubjectivity." "The function of language," Lacan declares, "is not to inform
but to evoke."

> What I seek in speech is the response of the other. What constitutes me
> as a subject is my question. In order to be recognized by the other, I
> utter what was only in view of what will be. In order to find him, I call
> him by a name that he must assume or refuse in order to reply to me.

Indeed, language so determines the subject's identity that his being
and becoming are functions of verb tenses: "What is realized in my
history is not the past definite of what was, since it is no more, or
even the present perfect of what has been in what I am, but the future
anterior of what I shall have been for what I am in the process of
becoming" (86).[47] Language is not immaterial but is in fact a "subtle
body." "Words are trapped in all the corporeal images that captivate
the subject" (87). Thus we use such expressions as "the incarnate
word," "pregnant with speech," and the "corpus" of an author's
writings. Given this understanding of language, Lacan asserts that the
twofold goal of analysis can be simply stated as "the advent of a true
speech and the realization by the subject of his history in his relation
to a future" (88). This implies that the primary task for the analyst is
to overcome the false equation of the subject's ego with the "presence" that speaks to him. When this has been achieved, it becomes

possible to understand the meaning of the analysand's discourse in terms of the relation "between the subject's ego (*moi*) and the 'I' (*je*) of his discourse" (90).

As he moves towards the conclusion of his paper, Lacan takes the risk of explicitly offering up his own speech for the kind of analysis he has been directing at the speech of analysands and the language of Freud's texts. He also makes it plain that he has been speaking all along to two audiences at once: those analysts who share with him a common "technique of speech" and those who understand nothing of that technique but who nonetheless can be addressed "through" the Rome audience (93). To the professional analyst, he offers a series of remarks concerning the duration of the therapeutic session and the importance of using the termination of the session as a strategic point of treatment, rather than as a mechanical or routine matter of scheduling.[48] But as he proceeds to gather together the major themes of his paper – the symbolic as the only true life, the power of the death instinct to give meaning to life, the role of psychoanalysis as a mediator between knowledge and care, the need for psychoanalysis to recognize the field and function of both biology and linguistics – Lacan rhetorically identifies himself with Prajapâti and his listeners with the Devas and Asuras. Lacan's rhetorical finale builds on a crescendo of allusion to Zen (100), the pre-Socratics (102), Heidegger (103), Eliot, the *Upanishads*, and the Bible (106).

As though to condense this long and difficult paper into a single image, Lacan forges a striking metaphor for the analyst's vocation. The Tower of Babel coils round the darkness of humanity in the world [*mundus*], all of which can simultaneously be seen as Moses's brazen serpent of healing that (uncannily but nevertheless typologically) recalls the serpent coiled around the Tree of Life:

> Let [the psychoanalyst] be well acquainted with the whorl into which his period draws him in the continued enterprise of Babel, and let him be aware of his function as interpreter in the discord of languages. As for the darkness of the *mundus* around which the immense tower is coiled, let him leave to the mystic vision the task of seeing in it the putrescent serpent of life raised on an everlasting rod. (106)

This brilliant trope is a composite of the visual and the verbal and serves to affirm the inseparability of psychoanalytic theory and practice. It relies heavily, however, on the tradition of suggested meaning [*dhvani*], which also travels under the names of Socratic irony, full

speech, condensation, and Freudian poetics. Lacan invites his reader
to recall Brueghel's magnificent paintings of the Tower of Babel
simultaneously with the text of Genesis 11, which begins with a recollection of a time when there was but one language and one speech
in the world. Now, however, there is a centripetal "whorl" about a
darkness at the heart of humanity that might be at once the unconscious and the death instinct. Lacan both invokes and distances
himself from the mystic vision – or the typological interpretation of
Scripture – that would see the serpent coiled (like Brueghel's Tower)
around the Tree of Life, while it also forms the healing serpent of
Moses, which enables those who are bitten by it to live (Num. 21: 8–
9). Here is language manifesting the unconscious, the death instinct
enveloping life, an elaborate biblical text about language generating
the possibilities of psychoanalytic cure. Before his dramatic final
quotations from Prajapâti by way of Eliot, Lacan offers this summary,
which more than justifies his appeal to language that constantly tries
to leap beyond itself into painting even as it wraps itself around –
thus giving a body to – the unconscious and the death instinct:

> The psychoanalytic experience has rediscovered in man the imperative
> of the Word as the law that has formed him in his image. It
> manipulates the poetic function of language to give to his desire its
> symbolic mediation.

Here is a vast appropriation indeed. Not only has Lacan become
Prajapâti, but psychoanalysis has taken over the functions of the Old
Testament law and the New Testament logos in order to raise the
"poetic function of language" to the position of managing the link
between desire and the symbolic. Poetry could have no more exalted
function.

IV

"The Freudian Thing"

"The Freudian thing, or the meaning of the return to Freud in
psychoanalysis," which Lacan delivered as a lecture in an abbreviated
version in 1955, invokes Vienna as strongly as "The function and
field of speech" invokes Rome. In a Straussian tone that may be easily

mistaken for frivolous light-heartedness, Lacan salutes the city of dreams as a place where opera creates harmony out of a convergence of multiple cultural voices and where the Freudian revolution occurred, a revolution analogous to Copernicus's in that it initiates a reassessment of what is central.[49] Just as heliocentrism finds one cosmological center by displacing another, so too psychoanalysis finds "the very centre of the human being" in a place different from that "assigned to it by a whole humanistic tradition" (114). Now, however, even in Vienna, Freud is displaced or in eclipse; and it falls to Lacan, an outsider, to herald a return to the prophet's textual center.

Lacan repositions the Freudian revolution, its eclipse, and his call for a return to Freud in the broad context of the cultural history of Europe and America since the First World War. The initial sounds of Freud's message were drowned by the noises of the collapse of the social structure of Europe and by ensuing conflicts leading to war. The noises of the conflict that followed – "the tocsin of hate, the tumult of discord, the panic-stricken breath of war" (115) – nevertheless carried Freud's voice on their waves. Here Lacan would seem to be referring both to the circumstances surrounding the reception of Freud's thought in France, which have been so carefully reconstructed by Elisabeth Roudinesco, and to Freud's recurring allusions to the First World War.[50] (In *The Psychopathology of Everyday Life* (1901) Freud prophetically observed that misreading, more than any other parapraxis, was encouraged by war conditions (SE, VI: 112–13).) In contrast to historically burdened Europe, America, while not being free of history, parades, in Lacan's view, "a cultural ahistoricism" that is, nonetheless, a consequence of the European historical weight that it carries and that defines its limited horizon. The emigrant experience, while presupposing history as its principle of being, also aspires to abandon that principle as it seeks to base human function on the alternative principle of difference, which, Lacan insists, is a reactionary principle.[51] Although Freud, when he was invited to Clark University in Massachusetts in 1909 to deliver *Five Lectures on Psycho-analysis* (SE, XI: 9–55), considered his visit to America a fulfillment of the history and promise of psychoanalysis, Lacan prefers to highlight Freud's supposed words to Jung as they entered New York harbor: "They don't realize we're bringing them the plague" (116). Lacan recalls these words, presumably, to emphasize the shock of the primary discoveries of psychoanalysis, which in its recovery of what has been repressed has a heavy investment in the reconstitutive powers of history.

The return to Freud involves, first, "showing what psychoanalysis is not" and, second, revitalizing Freud's "primary meaning" (116). If in the process of this return any inflexibility in Freud is to be found, it is his inflexible flexibility, or his determination to retain the original, startling vitality of psychoanalysis. In this sense, Freud's texts are classics that endure such commentary as situates them historically and brings to them the continuing test of making them answer real and pressing questions. Furthermore, Lacan confesses that reading Freud's texts has made him repeatedly experience the kind of surprise that comes only from genuine discovery. In this sense, the experience of reading Freud is a witnessing of "research in action" (117), which increases in its vigor as students continually discover the transforming effects of their study of Freud's texts on their psychoanalytic practice.

Having situated his discourse in time and place, Lacan proceeds to elaborate on what he means by a return to Freud. This magnificently artful text is divided into thirteen sections, which range in tone from the charming urbanity of the first Straussian section, through the aggressive argumentation of the second, to the careful exposition of Saussure and Freud in the fifth, to the heavy sarcasm at the expense of ego psychology in the seventh, on to an elegant summary of Lacanian theory in the eleventh, and concluding with a visionary projection of the future training of analysts in the thirteenth section. This rhetorical modulation of the text is in turn punctuated by two internal monologues. In section three, truth speaks for itself, and in section seven Lacan's desk speaks about the ego.

In the course of this essay the word "thing" comes to signify truth, objectification (or *chosisme*), the ego, the other, the way psychoanalysis is practiced or, at least, the favored (and not necessarily truthful) way it is practiced. Here Lacan is reworking some of the same ground as Heidegger in his essay on "The Thing" (1950). There Heidegger distinguishes between a thing, which stands on its own or "stands forth," and an object, which "remains inside consciousness."[52] While the thing is resistant to consciousness, the object is characterized by "nearness," not in the sense that the object is accessible in space but rather that it occupies the region of spoken language. But to occupy that region is not to be readily available or securely present, rather the object in the region of spoken language is always marked by its physical non-presence there. Whereas Heidegger, in "The Thing," is drawn by the mysterious unapproachability of the fourfold, the region of things, the gathering-together of earth and sky, gods and mortals [*das Geviert*], Lacan resists and subverts those efforts within psychoanalysis either to specify the truth or goal of psychoanalysis – turning the thing into an object – or to abstract a single message from Freud's texts – turning the object into a thing – and instituting it as the psychoanalytic doctrine.

Freud's "thing" – his discovery – above all "puts truth into question" (118), which can easily be misread as a move to abandon truth entirely. Here Lacan is quick to resist Nietzsche's view that "Truth is that sort of error without which a particular type of living being could not live. The value for *life* is ultimately decisive."[53] In place of this "shoddy Nietzschean notion of the lie of life," Lacan asserts the peace that falls on the analysand with the recognition of a truth that had previously been an "unconscious tendency." Indeed, so much attention in psychoanalysis, he argues, has been given to such mechanisms of defense as displacement and regression that attention to truth, which these defenses are aligned against, has been forgotten. In this way psychoanalysis has itself become an accomplice of the ahistorical and of processes of forgetting. The site of theory has been lost amongst the technical details of process. But without truth (the truth of theory and the theory of truth) it would be impossible for either analyst or analysand to discern the face from the mask or the Minotaur from the labyrinth. As though in anticipation of Philip Rieff,[54] Lacan declares that Freud is not a moralist (119) but a discoverer of truth in its startling and beautiful nakedness. Here, in his allusion to "the proverbial emblem" (120) [*l'emblème proverbial* (*É*, 408)] of the moment when truth is suddenly illuminated, Lacan creates a composite emblem of his own. Truth is usually represented in the emblem tradition as a naked woman looking at the sun (or holding it in her right hand), while holding an open book (sometimes with a quill pen) in her left hand. She rests her foot on a globe of the world.[55] In Lacan's emblem the dramatic emphasis shifts from truth herself, surprised in her nakedness, to the discoverer who illuminates her with his light. Lacan makes this emblem "proverbial" by fusing it with a composite proverb from such texts as these: "The truth shows best being naked." "Truth will come to light." "Truth lies at the bottom of a well." "None can guess the jewel by the casket.'

In section three of his essay, titled "The thing speaks of itself," Lacan replaces his composite proverbial emblem with an imaginary monologue in the manner of Erasmus's *The Praise of Folly*.[56] Here truth, who speaks "in Freud's mouth" (121), asserts her power, takes the beast by the horns, and proclaims her nakedness as a freedom from those mere properties of truth that men have employed to hide her. As the monologue continues, Lacan manages to retain Erasmus's multiple rhetorical ironies and to appropriate much of his argument. Folly (or madness) in Erasmus's text is not a property or a normative condition. Rather than claiming that some persons are fools and others are not, his *Moriae* declares that "So provident has that great parent of mankind, Nature, been that there should not be anything without its mixture and, as it were, seasoning of Folly.'[57] Both Erasmus's Folly and Lacan's Truth sense the defensive embarrassment in their auditors as their errors and misperceptions are exposed and corrected. Philosophers are particularly singled out for their substitution of self-love for philo-sophia. Although it was not their intention, their "discourse of error" (121) has unwittingly served Truth's purposes. The "sudden transformations of errors into truths" simultaneously highlight the scandal of the perpetuation of error and the shock of Truth's discovery. Truth trusts Hegel's claim that reason is so cunning that "it will do its job without your help." Indeed, Truth promises or threatens that "Whether you flee me in fraud or think to entrap me in error, I will reach you in the mistake against which you have no refuge" (122). In the meantime, however, she wanders about in forms that seem at first glance least true: dreams, conceits, jokes, and riddles.[58] Things – even Cleopatra's nose – are now the signs of truth, or the signs of her speaking discourse.[59] In anticipation of the myth of Actaeon's hounds that is soon to follow (124), Truth tells her auditors that they will need a sharper scent than all of their Aristotelian categories to guide them in pursuit of her whose ways "pass not only through a crack too narrow to find" but also "through the inaccessible cloud of the dream," "the fascination of the mediocre," and the "impasse of absurdity." This path of Truth's trajectory might well be a catalogue of Lacan's stylistic strategies, even as the "crack too narrow to find" anticipates Derrida's strikingly similar image of "the crevice through which the yet unnameable glimmer beyond the closure can be glimpsed."[60]

Truth's last words are an enactment of her declaration that her way in the world passes through dream and things, which are in turn her dream of language and her signs of things. The net of allusion in these final sentences is cast very wide. In dramatic form, Lacan is continuing to play Truth's monologue off against Erasmus's Folly and perhaps the hypostatization of wisdom in the Book of Proverbs. In terms of philosophical tradition, his treatment of Truth's working through a world of things owes a great deal to Lucretius's *res* in

De rerum natura. In his fascinating account of dreams (IV: 756ff.), Lucretius describes the way images flash through the dreamer's mind at high speed, while being drawn from a multitude of sources at once. This would seem to be precisely the effect Lacan is after in his complex sentence on the blood-hounds of Sophocles:

> Seek, dogs that you become on hearing me, blood-hounds that Sophocles preferred to unleash upon the hermetic traces of the thief of Apollo than on the bleeding sockets of Oedipus, certain as he was of finding with him at the sinister meeting at Colonus the hour of truth. (123)

Although Lacan has yet to refer to it directly, he alludes again here to the myth of Actaeon's hounds. In Ovid's version of the story (*Metamorphoses*, III: 138ff.) Actaeon accidentally, after a day of hunting, comes upon Diana, naked in her bath. To prevent him from telling others what he has seen, Diana transforms him into the stag that he himself had hunted, whereupon his hounds turn on him. Unable to cry, "I am Actaeon," he is devoured by the hounds as he hears his companions in the distance calling his name. In Truth's monologue the emphasis falls on the first part of the narrative. Truth's auditors become hounds as they approach her on hearing her speak. Not content to identify Truth with Diana, Lacan superimposes (also without naming her) the priestess of Apollo at Delphi. The associative connection would seem to be between the hounds of Actaeon and Apollo's double identity as shepherd and thief of Delphi, which he stole from Python. The truth that Teiresias brings from Delphi in Sophocles' *Oedipus Tyrannos* precipitates Oedipus's downfall, quester after truth though he has been; but it also leads to the mysterious and wonderful circumstances of his death in *Oedipus at Colonus*. By means of this network of allusion, Lacan manages to pack into one sentence his fascination with the power of speech, his distrust of fixed or determinate identity, his observation of the displaced and deferred ways of truth, and his anticipation that those who hear the words of Truth may risk either being transformed by her or becoming her devourer. Finally, we should recall that Truth all along has been speaking "in Freud's mouth." When Lacan first delivered this paper, he spoke the words of Truth for Freud at the psychiatric conference in Vienna to an audience who had seen the prophet's message eclipsed by the very institution that he founded. But even as he heralds a return to Freud by speaking himself the startling truth of Freud, Lacan also appropriates the Freudian discovery and renames it, making Actaeon dominant even over Oedipus. Lacan would seem to favor the tragic hero of true speech over the blind hero of self-knowledge. Thus, he creates the hounds of Sophocles.

In section four – "Parade" – Lacan delays for a few more paragraphs his explicit presentation of Actaeon. Lacan's audience is first invited to imagine themselves at a "murder party" where a search for the truth takes place. It soon appears that the ego is the murderer of truth or its victim. In either case, it is the "drama of knowledge" (124) that most interests Lacan; and for this he invokes the metaphor of Actaeon. Lacan carefully divides his presentation of the metaphor into two parts. In the first part Actaeon is "in Freud" and would appear to be that driving passion for knowledge – or epistomophilia – which relentlessly leads him on to discover the goddess Truth/Diana.[61] The Diana whom Freud/Actaeon finds dwells in or beneath the surface of the earth ("chtonian" is her epithet), and she quenches her pursuer's thirst with "the smooth surface of death" along with "the quasi-mystical limit of the most rational discourse in the world." In order to understand Truth's discourse, her auditor or reader must be able to recognize the place in her text where "the symbol is substituted for death." The drama of knowledge conceived as a quest for that recognition is not performed under the sign of thanatos, however. Rather, this drive or desire is an instinct, which, in Freud's view, is distinguishable from the primary instincts of sexuality and death. In *Three Essays on the Theory of Sexuality* Freud puts it this way:

> This instinct cannot be counted among the elementary instinctual components, nor can it be classed as exclusively belonging to sexuality. Its activity corresponds on the one hand to a sublimated manner of obtaining mastery, while on the other hand it makes use of the energy of scopophilia. (SE, VII: 194)

Freud would seem to want his theory of the desire for knowledge to be both informed by and transcendent of his theories of the other instincts.

Because epistomophilia is not to be equated with the death instinct, Lacan wants to dissociate the second half of the Actaeon metaphor from Freud: "the Actaeon who is dismembered here is not Freud." Rather, it would seem to be the best of Freud's disciples – those who "can measure up to the passion that consumed him" – who are so devoured. Lacan's reference to Giordano Bruno, however, radically alters the sense of the metaphor as it is uprooted from its Ovidian context. Bruno's *De gli eroici furori* (1585), to which Lacan alludes, has been hovering over the text of "The Freudian thing" since the presentation of Truth's proverbial emblem in section three. Bruno's emblems, like Lacan's, are visual texts that have been replaced by language. Each of the sections of the *Eroici furori* includes an emblem that is described rather than engraved; the description is then followed by a sonnet that employs the images from the verbal emblem. In Bruno's text, the truth of truths resides in the absolute light of Apollo, which in turn is reflected in Diana, its shadow or moon. Diana becomes, in this version of the myth, the world of nature in which traces or "vestiges" of truth can be found. Bruno's Actaeon and his dogs search for these reflections of truth in nature. When he is transformed into the stag and devoured by his hounds, Actaeon becomes the thing he sought and attains the power to contemplate the naked Diana (II: 2).[62] The climax of the Actaeon motif in Bruno's text is strikingly Lacanian: the hunter looks into a pool and sees in its "mirrors of similitude" (I: 4) the face of divine beauty. The text persistently maintains the ambiguity of the significa- tion of the reflection: in one sense, Actaeon sees his own reflection, like the child before the mirror; in another sense, he sees a reflection of the face of Truth/Diana. He may in fact see both at once.

Above all, however, language – especially speech – is Truth's medium. But this assertion, too, is subject to extreme readings. Some will cry in dismay, "Logomachia" (or now, after Derrida, perhaps, "logocentrism"); others will insist, "Everything is language" (or again, after Derrida, "There is nothing outside the text"). Lacan, however, wants to feel the pull of these two extremes without succumbing to either. The two words, "it speaks" [*ça parle* (*É*, 413)] serve both to resist these polar positions and to summarize Freud's discovery. Although this "it" that speaks is in one sense as unname- able as Othello's "cause," Lacan has taken great care to rescue this thing from vagueness, however ambiguous it remains. This thing is Truth, who works through the unconscious and becomes manifest in language, which is the medium of the unconscious. In anticipation of the next section of his paper, Lacan directs his auditors to turn to Saussure for the linguistic component that psychoanalytic theory needs.

In section five Lacan accomplishes this appropriation of Saussurean linguistics. Here the most important insight for psychoanalysis is the distinction between the overlapping networks of the signifier and the signified. Unlike Derrida, who will analyze in minute detail Saussure's *Cours de linguistique générale*, Lacan here requires only the outline of Saussure's theory. Having established that language is a system of signs, Saussure proceeds to investigate the nature of the sign. The relations between signs and what they signify are arbitrary and loosely governed by convention. Not only are signs different from what they signify; but also, what makes possible their definition is their difference from each other. Language, therefore, in Saussure's view, is a systematic structure of difference. From these basic observations, Saussure develops the distinction between the structure of language independent of its place in history – the synchronic structure – and the structure of language in different periods of history – the diachronic structure. The consequence of these distinctions, in Lacan's view, is that "the unity of signification . . . proves never to be resolved into a pure indication of the real, but always refers back to another signification." Furthermore, signification "always proves to be in excess over things that it leaves floating within it" (126). Language, desire, and the human subject are all fractured by division and difference: the signifier from the signified, the lack from the longing, and the ego from the unconscious. Alone, the first of each of these differentiated pairs gives a false expectation of definition, attainability, and identity. This expectation is further enshrined in the legal and grammatical fictions of the "I" and in such concepts as unified consciousness and the *belle âme*. These fictions are in fact fragments or metonymies of the subject. Indeed, a crucial aspect of Freud's discovery was "the manifest disorder to be found . . . in the organism's pseudo-totality" (127). The ethic of psychoanalysis, Lacan emphasizes, has nothing to do with the *individualism* that distinguishes Marxism and American ego psychology from Freud's project. Far from being anti-humanistic, however, psychoanalysis explores the world of the human subject through language, which is the human thing.

The focal point of Lacan's theory of the place of linguistics in psychoanalysis is a single sentence from Freud's *New Introductory Lectures in Psycho-analysis*: "Wo Es war, soll Ich werden," which is translated by Strachey as "Where id was, there ego shall be" (SE, XXII: 80). This sentence appears in the context of Freud's argument that it is the intention of psychoanalysis "to strengthen the ego, to make it more independent of the super-ego, to widen its field of perception and enlarge its organization, so that it can appropriate

fresh portions of the id." Although Lacan takes great pains to correct
W. J. H. Sprott's 1933 English translation, his real but unstated quarrel would appear to be with Freud's own text. In both the *New Introductory Lectures* and *The Ego and the Id* (to which Lacan also refers),
Freud's fundamental task is to restate the project of psychoanalysis. In
both texts he does so by emphasizing the role of psychoanalysis in
strengthening the ego: "Psycho-analysis is an instrument to enable the
ego to achieve a progressive conquest of the id" (SE, XIX: 56). After
two dense paragraphs of grammatical speculation reminiscent of
Freud's own philological exercises, Lacan finally insists that what is
at stake is not a matter of "grammatical conception" (129) but rather
a matter of developing an analogy that enables the analyst to read a
symptom in such a way as to recognize its function as a signifier.
Nevertheless, it is to Lacan's purpose to violate his own Saussurean
principles in order to declare the "true meaning" of Freud's sentence
as "Where subject was, must I emerge" [*venir au jour*] (128), which
links the "I" to an indefinite future rather than shaping that future
according to an early image of what the ego shall be.

The initial obstacle to the recognition of the symptom as signifier is
the inherent resistance of discourse itself. Here Lacan's argument
briefly touches on the same ground covered by Paul de Man's essay
"The Resistance to Theory" (1982).[63] De Man argues that reading
as a theoretical problem brings into prominence the conflict between
the intuition or desire that language should be about some *thing* beyond itself and the repeated (perhaps inescapable) realization that it
is obsessively self-referential. This self-referentiality of language –
"language about language" – stands solidly in the way of making
present what language is ostensibly "about." Lacan relates this theoretical problem to the immediate task of the analyst's speaking to
the analysand. On the one hand, presumably as a check on counter-
transference, the analyst proceeds to objectify the subject; but on the
other hand, he seeks to engage the subject in such a way as to make it
possible for the subject to speak. Just as the analyst speaks to the
subject but about something else, so the analysand, when he speaks
about himself, speaks as though about "something other than that
which is in question." It is as though "the thing" speaks to the
analyst, and this thing would remain forever inaccessible to the
subject were it not for its power to elicit a response in the analyst.
Then, "having heard its message in this inverted form," the analyst
returns the message to the subject, giving "him the double satisfaction of having recognized it and of making him recognize its

truth" (131). But is it after all possible to equalize the thing and the intellect [*adaequatio rei et intellectus*]? Lacan ends this sixth section of his discourse in the confidence of that possibility. Resistance, however, continues to be a positive value in Lacan's theory, just as it was for Freud, who became suspicious of the easy acceptance of psycho-analysis in America.[64]

In section seven, however, Lacan promptly checks this optimism, demonstrating in his own text the resistance of discourse. Here he names the presiding trope of his paper – prosopopoeia – while invit-ing his auditors to consider the consequences if one of them were to dream that he was the desk from which Lacan is speaking (133). Prosopopoeia is a curious figure, which can be described as "the cata-chrestic trope that covers our ignorance of nature, death, and God. Prosopopoeia makes everything we say of these, like what we say of the human heart, an allegory."[65] When Heidegger writes about "the thing" and "the fourfold," he must resort to prosopopoeia.[66] Since *prosopon* signifies mask or face, prosopopoeia is that trope that masks an enigma.[67] On the one hand prosopopoeia may personify the non-human, as in Freud's observation that "it is in fact natural to man to personify everything that he wants to understand in order later to control it (psychical mastering as a preparation for physical master-ing)" (SE, XXI: 22). But on the other hand prosopopoeia may work to transform the human, or an aspect of the human, into an object or a thing. Lacan's term for this is *chosisme*, which might be translated, however awkwardly, as "thingification" (or perhaps "concretism").[68] The particular danger in *chosisme* is that its tropol-ogical character may be forgotten, as Lacan insists it has in ego psychology and in the behaviorial sciences, where prosopopoeia has been almost totally repressed. These sciences of unself-reflective *chosisme*, particularly as they are practiced in America, take the brunt of Lacan's sarcastic humor and protest.[69]

Is there so great a difference, Lacan asks, between the desk and us, as far as consciousness is concerned? What makes this question worthy of consideration, as by now is usual in this paper, is a power-ful image followed by its explication. First, Lacan invites his auditors to imagine one of them placed with a desk between two parallel mirrors, which reflect both the observer and the desk to infinity. The effect on the observer, when he sees his image so reflected and repeated in the same way as that of the desk, is to find himself observed "by the eyes of another" (134). This other (the observer's image) is what makes it possible for him (the observer) – and/or it (the image) – to "see itself seeing itself." For a moment, at least, this would seem to put the observer and the desk, companions in reflection that they have become, on the same level of *chosisme*. However, in an exceedingly complex performative sentence, Lacan pronounces this reflection a "mirage of consciousness" and an "inanity." What he is willing to accept, however – and this may be his central thesis – is "that the ego, and not the desk, is the seat of perceptions but in being so it reflects the essence of the objects it perceives and not its own, in so far as consciousness is its privilege, since these perceptions are very largely unconscious." The task is to get access to the unconscious presence of reflections in the ego of the essence of objects. Such is the thing Lacan seeks.

In section eight the desk speaks of the ego in a multiply ironic counterpart to Truth's Erasmian monologue. The desk begins by asking what makes the ego treated in analysis better than a desk. As the desk's monologue proceeds, Lacan's text succeeds in realizing the potentials of surrealism as a mode of parody. At one point, the desk launches a frontal attack on any ego psychologists who may be within range: "Is it not clear that there is no other way of distinguishing the healthy part of the subject's ego than by its agreement with your point of view, which, in order to be regarded as healthy, becomes the measure of things ... all of which confirms ... that the purpose of analysis is achieved with identification with the analyst's ego?" (135). Here, of course, it is important to recall that the "given" of the monologue is that one or more of Lacan's auditors is being imagined to have a dream in which he is a desk who speaks. Thus, when that thing within the auditor-analyst speaks as a thing-as-desk about the ego-as-thing, the thing within who speaks is that presumably unconscious reflection of the essence of things that has invaded the monologue from the previous section of Lacan's paper. For the ego psychologist (who may indeed be this particular dreamer), the desk is the ideal patient:

> Since with me not so much trouble has to be taken, the results are acquired at once, I am cured in advance. Since it is simply a question of substituting your discourse for mine, I am a perfect ego. (136)

At this point Lacan interrupts the monologue to confess that the desk has been under his command all along and has thus been deprived of its say. So wide is the net of Lacan's irony, however, that even his explicit rhetorical analysis of the desk's discourse remains caught in

the mesh of his surrealistic satire. In Lacan's technical vocabulary
here, his discourse and the desk's are exercises in pleonasmic anto-
nomasis (136): in more words than seem at first necessary Lacan
both substitutes a thing for a subject (desk for ego) and a subject for a
thing (the agent of desire for the ego image). By a *reductio ad absurdum*
the inherent *chosisme* of ego psychology has transformed the psychologist and the privileged ego into a piece of furniture. But all of this
has taken place under the sign of "the Freudian thing." Lacan seems
to need pleonasm in order to suggest, without explicitly saying so,
that Freud's own texts often invite such a transformation. This would
seem to be why Lacan again quotes the motto from *New Introductory
Lectures*, "Wo Es war, soll Ich werden," which allows him to point
to the place in those lectures where Freud claims that the intention
of psychoanalysis is to strengthen the ego (SE, XXII: 80) without
overtly citing that claim.[70]

Part of what is being played out at this point in Lacan's paper is the
significance for psychoanalytic theory of the dynamics of pronoun
choice and grammatical gender. To go from the English to the
French text of the desk's monologue is to be immediately struck by
the extent to which things are already personified in French even
before they are appropriated by prosopopoeia: *la chose*, *la résistance*, *le
pupitre*, *le moi*, *le je*, *le Ich*. Lacan wants to claim that such linguistic
features as these indicate both the processes by which the world of
things is reflected in the unconscious and the availability of those
processes in language. The larger units of Lacan's discourse – his
tropes and textual disruptions – serve to magnify these reflections.

Beginning with section nine, "Imaginary passion," Lacan's polemical mode gives way to a more direct exposition of his principal
theories. Here again the pronouns are important rhetorical markers:
"my fellow-man," "my desires," "I think," "I believe," "I conceive."
The effect of these simple words is to abandon the language of the
ego for that of active desire, to leave the world of things for that of
intimate subjects, all of which further serves, however retrospectively,
to highlight the rhetoric of the ego: "One can see to what the
language of the ego is reduced: intuitive illumination, recollective
command, the retorsive aggressivity of the verbal echo" (139). After
eight sections in the aggressive language of the ego's retort or echo,
Lacan invites his auditors now to consider the ego [*le moi*] as a locus
of passion.

This first involves a recapitulation of the argument of the paper on
"The mirror stage." The fundamental passion of the ego is a longing

for the narcissistic image of *amour-propre*, which is a love not for one's own body but for the always unattainable image of it. This makes *amour-propre* from the start a desire for an other. Initially, however, because of the misprisions of the mirror stage, this desire is a demand for the unconditional surrender of the other, based on the false expectation of a unity or solidity in the other, on the analogy of what is expected as the future of one's own ego. Once it is possible to recognize that the other likewise desires an other, a truce in the war of "you or I" is possible. The consequence of this recognition for the analytic situation is that psychoanalysis becomes a "game for four players" in which two subjects are "each provided with two objects, the ego and the other" (139). In the analytic situation the analyst must also recognize two others, the one who speaks to him and the Other he becomes himself to make that speaking possible. Already this begins to suggest how far inward otherness extends. As "the locus in which is constituted the I who speaks to him who hears," the other "extends as far into the subject as the laws of speech" (141): that is to say, into the very structure of the unconscious itself.

At this point Lacan folds his theoretical summation back into the presiding question of this paper: where is truth in all of these processes of symbolic processing and repression? The momentary answer to this question takes the form of a sentence that simultaneously illustrates the processes of speech it ostensibly describes: "Too early" (143) the child receives the sour grape of speech from "a father" or authority figure, which serves to authenticate "the nothingness of existence," in that the child has been previously fed by the mother on the milk of her despair. Having suckled on the mother's words of "false hope," the child receives the speech, or law, of the father as though it were the grapes of wrath. Lacan does not immediately allegorize this sentence by saying that the alternative tastes of mother's milk and father's unripe grapes produce the multiple splits in the child, as, for example, between his longing for an integrated or individuated ego and his being as a divided subject; between his unconditional desire for an undifferentiated other and his own alterity; between his dream of stable, referential language and the arbitrariness and bifurcations of signifying processes. While allowing this to be inferred, Lacan moves on to make his fundamental point that speech is the center of gravity of transference, or both its center and its gravity. This, if not the Freudian thing itself, at least makes possible an approximation of an equalizing of the thing and its intellection [*adaequatio rei et intellectus*].

Lacan concludes his paper by reminding his auditors that Freud considered the study of languages, institutions, literature, and works of art as necessary for an understanding of "the text of our experience" (144). In addition to the methods of the linguist and historian that Freud brought to psychoanalysis, Lacan adds those of the mathematician, in anticipation of his later work. In this championing of the hybridization of disciplines, Lacan offers as a definition of "true teaching" the necessity of innovation. Freud's thing, his truth, was such a teaching. Now the task continues to be what it was for Actaeon when he surprised Diana: a recognition of the complexity of truth, its humbleness and estrangement, its indifference to sex, its relation to death [*parente de la mort*], its bracingly inhuman quality – all aspects of Diana, after all, as she is surprised by Actaeon in his guilt or knowledge. But Lacan concludes by wishing that the huntsman may "let the pack pass by without hastening your step" in the hope that Diana "will recognize the hounds for what they are" (145).

V

"The Agency of the Letter"

The titles of Lacan's papers often do more than announce his topics. They may anticipate significant puns, such as the play on "stage" and "stadium" in chapter one, or they may subtly introduce key terms, such as "aggressivity" or "thing," which are subjected to careful scrutiny in the discourse of chapters two and four. It is not surprising, therefore, that when Lacan writes about the literalness of the language of the unconscious in "L'instance de la lettre dans l'inconscient ou la raison depuis Freud" problems will arise concerning the appropriate translation of his title. Alan Sheridan's translation of the phrase "l'instance de la lettre" as "the agency of the letter" has met with considerable resistance.[71] *Agency* has the sense of function or instrumentality; whereas *l'instance* suggests urgent solicitation or entreaty, as is also implied in the quotation from Leonardo with which Lacan begins. For this reason, the rendering of the title by Jan Miel in the 1966 *Yale French Studies* translation, "The insistence of the letter in the unconscious," has a certain appeal. *Instance*, however, more in French than in English, recalls Freud's *Instanz*, which he uses to designate the substructures of the psychical apparatus. *Instanz* is translated usually as *agency*, which in the context of Freud's writing suggests dynamic structure (SE, IV: 144–6). Lacan would seem to want all of these associations for his *l'instance*: the solicitating appeal of the letter, its demanding urgency, its functionality, and its embeddedness in the psychical apparatus. Before passing beyond the first word of Lacan's title, the reader is already being engulfed by the argument to follow.

Lacan delivered this paper first as a lecture in 1957 at the Sorbonne at the invitation of the Philosophy Group of the Fédération des étudiants ès lettres. The site of what has been called Lacan's first "intervention" in the University was appropriately the Amphithéâtre Descartes.[72] His lecture is at once a subversive intervention into *the* great French institution of traditional knowledge, the Sorbonne, and a continuation of his assault on the inheritance of Descartes. As the subtitle of his paper implies, reason (or its Cartesian status) has changed in the wake of Freud's discovery of the unconscious. Not only the title and the place, but also the date of Lacan's performance was significant. The year before, Jakobson and Halle had published their influential *Fundamentals of Language*; and in 1957 Noam Chomsky's *Syntactic Structures* appeared at last in print after having created great excitement and anticipation by its circulation in mimeographed form. Although Lacan now seems to have underestimated the revolutionary importance of Chomsky's work, he was clearly caught up in the intellectual excitement surrounding the new prominence of linguistics.[73]

Lacan is simultaneously concerned with returning to the language of Freud's own writings, with discovering in those writings a means of access to the language of the unconscious, and with re-creating in the language of his own texts the recurring shock of Freud's discovery and the uncanny feel of the unconscious. To do all of this Lacan fashions a language for his texts "somewhere between writing (*l'écrit*) and speech" (146). From writing, Lacan wants the means to tighten up the reader's access to his text. On the one hand, this results in assuring that the reader is left with "no other way out than the way in"; on the other, it manifests a preference for textual difficulty. From speech Lacan wants the sense of urgency and the perennially new, even at the risk of masking the difficulty of his topic. In 1956 Lacan had translated Heidegger's paper on the "Logos" for *La Psychanalyse*. In that paper Heidegger sets out to reach "into the essential origins of language."[74] What makes that enterprise difficult, Heidegger insists, is not that what is sought is remote or abstract, but rather that it is so close at hand that it cannot be easily grasped. In this respect the essence of language is like reading in its difficult pursuit of what is near at hand. For both Heidegger and Lacan, reading, like the logos, involves a gathering together or a "bringing-together-into-lying-before," a gleaning at harvest time or a gathering of fruit from the vine and the soil.[75] Such writing about language as this, with its metaphors of the soil, the grape, and the harvest, would seem initially incompatible with the rigorous terminology of a newly prominent science of linguistics. It is, however, not uncharacteristic of Lacan to be drawing on both Heidegger and Jakobson simultaneously. Reading, after all, is a "gathering together." It would seem that Lacan wants his readers (1) not to find an easy escape from his language, (2) to find in his language a means of conveyance back to the language of Freud's texts and to that of the unconscious itself, (3) to encounter at every turn the difficulty of reflecting on what is none other than one's own means of reflecting, the divided mental processes with which we desire and pursue knowledge, (4) to be critically suspicious of the ways all of these concerns have been made easy or accessible by abandoning their attendant problems and resistances. Difficulty, in short, is here a sign of theoretical legitimacy. It reminds desire of the necessity of its perpetual pursuit.

Lacan seems to have expected a sympathetic response to his emphasis on language in this paper, particularly because he is appealing to the literary training of the *étudiants ès lettres*. In making such an appeal, Lacan is following Freud's argument in *The Question of Lay Analysis*, where he writes, "Analytic instruction would include branches of knowledge which are remote from medicine and which the doctor does not come across in his practice: the history of civilization, mythology, the psychology of religion, and the science of literature" (SE, XX: 246). Freud also welcomed the corresponding appropriation of psychoanalysis by those humanistic disciplines that he drew from (SE, XX: 62), which anticipated his own and Lacan's current importance for literary studies.[76]

Lacan begins the first of the three numbered sections of "The agency of the letter" by recalling that psychoanalysis discovers the whole structure of language in the unconscious, which requires a thorough reassessment of the limited view of the unconscious as simply the locus of instincts. Although Lacan announces here clearly enough the revisionary character of his theory of the unconscious, it may not be immediately obvious that his invocation of linguistic theory is not merely an application of Saussure and Jakobson but a revision of their theories as well. Even in his medium of presentation, his hybridization of speech and writing, Lacan departs from Saussure's linguistic axiology. Saussure's antagonism to writing throughout *The Course in General Linguistics* is reflected in such phrases as "the tyranny of the written form," the "erroneous" and "pathological" changes in pronunciation that result from the introduction of writing, the "dead letters" that await resuscitation by speech, the "monstrosity" of orthography, the "external" and "abnormal" changes in language brought about by writing that are "not the result of its natural evolution."[77] Lacan, on the other hand, by locating himself "half-way between" speech and writing, proposes to take the letter of language literally ('Mais cette lettre comment faut-il la prendre ici? Tout uniment, à la lettre" *É*, 495). To read the unconscious is to read it by the letter, every jot and tittle. Even before he names the founder of modern linguistics, Lacan has already radically disrupted Saussure's theory of language by giving such prominence to the letter. Just as he positions himself between speech and writing, Lacan also arbitrates between the innate and behavioral views of language acquisition. Language is not the same as those functions of mind and body that serve it. Rather it exists "prior to the moment at which each subject at a certain point in his mental development makes his entry into it" (148). In this respect it is virtually indistinguishable from culture. Here Lacan is laying the groundwork for his theory that the letter is simultaneously a metonymy and a metaphor for language, culture, and the unconscious.

Linguistics, in Lacan's view, not only has reclassified and regrouped the sciences, it has brought about a revolution in knowledge. As he proceeds to offer an algorithm for the foundation of the linguistic revolution, Lacan keeps that revolution going by radically revising Saussure's theory of the sign even as he appears to be explicating it. Although Lacan insists on giving Saussure credit for the formulation "the signifier over the signified" (149), Saussure in fact gives the signified the hierarchical place. There is a curious irony, however, in Saussure's resorting to diagrammatic representations in the presentation of his theory of language. At one point in his text he argues that "Whether we are seeking the meaning of the Latin word *arbor* or the word by which Latin designates the concept 'tree,' it is clear that only the connexions institutionalized in the language appear to us as relevant."[78] Even before this sentence is complete, Saussure begins to punctuate his text with diagrams, including a graphic representation of a tree. Lacan, apparently sensing this irony, replaces Saussure's

illustration with two of his own. The first reverses the places Saussure
assigns to the drawing of the tree and the sign for tree (*arbor, arbre,
tree*); and the second introduces a diagram of two doors over which
appear the labels "ladies" and "gentlemen." The purpose of this
diagram is to demonstrate how the "signifier enters the signified" and
shapes its signification. The signified's function as a definable referent,
distinguishable from others, is dependent upon the signifier.

This structure of signification, in order to be imagined, requires the
metaphor of the signifying chain, the "rings of a necklace that is a
ring in another necklace made of rings" (153). Part of what Lacan is
after here is the idea that the S/s units of signification are reducible to
ultimate differential elements (the individual rings) but are, nevertheless, parts of a closed order (the necklace). Furthermore, it is possible
to move from one ring to the one that is looped through it, as one
moves from one meaning to another; but also the entire structure
loops back upon itself. Each individual pair of looped rings anticipates the structure of the entire necklace, serving as a metonymy for
it, while the necklace itself serves as a metaphor for language.
Furthermore, in the midst of the dynamism or play of the chain-as-
metaphor there is the sense that its structure can be grasped whole. It
constrains speakers while leaving them free. In this respect, metaphor
for the structure of language that it is, the signifying chain manifests
Lacan's mode of theoretical creativity. As in his entrance into
Saussure to find a place for his own linguistic theorizing, Lacan
repeatedly finds his creative freedom within a pre-existing text or
structure. He would seem to want that same destiny for all children,
born as they are into language before their mental development
enables them to manipulate its rings. Signifying, then, is a process of
insisting, rather than consisting. No single ring contains the meaning
"of which it is at the moment capable" (153), while each ring insists
that one move on to the next.

The critical limitation of the interlocking rings in the necklace as
a metaphor for language is the sense of its linearity, despite the individual circular elements of which it is made. Here Lacan picks up
on Roman Jakobson's observation that of the "two varieties of combination in language – concurrence and concatenation – it was only
the latter, the temporal sequence," which Saussure recognized.[79] In
addition to the linear structure of language, there is what Lacan finds
analogous to polyphony or reminiscent of the sounds of poetry.
Concurrence counters the forward, linear drive of discourse and its
apparent monophony by recalling earlier sounds to the ear. It also

opens up a vertical structure of "a whole articulation of relevant
contexts" that seem to cut across the linearity of the signifying chain.
Although he is not this explicit, Lacan would seem to be arguing that
at those points of intersection of the linear and the vertical in
language – or of two or more melodic lines in music – there are
"anchoring points," as when the otherwise linear and separate
melodic lines sound together. If we follow the injunction of his paper
and read Lacan here by the letter, these points are like upholstery
buttons [*points de capiton*], which tack down simultaneously the
forward movement of discourse and its vertical textuality. One thread
at least in Lacan's theory is familiar. As one reads any text, being
carried forward by its various linear structures of argument and
rhetorical expectation, there are also reiterative images – such as
Lacan's mirror or his hounds of Actaeon – that make the reader pause
and take stock, turn back and reflect, compare and reconsider. These,
one might say, are linguistic turns or theoretical moments, when self-
reflection and the demands of critique overwhelm the forward thrust
of the text. Another thread in Lacan's argument is left loose, however; this is the possibility that truth in discourse manifests itself
in those moments when the upholstery button of the letter pins down
both the linear and the vertical at once.

As though anticipating Jean Starobinski's work on Saussure's
anagrams, Lacan finds in *arbre* the very bar (*barre*) that makes possible
the "incessant sliding of the signified under the signifier."[80] Lacan
offers an impressive list of examples in which *arbre* may be seen
sliding under the *barre*: these range from the trees in the Garden of
Eden to Valéry's speaking tree in "Au Platane." The allusion to
Valéry has a surprising pertinence. As early as 1892, a decade before
the texts of Freud and Saussure that Lacan is here piecing together,
Valéry may be seen to have anticipated not only Lacan's Saussurean
complement to Freud but also Lacan's use of mathematical models
and his revision of Saussure concerning the hierarchy of the signifier. Valéry develops a theory of "subtler numbers," or $N + S$ ("nom-
bres plus subtils"), to account for the diverse interchanging and
combining of sensations or ideas in the mind. There is an inescapable quality about language for Valéry, an "in-everywhere" and "in-
everything" [$Εν παντα$ (E, 504)]. Insisting that "all things are signs
of the mind," he thinks of psychology as providing a means to
discover the conditions and possibilities of substitutions that occur in
memory, association, and comprehension. These he would represent
by equations and other mathematical symbols.[81]

Perhaps Lacan's boldest move to reveal that what appears to be new thought is already under way in earlier texts is his recollection of Quintilian's account of metonymy and metaphor, as though vaguely remembered from "some grammar of our childhood." Despite this casual way Lacan introduces Quintilian, he in fact proceeds to follow him more closely than the modern linguistic sources (Saussure and Jakobson) that are more overtly cited. In *Institutionis Oratoriae* (VIII. vi. 8–27) Quintilian not only links metaphor with metonymy; his thought also proceeds through the same steps that Lacan follows. Quintilian first defines metaphor as the substitution of the object of comparison for the thing described (vi. 9), but he then moves on to offer a purely linguistic definition of metonymy as "the substitution of one name for another" (vi. 23). Quintilian's principal examples include the substitution of the name of the inventor for the invention, or the author for his texts (vi. 26). If this definition and its accompanying examples were turned back on Lacan's text, metonymy would appear to be one of his favored tropes. "Freud" and the "letter" are both Lacanian metonyms for the unconscious. Following the example of Quintilian's definition of metonymy, Lacan offers a parallel definition of metaphor, which also recalls Dali's paranoic knowledge. Metaphor springs from "two signifiers one of which has taken the place of the other in the signifying chain," while the one replaced continues to have an occult presence "through its (metonymic) connexion with the rest of the chain" (157). These preliminary definitions lay the foundation for the second part of the paper, which is the heart of Lacan's theory of language and the unconscious in *Écrits*.

Freud was himself a passionate philologist, and his attention to language increases in intensity when his topic is the unconscious. This linguistic concentration, as in *The Interpretation of Dreams*, in turn is reflected in the texture of Freud's own discourse. Furthermore, Lacan argues, Freud had already anticipated Saussure's observation of the problematic relationship between the signifier and the signified, especially the unexpected tendency of the latter to be reshaped by the former. (Indeed, both Freud and Lacan would seem to anticipate Derrida's discussion of hieroglyphics in *Of Grammatology*: "the so-called 'ideogram' is a letter" (160).) Nevertheless, the mistaken idea that symbolism is based on natural analogy is prevalent in psychoanalysis. Dream interpretation is founded on the principle of distortion or transposition [*Entstellung*], which in Lacan's modification of Saussure amounts to the sliding of the signified under the signifier.

There are two sides to this process, condensation and displacement. Following in part the example of Jakobson, Lacan links these forms of distortion with metaphor and metonymy.[82] Condensation is the imposition of one signifier upon another. Even in Freud's word for condensation [*Verdichtung*], which includes the German word for poetry [*Dichtung*], the process of condensation is already taking place. Freud's term, Lacan says, "shows how the mechanism is con-natural with poetry" (160). Whereas the word "metaphor" in English, French, and Greek has the linear sense of one signifier or signified being carried along or conveyed to another – hence the usual term "vehicle" for the second element in metaphor – *Verdichtung* implies a vertical sense of pressure or of thickening. Displacement [*Verschiebung*] suggests dislocation, deferring, postponement; and for this reason Lacan finds it "closer to the idea of that veering off of signification that we see in metonymy" (160).

After all that Lacan has said about the sliding of the signifier under the bar to invade the place of the signified, it should not be surprising that definitions of these terms are in many ways unstable. Quintilian, for example, sometimes writes about metaphor in explicitly linguistic terms: "A noun or a verb is transferred from the place to which it properly belongs to another where there is either no *literal* term or the *transferred* is better than the *literal*" (VIII. vi. 5). At other times he refers to the substitution of an object for a thing (VIII. vi. 8). Initially, Jakobson clearly distinguishes metaphor from metonymy in order to sustain his primary distinction between two types of aphasia, one that impairs the faculty of selection and substitution and the other that impairs combination and contexture. But when he links these distinctions up with Freudian theory, his term "contiguity" becomes "Freud's metonymic 'displacement' and synecdochic 'condensation,'" while his "similarity" slides into "Freud's 'identification and symbolism.'"[83] Lacan, on the other hand, abandons Jakobson for Quintilian and associates condensation with metaphor and displacement with metonymy.[84]

The importance of these tropes, after all, for both Lacan and Freud, is their operation in "dream-work." Freud emphasizes that the essence of the dream lies in the processes of dream-work, "which transforms the latent dream into the manifest one," rather than in the latent content itself. Thus, condensation is the "first achievement of the dream-work" (SE, XV: 170–1). Lacan prefers a more homely image. For him the dream is like a game of charades in which the dumb-show is to be penetrated by the identification of some "well

known saying or variant" (161). Although, especially here in this
paper that points to the insistence of the letter, Lacan is finely tuned
to the powers of language, he also reveals his own powerful attraction to the visual, which perhaps is what most distinguishes his
imagination from Freud's. Thus, he turns to the process of applying
color to the stencil-plate for an image of dream elaboration, which
continues his elaboration of metaphorical processes in terms of visual
images. While Jakobson observes that the Romantic tradition in
poetry has almost thoroughly eclipsed metonymy with its preference
for metaphor, Lacan continues in his most congenial, high baroque
vein, favoring metonymy while seeing metaphor as its inevitable
complement. What Lacan is insisting on throughout his paper is a
literal reading of Freud, just as Freud himself insists on reading
dreams literally. Indeed, Freud refers to "dream-thoughts and dream-
content" as languages that obey "syntactic laws" (SE, IV: 277),
anticipating Lacan's most famous aphorism, "the unconscious is
structured like a language."[85] Yet from its beginnings, psychoanalysis
misconceived the role of the signifier. In part this resulted from the
development of dream interpretation before Saussure announced his
linguistic discoveries. But even more important for Lacan is the
general neglect of the art of reading literally.

In order to recover the universal laws of dreams and the
ubiquitousness of the unconscious, the topography of the unconscious needs to be mapped. Lacan chooses to do this by way of
algorithms and pseudo-mathematical symbols. Although Lacan had a
long-standing interest in mathematics, his equations and other mathematical functions serve more to fix his ideas and to fulfill mnemonic
and pedagogic purposes than to advance his theoretical project.[86] It
may be that Lacan resorts to algorithms because the word "signifier"
is itself a signifier, but what it points to is the formal network of
differences that is language. Indeed, the capacity of a signifier to
signify arises precisely from the difference between that signifier and
others and between that signifier and what it signifies. These qualities
do not as obviously apply to the word "signifier" itself. Thus, the
utility of the algorithm is its purely formal character, which leaves
open the determination of meaning. Lacan offers three such algorithms (164). The first represents the effects of the signifier on the
signified. Lacan's word for "effects" is *l'incidence*, which suggests an
unexpected "falling in" or decomposition, implying that the signified
unexpectedly occurs as an effect of the decomposition of the signifier.[87] The second algorithm represents the structure of metonymy.

Rather than being simply one among many rhetorical figures or tropes, metonymy capitalizes on a key feature of the signifier. Here one might say that metonymy is a metonymy for the signifier in its capacity of highlighting its differential partiality as an element of a signifying chain. No sooner does one chain (S) appear to be completed by another (S′) than yet another begins. The third algorithm represents the structure of metaphor. Here one signifier takes the place of another, supplanting it in the signifying chain and driving it into the realm of the signified below the bar. Where little s was there shall big S be.

None of Lacan's algorithms sustains a close examination in terms of his use of mathematical signs and functions. The curiosity of the word "algorithm" may itself have appealed to Lacan. The term "algorism" (the decimal number system) is derived from the Arabicized Persian al-Khwarizmi, the surname of the mathematician whose work on algebra in its European translation made Arabic numerals widely known. "Algorism" was refashioned as "algorithm" by association with the Greek word for number [ἀριθμός]. The word serves to illustrate at once several Lacanian rhetorical fascinations, from prosopopoeia to metonymy.

If the unconscious is the nucleus of our being, desire is its moving force. Among the enigmas of desire are its frenzied mocking of the infinite and its envelopment of knowledge and power with orgiastic pleasure. What distinguishes the energy of desire is metonymy, its "being caught in the rails – eternally stretching forth towards the *desire for something else*" (167).[88] Unconscious desire, operating as always in its symbolic mode, is both indestructible and not subject to need. Always on the move, it travels according to Freud's "dialectic of return" (SE, VII: 228), Hölderlin's "return home," and Kierkegaard's repetition. What threatens to bring the train of desire to its final destination, however, is Freud's theory of the ego, which Lacan actually repressed from his text of "The Freudian thing" (128–9). Here (168–9) Lacan offers a rare confession of his departure from Freud in order to challenge all psychoanalytic theories of the ego's centrality. But as Lacan progresses to his observation about the disturbing character of new truth, which leads him to distinguish between the "real" that we are used to and the "truth" that we repress, it remains open whether Freud represses what challenges his theory of the ego or whether Lacan here represses what to him is an uncomfortable aspect of Freud's theory. Lacan is quick, however, to admit that epistemophilia is not only the desire to know but also the desire singularly to possess knowledge in order to be "the only one to *know*" (169). Here he offers, twenty years before Harold Bloom, a concise statement of the anxiety of influence:

> Now it is quite specially necessary to the scientist, to the seer, even to the quack, that he should be the only one to *know*. The idea that deep in the simplest (and even sickest) of souls there is something ready to blossom is bad enough! But if someone seems to know as much as they about what we ought to make of it . . . then the categories of primitive, prelogical, archaic, or even magical thought, so easy to impute to others, rush to our aid! (169)

In such moments as this the desire for knowledge, the lust for power, and the resistance to belatedness all rush in at once.[89] Lacan's description here is an account of Freud's pioneering situation, but it is also equally a situating of Lacan's own position. The transmission of the shock of recognizing the unconscious processes is always subject to derailment.

The final section of this paper returns to the text of Freud's that simultaneously promotes Lacan's theory of perpetual futurity of desire and frustrates the reading that Lacan wants to give to it. In "The Freudian thing" Lacan read "Wo Es war, soll Ich werden" to signify "Where the id was, there the ego shall be;" but here he modifies that translation to read, "*I* must come to the place where *that* was" (171, emphasis added). Here Lacan wants to stress "the self's radical ex-centricity to itself," which encompasses at least the linguistic disruptions of the unconscious, the differential and deferring operations of signification, the discrete but intertwined processes of metaphors and metonyms, the driving force of desire, and the mirage of the ego as a determination of the subject's future. The most immediate source of these reflections is the perennial experience of attempting to speak or write in such a way that the integrity of thought, the demands of a given language, the rhetoric of the occasion, and the response of listeners or readers are all simultaneously engaged. Were the speaker and listener unified, stable objects, the task of speaking and writing – or of performing in all ways as a subject – would be radically simplified. Freud's tragic insight, of course, is that this is never so. Even before speaking or writing for another, the speaker already confronts another: his or her own projected identity. The recollection of the joke of the two Jews going to Cracow and the example from Gide's biography (173) simply intensify this point.

Freud, through his investigations of the insistence of the letter as it manifests itself in the signifying processes of the unconscious, should rightly be seen as heroically working against madness. But Lacan points out that the "supreme agent forever at work," digging the tunnels of madness, is none other than reason itself (174). One way of reading this is to see that the ideology of monolithic and undifferentiated reason, identity, and meaning brings madness into being and labels it as the combined process of the unconscious, language, and desire that Lacan has all along been celebrating. Read another way, burrowing reason has at last been driven underground by the Freudian revolution, forced by alterations in the relation between the subject and the signifier to change history and to modify "the moorings that anchor" being. In the face of the betrayal of Freud by psychoanalysis itself, Lacan looks to a Heideggerian recovery of Freud. That would seem to be what he evokes in his concluding comments on "humanistic man." Heidegger's "Letter on Humanism," which had been published ten years earlier than Lacan's paper, warns that "Every determination of the nature of man which takes for granted a view of the essent, without inquiring into the truth of Being, is consciously or unconsciously, metaphysical . . . Humanism, in determining the humanity of man, not only fails to inquire into the relation of Being to man but is even a hindrance in the way of such inquiry."[90] Lacan is determined to break through such a hindrance and to keep alive Freud's relentless questioning of the truth of Being.

VI

"The Signification of the Phallus"

Lacan's "The signification of the phallus," which he delivered at the Max-Planck Institute in Munich in 1958, studies the phallus as exemplary of the waywardness of the signifier, especially its detachable difference from the signified and its ultimate capacity to invade and to reshape meaning. Two dictionary definitions of "phallus" begin to give a sense of the problematics of Lacan's topic:

> *Phallus* 1. The rudiment of embryonic or fetal tissue that develops into the penis or clitoris. 2. The penis or clitoris. (*Dorland's Illustrated Medical Dictionary*, 1981)

Phallus 1a. An image of the male generative organ, symbolizing the generative power in nature, venerated in various religious systems; *spec.* that carried in solemn procession in the Dionysiac festivals in ancient Greece . . . b. The male generative organ, often in the context of its symbolical significance. (*OED*, 2nd edn. 1989)

Lacan begins his paper with the abrupt announcement that "the unconscious castration complex has the function of a knot [*noeud*]" (281). If we are to imagine this to be a Gordian knot in the signifying chain of Freudian and Lacanian discourse, which is waiting to be cut, then the theory of the castration complex is no less critical for psychoanalysis than the move beyond the pleasure principle. Lacan lists two twists in this knot: first, the place of the castration complex in the dynamic development of psychoanalytic theory, and second, its operation in the sexual development of the human subject. More loops and twists immediately follow: (1) the antinomy according to which men assume the attributes of their sex through the threat of privation of those very attributes, (2) the corresponding antinomy of absence or privation that manifests itself as penis envy [*penisneid*] in the unconscious of women, (3) the relationship between these per-mutations of the castration complex and such other highly charged theories as incest prohibition and the "phallic mother," (4) the controversies within the psychoanalytic community itself over Freud's theories of the phallic stage in human development, especially Ernest Jones's famous charge of phallocentrism against Freud, and (5) Lacan's appropriation of phallic theory to designate the processes of signification itself.

The principal difficulty in reading "The signification of the phallus," however, is not just that all of these issues are tied together in a complex theoretical knot, but also that the issues became politically charged even as Freud began theorizing about them.[91] What is most remarkable about Freud's earliest writings on the castration complex, especially in light of the controversies they aroused, is his artful creation of the child's point of view in order to suggest how early one becomes a passionate novice in sexual theory. Indeed, the tentative efforts of the child's theorizing imagination are what Freud celebrates in *The Sexual Theories of Children* (1908), which is Lacan's primary reference in this paper and the Freudian text that first puts forward the castration complex. Freud very carefully introduces these theories by warning his reader that they are erroneous:

These false sexual theories . . . all have one very curious characteristic. Although they go astray in a grotesque fashion, yet each one of them contains a fragment of real truth; and in this they are analogous to the attempts of adults, which are looked at as strokes of genius, at solving the problems of the universe which are too hard for human comprehension. (SE, IX: 215)

These theories are manifestations of a desire for knowledge that far exceeds any hope of satisfaction, and their fragmentary truth consists in how they match the child's perception and limited understanding at the time they are formed. Although they are "false" and "grotesque," these theories become instrumental in the psychic development of the child precisely because they are the child's self-reflective theories of its own development. Finally, in their relentless self-reflection and self-criticism, no less than in their passionate intensity, the sexual theories of children are noble models of theoretical activity, worthy of respectful attention and even cautious emulation. The theories are true at least in so far as they are accurate reflections of the child's understanding of sexuality.

Throughout the text of *The Sexual Theories of Children*, Freud alternates between a language of direct, child-like observation and a language of more abstract, mature critical intelligence. In this respect his writing matches the usual double point of view of a pastoral romance or a *Bildungsroman*, in which the reader is invited to identify simultaneously with the youthful personality of a character and with the more mature persona of the narrator. Because Freud's cautions about these theories have been largely forgotten in the wake of the controversy they generated, it has become difficult to hear the imagined voices of Freud's children, despite their simplicity and tentativeness. Lacan seems intent on recovering those voices as they may be heard in such Freudian passages as these:

When a small boy sees his little sister's genitals, what he says shows that his prejudice is already strong enough to satisfy his perception. He does not comment on the absence of a penis, but *invariably* says, as though by way of consolation and to put things right: "Her_____'s still quite small. But when she gets bigger it'll grow all right." (SE, IX: 216)

It is easy to observe that little girls fully share their brother's opinion of [the penis]. They develop a great interest in that part of the boy's body. But this interest promptly falls under the sway of envy. They feel themselves unfairly treated. (SE, IX: 218)

That the baby grows inside the mother's body is obviously not a
sufficient explanation. How does it get inside? What starts its development? That the father has something to do with it seems likely; he
says that the baby is *his* baby as well. Again, the penis certainly has a
share, too, in these mysterious happenings; the excitation in it which
accompanies all these activities of the child's thoughts bears witness to
this. Attached to this excitation are impulsions which the child cannot
account for – obscure urges to do something violent, to press in, to
knock to pieces, to tear open a hole somewhere. But when the child
thus seems to be well on the way to postulating the existence of the
vagina and to concluding that an incursion of this kind by his father's
penis into his mother is the act by means of which the baby is created
in his mother's body – at this juncture his enquiry is broken off in
helpless perplexity. For standing in its way is his theory that his
mother possesses a penis just as a man does, and the existence of the
cavity which receives the penis remains undiscovered by him. It is not
hard to guess that the lack of success of his intellectual efforts makes it
easier for him to reject and forget them. (SE, IX: 218–19)

Without being yet named as such, nascent theories of the castration
complex, penis envy, the phallic mother, disavowal, and epistemophilia are here being activated.[92]

Immediately after offering a topical outline of phallic discourse
(282), Lacan cites Longus's pastoral romance of *Daphnis and Chloe*,
apparently in order to stress precisely Freud's warning that the sexual
theories of children are instances of *méconnaissances*, misprisions without which knowledge or insight is not possible. In book III of
Daphnis and Chloe, a young woman named Lycaenium, who is described as too fine and delicate for country life, is married off to
Chromis, a landed man in his declining years. When she sees young
Daphnis, Lycaenium is determined to win him away from Chloe. Her
eventual seduction of Daphnis (III. 18–20) takes the form of an
"amorous lesson" in sexual initiation. From Lycaenium's point of
view this is her sexual conquest of Daphnis, while from his point of
view it is a preparation for his making love to Chloe, when he is able
to profit from Lycaenium's "lesson" (IV. 40). An oddly appropriate
feature of the text, from a psychoanalytic point of view, is that until
quite recently modern translations of Longus's pastoral romance re-
vert to Latin for the scene of Daphnis's sexual initiation, as though
to hide yet again what the amorous lesson sets out to reveal.

The artful naïveté of Longus's pastoral style is remarkably similar
to Freud's, and Daphnis's sexual theorizing anticipates that of Freud's

imaginary children. Lycaenium tells Daphnis that since she is a grown woman and not sexually innocent, their intercourse is painless for her. For Chloe, she warns, the experience will be otherwise. Being a virgin, Chloe will struggle, cry, weep, and bleed. "But do not be afraid," she tells him. Whether or not this is Lycaenium's intention, her amorous lesson inhibits Daphnis's desire for Chloe: "He did not want her to cry out, for to do so would make him seem to be her enemy; nor did he want her to cry, for to do so would make him seem to be one who wished to hurt her; nor did he want her to bleed, because in his innocence he dreaded blood and thought it only came from a wound." The knowledge Daphnis acquires from Lycaenium, however mixed with *ménconnaissances*, becomes for him nothing less than a means of prolonging desire. Indeed, the version of the story that appears in Theocritus's *First Idyll*, which is probably Longus's principal source, represents Daphnis as initially refusing love and being punished by Aphrodite with perpetually unattainable desire. Uncharacteristically, however, Lacan misreads or misremembers Longus's story. As though, perhaps, to make it a more schematic reflection of Freud's theoretical knot, he makes Lycaenium "an old woman" (283).[93] In the Greek text she is described as "young, fair, and buxom" (III. 15), not, it would seem, a phallic mother, but rather a facilitator of Daphnis's epistemophilia.

While Longus's pastoral helps Lacan recover the erroneous but important theorizing of Freud's exemplary children, Lacan's allusion to "the famous painting in the Villa di Pompeii" (288) serves as an emblematic representation of his argument that privation is the distinguishing mark of the phallus's signifying power. Here Lacan is referring to the frieze in the Villa of Mysteries, depicting an initiation ritual into the cult of Dionysus. Apparently because these mysteries posed a threat to the order and authority of the Roman state and the traditional powers of the paterfamilias, they were violently suppressed during the second century BC. One effect of the official suppression was that the mysteries became a household cult, where they were practiced in secrecy, as they obviously were in the villa where their visual record miraculously survives. Of the six panels that make up the frieze, the one Lacan alludes to is at the far end of the hall, which confronts viewers as they enter the room. There, to the right of the ritual of mask and bowl and the sacred marriage of Dionysus and Ariadne, a young woman lifts a veil from the sacred *iknon*, or winnowing-basket, which would have contained, along with the other sacred objects, the phallus that is to be revealed to initiates.[94] Not only is the phallus not visible to the viewer of the picture, the initiate herself appears to have averted her eyes from the basket just as she lifts its veil. Dominating the scene is a winged female flagellator, who would appear to be Agnoia or Ignorance. Agnoia both looks away from the *iknon* and gestures defensively towards it as she prepares to strike the initiate. Rather than being a participant in the ritual herself, Ignorance serves to externalize the fears of the initiate at the moment she uncovers the phallus. The frieze represents visually the root sense of *mystery* as a closing up of the organs of knowledge and speech, the eyes and the lips.

Part of the potency of Lacan's allusion derives from the importance the image of Pompeii had for Freud, for whom it is associated with repression, burial, and childhood (SE, IX: 85). But Lacan, in his recollection of the Villa of Mysteries, makes the connection between the buried sexual theories of childhood and the phallic initiation of the woman in the Dionysian cult, which takes him beyond Freud's own tentative theory of the phallus. Indeed, the frieze locates the phallus in its place within the unconscious: in an ancient buried city in a villa where the suppressed mysteries were secretly practiced, in a painting of a frightened initiate flagellated by her own ignorance as she lifts the veil from a basket that conceals from view the Dionysian phallus, itself detached and displaced as a ritual object in a cult of mystery. Even before he mentions Pompeii, Lacan has described the signifying function of the phallus in a way that forestalls the possibility of theoretical phallocentrism:

> For the phallus is a signifier, a signifier whose function, in the intra-subjective economy of the analysis, lifts the veil perhaps from the function it performed in the mysteries. For it is the signifier intended to designate as a whole the effects of the signified, in that the signifier conditions them by its presence as a signifier. (285)

The phallus is an emblem of the signifier *par excellence* precisely because its only presence is a dismembered absence – deferred, concealed, and buried.

Lacan's references to Freud in this paper are many and rapid. In no more than two pages of his own text he moves from *The Sexual Theories of Children* (1908) to *Civilization and Its Discontents* (1929–30) to *Analysis Terminable and Interminable* (1937). Along the way he pauses over Freud's theory of the phallic mother, which appears in *New Introductory Lectures in Psycho-analysis* (1932–3). There Freud announces provocatively that "the discovery that she is castrated is a turning-point in a girl's growth" (SE, XXII: 126). Such a sentence as this can far too easily be lifted out of the general context in which Freud advances these theories. That context includes (1) his assertion that these theories are what he names *méconnaissances* and Freud calls "false sexual theories" and (2) his insistence that the sexual identity of boys as well as girls arises under the burden of privation. Absence in both Freud's and Lacan's theories – as well as those of boys and girls – is thought to generate desire, development, and knowledge. But especially in the lecture on femininity in *New Introductory Lectures*, what draws Freud's concerned attention is the problem of what causes hostility towards the mother. Freud speculates – this is in 1932–3 – that when girls and boys come to recognize that the mother lacks what she is expected in terms of the children's phallic theory to have – a penis – this "discovery of women's lack of a penis" causes them to be "debased in value for girls just as they are for boys and later perhaps for men" (SE, XXII: 127). Rather than being itself merely phallocentric, Freud's theory is both an attempt to get at the aetiology of phallocentrism and to discover a means of lifting its veil.[95] Lacan is principally concerned with what happens when a desire for knowledge uncovers not a presence but an absence – "a privation" [*une privation* (*É*, 685)] – a discovery that unmasks all processes of signification, thus making the phallus the exemplary case of the arbitrariness of the signifier and of its disruptive invasion of signification.

VII

"The Subversion of the Subject"

"The subversion of the subject and the dialectic of desire in the Freudian unconscious" is the final paper in the English edition of *Écrits*, and it serves appropriately as a conclusion to that volume. But it is also one of Lacan's most theoretically ambitious papers, opening up as much as closing down the range of his theoretical project. Presented, like "The agency of the letter," to a philosophical audience, this text works to place Lacan's return to Freud in the context of the Western philosophical tradition, while serving at the same time as a continuation and elevation of Lacanian theory. The paper brilliantly displays Lacan's rhetorical techniques of condensation, exposition, and elaboration. As a condensation of Lacanian theory, it operates mainly through a succession of elaborate graphs in order to arrive at a single, composite theoretical image for which the term "anagogic monad" may be an apt approximation.[96] The aim of such a monad (Lacan's "completed graph" (315)) is to include in a single figure the entire theoretical structure that he has been so far building piece by piece. Such an emblematic condensation, however, is placed within a linear exposition or argument that progresses through a sequence of such topics as the structure of psychoanalytic knowledge (292–7), the language of the unconscious (297–8), the concept of the subject (298–304), the Other (304–9), the dialectic of desire (310–17), and the jouissance of love and philosophy (317–24). Overarching the condensation and exposition, there is a theoretical elaboration or escalation that lifts Lacan's previous work onto a new plane of theoretical investigation. Part of this elaboration is achieved simply by the intensity and compactness of the paper's language, which attempts to say it all in a brief space. But also there is here a fuller discussion of jouissance and a new discussion of love that takes this text beyond the reach of the earlier papers in *Écrits*, especially in its concluding discussion of Plato's *Symposium*.

The graphs, like the algorithms in "The agency of the letter," are mnemonic devices and do not constitute any sort of mathematical code or psychoanalytic metalanguage. Indeed, Lacan admits that he may incur opprobrium for their pseudo-mathematical character (318). As this paper unfolds its argument in linear time, the graphs provide anchoring points of spatial condensation as though to offer models of the signifying structure of the unconscious in a developing, tentative image or graphic sequence. The graphs lie somewhere on the horizon of the intelligible, falling in an uncharted area circumscribed by mathematics, the impossible but perennial desire for a psychoanalytic metalanguage, emblematic imagery (combining the visual and the verbal), and the disposable art of the rough sketch. The reader is clearly not free simply to invent their significance, nor are Lacan's explanations sufficient to make the graphs fully comprehensible. Rather, they function both retrospectively and prophetically at once, recalling to the reader's memory earlier arguments as far back as "The mirror stage," while anticipating theoretical work that Lacan has only just begun to write up. (In his explanatory note, he warns his readers that his "teaching has always been ahead of [his] published work" (292)).

The graphs are also performative in the sense that they entice the reader to see in each of their first three tentative stages the kind of anticipatory theory – which is ultimately a theory of desire – that they promise without ever quite delivering. In this respect they are part of Lacan's figurative arsenal that includes the torus, the Moebius strip, and the Barromean knot. The outline of the "completed" graph moves from the future of the subject – ($) – back to the point from which that future is projected – I(O) – or from the slippage of the signifier under the bar as it invades the realm of signification back to a point at which the "I" is conceived as an ego ideal, formed during the mirror stage but falsely assumed to lie in the future. This outline, then, stretches from a theory of signification back to a revision of the understanding of the "I" or human subject that has been falsely anticipated as a stable unity or ego. Arching across this outline is the vector of the signifying chain, which moves in graph I from S to S', or as Lacan rewrites it in the completed version, from signifier to voice and from jouissance to castration. What are most important here are the anchoring points at which the vector(s) cross the line of the subject at s(O), O, S(∅), ($◆D). These semiotic upholstery buttons [*points de capiton*] keep the movement of signification from being otherwise endless and arbitrary. Although Lacan is not this specific about them, these would appear to be key moments during which the subject's speech (the analysand's, for example) captures significant episodes – or moments of truth – in its reflective and reverberative history. These are also moments of multiple otherness. The O might well be the recognition that the ego ideal is an always alien and unattainable imaginary "I," while the s(O) might be understood as the inescapable other (or alterity) that is a constituent feature of the subject. The path of the vector – s(O) → O – implies that the otherness was always a part of the subject, though perhaps only discovered later at point O. The recoil back from O to e is the effect of a "short circuit" (307) by which the ego is articulated as a metonymy of the signifying powers of the subject. Finally, the graph expands – $O($◆D)S(∅)($◆O)s(O) – with the introduction of the Other whom the divided subject desires. An initial sense of that Other arises from the subject's primary conception of its own otherness (O), but it is also as an other that the subject desires. Thus, the initial formulation of desire reflects a double and a projected lack: "What do you want?" [*Che vuoi*?]. Only by the most carefully applied and meticulously restrained psychoanalytic skill does this question become, "What does he want of me?" (312.) The

vector from jouissance to castration propels the subject from auto-
eroticism to ecstacy and toward the pole of the Other, where the
privation of the castration complex leads to a reciprocal understanding of the divisions within signification and the subject. But this
capping vector awaits discussion until the final section of the paper.

It would, of course, be a perversion of the graph to imply that such
a reading as this constitutes its fixed meaning. That would be not only
a violation of its participatory mnemonic function but also an abandonment of the most basic principles of signification that Lacan
employs. Indeed, Lacan himself leaves such portions of the graph
as $i(o)eI(O) undescribed, as though to await future theoretical
developments. He also punctures any pretense of high theoretical
seriousness with jokes, colloquialisms, metaphors from poker, and
near obscenities.

As exposition, the paper sets out to account for the situation of the
human subject in relation to knowledge. Despite its vicissitudes,
psychoanalysis is best placed to provide such an account. Flanked on
one side by the philosophical tradition of Descartes and Hegel and on
the other by the empiricist dream of science, psychoanalysis has a
heavy investment in the "connaturality implied in knowledge" (294).
The word "connaturality" [*connaturalité (É*, 795)] itself helps with the
epistemological placing of psychoanalysis. On the one hand it recalls
Aquinas's famous distinction between knowledge *per cognitionem* and
knowledge *per connaturalitatem*, and Lacan soon cites Aquinas (297);
knowing by cognition only is a detached knowledge *about* a topic,
while connatural knowledge implicates the knower in what he knows.
Such a kinship of the knower and the known presupposes that knowledge of this sort is driven by love.[97] But on the other hand, "connaturality," like *connaissance*, implies too easily the association of
knowledge with birth [*naissance*]. In its mediating position between
philosophy and science, psychoanalysis is a structured form of participatory knowledge, connatural with the unconscious. It is, however,
on the "frontier between truth and knowledge" (296) that psychoanalysis operates. Herein lies Lacan's principal quarrel with Hegel,
for whom the fully conscious self [*Selbstbewusstsein*] has the potential
of achieving absolute knowledge. This total investment in consciousness enables Hegel to announce, at the end of the *Phenomenology
of Spirit*, the twin goal of life and thought: "Absolute Knowing, or
Spirit that knows itself as Spirit."[98] One consequence, however, of
Freud's discovery of the unconscious has been "the re-entry of truth
into the field of science at the same time as it gains recognition in

the field of its praxis: repressed, it reappears" (297). Knowledge is no longer, since Freud, immune to the subversion of truth, just as the subject is no longer a self-knowing consciousness. The barrier between cognition and connaturality has been permanently breached and the subject forever subverted.

The agent of this subversion is the Other. At its most immediate and inescapable this Other is a component of the subject, which may manifest itself as (or through) the unconscious, as the ego ideal projected always at the horizon of futurity, or as a terrifying form of negativity revealed in such anguished utterances as "I feel that I do not exist" or in Freud's dream of the dead father (300). Once the structure of language is discovered within the unconscious, this Other of the subject is also that structure. This linguistic Other is not, however, clearly separable from the Other as component of the subject, except perhaps as a distinguishable element of psychoanalytic theory. Lacan asserts their linkage in a single, powerful sentence: "Being of non-being, that is how *I* as subject comes on the scene, conjugated with the double aporia of a true survival that is abolished by knowledge of itself, and by a discourse in which it is death that sustains existence" (300). The Other is also another subject whom *I* desire(s). This Other is not unambiguously discrete. At first it may be the unreflected upon object of *I*'s desire and thus a reflection of the Other that is already a component of the subject. Once, however, that Other comes to be known also as a subject, "desire becomes bound up with the desire of the Other," and, consequently, "in this loop lies the desire to know" (301). At such moments when desire is energized by the insight of the Otherness of the other – or by a sense of the mutuality of divided subjectivity – both love and philosophy are born. (Here Lacan anticipates his turn to Plato's *Symposium* at the end of his paper.) This final sense of otherness binds psychoanalysis to philosophy and Lacan to the audience he is addressing in his paper.

This desire for the Otherness of the Other, arising out of the subversion of the subject, implies a dialectic of desire. The two terms "dialectic" and "desire" take Lacan, again, back to Hegel. However much Lacan's understanding of Hegel may be deflected through Kojève, there are important passages in Hegel's *Phenomenology* that are remarkably close to Lacan's theory of the Other. For example, in his section (C(AA.)B) on "the actualization of rational self-consciousness through its own activity," Hegel writes, "It is in fact in the life of a people or nation that the *Notion* of self-conscious Reason's actualization – of beholding, in the independence of the 'other',

complete *unity* with it, or having for my object the free thinghood of
an 'other' which confronts me and is the negative of myself, as my
own being-for-*myself* – that the Notion has a complete reality" (para.
350).[99] Here, however, it is reason itself that makes possible its own
actualization in the other's independence. For Hegel self-actualizing
reason overcomes desire [*Begierde*]. The closest English approximation
to Hegel's *Begierde* would seem to be "lust." When Freud develops his
concept of wish [*Wunsch*], he also closely associates it with the body,
as in this passage from *The Interpretation of Dreams*:

> A hungry baby screams or kicks helplessly. But the situation remains
> unaltered, for the excitation arising from an internal need is not due to
> a force producing a *momentary* impact but to one which is in continu-
> ous operation. A change can only come about if in some way or other
> . . . an "experience of satisfaction" can be achieved which puts an end
> to the internal stimulus. An essential component of this experience of
> satisfaction is a particular perception (that of nourishment, in our
> example) the mnemic image of which remains associated thence-
> forward with the memory trace of the excitation produced by the
> need. As a result of the link that has thus been established, next time
> this need arises a psychical impulse will at once emerge which will seek
> to re-cathect the mnemic image of the perception and to re-evoke the
> perception itself, that is to say, to re-establish the situation of the ori-
> ginal satisfaction. An impulse of this kind is what we call a wish. (SE,
> V: 565–6)

For Hegel reason overcomes lust; and for Freud wish, propelled by
need, is dissolved in its fulfillment. Lacan's dés ir is a far more ex-
pansive and subversive concept than Hegel's *Begierde* or Freud's
Wunsch. As "the gain obtained over anxiety with regard to need"
(312), Lacan's "desire" recalls King Lear's similar economics of
psychic inflation:

> O! reason not the need; our basest beggars
> Are in the poorest thing superfluous:
> Allow not nature more than nature needs,
> Man's life is cheap as beast's.

Desire takes shape in the margin of philosophical and psychoanalytic
discourse, which has despised or neglected it. But its tenuous theoretical status also reflects the marginalization of desire in the subject,

too. There, "this margin being that which is opened up by demand" is, like Lear's cry, a "request for love" (311).

Lacan pictures the margins of desire as both cramped and "trampled by the elephantine feet of the Other's whim." Though they at first seem, like the margins of a text, to be linear spaces, the sidelines of desire are also vertiginous, where each longing opens itself up to what is deeper and more remote from the sort of cathexis that Freud describes or the sort of rational transcendence that Hegel thinks possible. Part of what may justify in this connection Lacan's extraordinary sequence of biblical references (316ff.) is the anticipatory character of biblical narrative, manifested in typology and midrash, which seem to be textual equivalents of desire, especially if one reads, as Lacan appears to do, the Bible as culminating in a kerygma of love as an openness to what is beyond the subject. (Old Testament passages cited as prophecy in the New, as well as typological linkages in the Old, continue to be listed in the margins.) That this textual longing has a configuration similar to the doctrine of grace – an openness to a source of love that is beyond the subject – makes Lacan's biblical readings even more theoretically serviceable.[100] Is there, then, a sufficiently vertiginous hole in discourse, an excess of demand over need, that "the subject disappears in it" (314)? Desire, with its perpetually receding horizon and expanding expectation, would seem to be such an excess beyond satiation. No erogenous zone or specular image can contain it.

The term "dialectic" is one that Lacan, appropriately, does not find particularly problematic. He says little about it. For Hegel, dialectical method is the only method that makes scholarship and science possible. With little overt allusion to Hegel, Paul de Man has written about theoretical "blindness and insight" and Frank Kermode about "the uses of error" in ways that appropriate and abbreviate dialectic.[101] What their condensed dialectic involves is simply the creative use of what was erroneous or incomplete – *méconnaissances* – in a previous theory. Lacan reads Hegel on "lust" and Freud on "wish"; he in turn develops a theory of desire. The conditions for theory development would seem to be clear: when the first proposal is found to be faulty, another, designed to supply what the first misconceived or lacked, is proposed in its place. The previous blindness or error is not totally displaced, however. It has given birth to the new concept, which cannot obliterate all traces of its origin. The new in its turn becomes subject to revision, and so theory goes on. Lacan wants to add that such is the career of the desiring subject, too, always reflecting with a

divided consciousness on its own Hegelian progress, but always
subject to unconscious subversions: longing for knowledge, yet self-
critically aware of its own approximations and failings. This raises de
Man's "blindness," Kermode's "errors" and Lacan's *méconnaissances* to
the level of dialectical properties. Whatever confidence Hegel may
have had in his *Philosophy of History* that German society of his own
time constituted the ultimate synthesis in the dialectical movement of
Western history seems now so incredible, in light of the intervening
history of Germany, that any synthesis arising from the dialectical
tensions of thesis and antithesis must now seem tentative. For Lacan,
synthesis is clearly the weakest term in the dialectic of desire, especially because desire is driven by privation and negativity, which
"is what predestines the phallus to embody *jouissance* in the dialectic of
desire" (319).

In place of a synthesis Lacan offers an elevation or elaboration of
his theoretical project, as he turns to the Alcibiades episode in Plato's
Symposium. In certain obvious ways this dialogue parallels Lacan's
argument, especially in its image of Socrates" ladder of love that
ascends from physical desire to the love of wisdom that is philosophy
(*Symposium*, 209e–211a). But the Alcibiades episode is often read less as
a model of desire than as a misreading or *méconnaissance* of Socrates.
Before Alcibiades's arrival at the banquet of Agathon, Socrates tells
how a woman of Mantinea, called Diotima, not only instructed him
in love but also instilled in him what was to become the Socratic
method. She tells him that love, born of contrivance (his father) and
poverty (his mother), is always poor and lives in want. Like his
father, love schemes to possess what is beautiful and good, all his life
yearning after knowledge. On the same day he will flourish and meet
his death, only to rise again with new vitality. Whatever he wins, he
loses; but he manages to be neither totally poor nor rich and neither
thoroughly ignorant nor wise. Such, then, are all lovers of wisdom
(philosophers); they are an "intermediate class." Diotima concludes,
"The object of love is in all truth beautiful and delicate and perfect
and worthy to be thought happy, but what feels love has a totally
different character" (*Symposium*, 203b–204d).[102] Alcibiades arrives at
the banquet of Agathon immediately after Socrates has repeated and
affirmed Diotima's lesson. Without the benefit of Socrates's lesson in
love, Alcibiades speaks at great length in praise of Socrates, confesses
his love for him, and recounts his attempt to seduce Socrates. In
Lacan's reading of this episode, what Alcibiades longs for in Socrates
is what he has not seen. Thus Alcibiades describes Socrates's face as

like "those figures of Silenus in statuaries shops, represented holding pipes or flutes; they are hollow inside, and when they are taken apart you see that they contain little figures of gods" [ἄγαλμα].[103] Socrates shows himself to be "the precursor of psychoanalysis" (323) by naming the object of the transference, Agathon. Socrates sees that Alcibiades has told his story of the failed seduction of Socrates in order to win Agathon. Unlike the neurotic, who refuses to "sacrifice his difference . . . to the *jouissance* of an Other," Alcibiades, for Lacan, "is *par excellence* he who desires, and he who goes as far as he can along the path of *jouissance*" (323). Plato momentarily distracts his reader with Alcibiades' good looks, while leaving it to Socrates to expose his lover's poverty and cunning.

Lacan's curious rehabilitation of Alcibiades may serve a larger purpose than the exposition of jouissance. Throughout *Écrits* Lacan cunningly plays Alcibiades to Freud's Socrates. Alcibiades, Lacan observes, "projected Socrates into the ideal of the perfect Master" (323), which Lacan has also done to Freud with as much cunning and resourcefulness as Alcibiades displays in crawling into bed with Socrates. Lacan's text, like Alcibiades's narration, is an instrument of a double seduction: it is a gift of love to his readers and to Freud, replete with displays of the highest (and on occasion the lowest) rhetorical arts of the seducer.[104]

NOTES

1 For a complete bibliography of his publications, see Jöel Dor, *Bibliographie des travaux des Jacques Lacan* (Paris: Inter Editions, 1983). David Macey has a useful annotated and abbreviated bibliography in *Lacan in Contexts* (London: Verso, 1988), 210–57.

2 From 1972 the texts of Lacan's seminars began to be established by his son-in-law, Jacques-Alain Miller. Elisabeth Roudinesco describes that project this way: "Through that 'establishment,' the seminar's author was no longer quite Lacan, without being completely Miller. In brief, the established text conveys the content of a doctrine which, although Lacanian, bears the trace of Millerism – that is, of a hyperrationalist tendency within Lacanianism": *Jacques Lacan & Co.*, trans. Jeffrey Mehlman (London: Free Association Books, 1990), 567.

3 See Malcolm Bowie's *Freud, Proust and Lacan: Theory as Fiction* (Cambridge: Cambridge University Press, 1987), especially the excellent observation that "literature, for Lacan, is a Protean object of desire and . . . his theoretical texts sometimes become overwrought in their attempts to trap and devour it" (155).

4   Alan Sheridan's bibliographical note, on which considerable specu-
    lation has been based, erroneously refers to an English translation of
    the Marienbad version as having been published in *The International
    Journal of Psychoanalysis*, 18 (January, 1937). Lacan himself admits in a
    footnote that he neglected to submit the paper for the report of the
    conference (*É*, 67).

5   Henri Wallon, "Comment se développe chez l'enfant la notion de
    corps propre," *Journal de psychologie* (November-December, 1931), 705–
    48, and *Les Origines du caractère chez l'enfant* (Paris: Bovin, 1934). For
    commentary on Wallon's work and his relationship to Lacan, see
    Roudinesco, 66–71, 142–4. In "Propos sur la causalité psychique"
    (1946), Lacan returns again to the mirror stage concept, again without
    referring to Wallon (*É*, 151).

6   Roudinesco, 143.

7   Salvador Dali, "L'âne pourri", *SASDLR*, 1 (July, 1930), 9–10.

8   One of the drawings is reproduced in Dawn Ades, *Dali* (London:
    Thames & Hudson, 1982), illus. 64. For Freud's comments on Dali,
    see his letter to Stefan Zweig (July 20, 1938) in *Letters of Sigmund Freud
    1873–1939*, ed. Ernest L. Freud, trans. Tania and James Stern
    (London: Hogarth Press, 1961).

9   Dali's praise of Lacan appears in his "Interprétation paranoïaque-
    critique de l'image obsédante: l'angélus de Millet," *Le Minotaure*, 1
    (June, 1933), 10. Lacan's paper, "Le problème du style et la conception
    psychiatrique des formes paranoïaques de l'existence" was published in
    the same issue (68–9).

10 David Macey also detects here an allusion to Claudel's pun on *co-
    naissance* as *knowledge* and *co-birth: Lacan in Contexts*, 63. For a full
    discussion of Lacan, Dali, and Surrealism, see Roudinesco, esp. 3–34,
    110–13, and Macey, 44–74.

11 For an account of Caillois, Lacan, and the founding of the Collège de
    sociologie, see Denis Hollier, *Le Collège de sociologie* (Paris: Gallimard,
    1979).

12 I have greatly simplified this difficult text by substituting definitions in
    brackets for some of Freud's more obscure symbols.

13 Martin Heidegger, *Introduction to Metaphysics*, trans. Ralph Manheim
    (New Haven: Yale University Press, 1959 (originally published 1935)),
    14.

14 On Lacan's difficult relationship with Sartre, see Macey, 103–7, and
    Roudinesco, 623–4.

15 Although paintings with this title in Vienna and in Munich have been
    attributed to Bosch, the consensus is now that his painting, com-
    missioned in 1504 by Philip the Fair, has been lost.

16 A good set of reproductions can be consulted in John Rowlands, *Bosch*
    (London: Phaidon, 1975), plates 17–26.

17 See Strachey's note on the composition of the *Outline* (SE, XXIII: 142).

18 Freud's single overt reference to Socrates in the Standard Edition is buried in a footnote (SE, X: 240n.), although he often alludes to Socrates without naming him. Alcibiades' love for Socrates in the *Symposium* forms part of the subtext for Freud's discussion of aggression and the origins of homosexuality in *The Ego and the Id* (SE, XIX:43).

19 See for example Maxim 105, which begins, "L'amour-propre est l'amour de soi-même, et de toutes choses, pour soi; il est plus habile que le plus habile homme du monde": *Oeuvres complètes*, ed. L. Martin-Chauffier (Paris: Gallimard, 1957), 322.

20 Lacan is drawing here on Melanie Klein's "The Importance of Symbol Formation in the Development of the Ego" (1930), which argues that "there is an early stage of mental development at which sadism becomes active at all the various sources of libidinal pleasure." This sadism is manifested, according to Klein, in "the subject's dominant aim . . . to possess himself of the contents of the mother's body and to destroy her": *The Selected Melanie Klein*, ed. Juliet Mitchell (London: Penguin Books, 1986), 95–6.

21 The published version of Kojève's seminar, *Introduction à la lecture de Hegel. Leçons sur la phénoménologie de l'esprit professées de 1933 à 1939 à l'École des hautes-études* (Paris: Gallimard, 1947), is a meticulously prepared set of notes by Raymond Queneau.

22 Roudinesco, 141. See also her excellent discussion of the general impact of Kojève's teaching (134–42), which concludes with the anecdote of Lacan's taking possession of Kojève's annotated text of the *Phenomenology* in 1968. For a comprehensive assessment of Kojève's thought, see Dominique Auffret, *Alexandre Kojève: la philosophie, l'État, la fin de l'Histoire* (Paris: Grasset, 1990).

23 G. W. F. Hegel, *Phenomenology of Spirit*, trans. A. V. Miller (Oxford: Oxford University Press, 1977), 116–17 (sections 191, 193, 194).

24 Cf., however, Malcolm Bowie's attempt to draw a sharp distinction between Marx's and Lacan's concepts of alienation on the grounds that Lacan's alienation is permanent while Marx's is not: *Lacan* (London: Fontana Press, 1991), 24–5.

25 For a detailed account of the relationships between the International Psychoanalytical Association (IPA) and the the Société française de psychanalyse (SFP), see Roudinesco, 277–369.

26 Lacan's allusion is to *Noctes Atticae*, 16. 17. 2. Lacan's attraction to Aulus Gellius is quite understandable: Gellius venerated all forms of learning, including philosophy, language, literature, history, and law; he was meticulously textual in what he wrote about other authors; and his careful and extensive citations preserve a great deal of archaic material that would otherwise have been lost.

27   See especially *The Order of Things* (London: Tavistock, 1970), 313. John
     Forrester has carefully tested Foucault's hypothesis in terms of the
     history of psychoanalysis in *Language and the Origins of Psychoanalysis*
     (London: Macmillan, 1980), 166–212, and "Michel Foucault and the
     History of Psychoanalysis" in *The Seduction of Psychoanalysis* (Cam-
     bridge: Cambridge University Press, 1990), 286–316.

28   *The Order of Things*, 361. When considering the reception history of this
     material, it is useful to keep in mind that *Écrits* and Foucault's *Les
     Mots et les choses* were both published in 1966.

29   One of the best accounts of Freud's characterization of himself as hero
     is Malcolm Bowie's essay on "Freud's dreams of knowledge" in *Freud,
     Proust and Lacan*, esp. 27–35.

30   A recent sign of this situation is the appearance of Joseph H. Smith's
     Arguing with Lacan: Ego Psychology and Language (New Haven: Yale
     University Press, 1991).

31   Søren Kierkegaard, *The Concept of Irony*, trans. Lee Capel (Blooming-
     ton: Indiana University Press, 1965), 276.

32   Vlastos, *Socrates* (Cambridge: Cambridge University Press, 1991),
     44.

33   Anthony Wilden did not share this view. See his monumental com-
     mentary on the "Rome discourse': *Speech and Language in Psychoanalysis*
     (Baltimore: Johns Hopkins University Press, 1968), 285, 290. Wilden
     reads Lacan as more closely parallel to R. D. Laing's existential theory
     of schizophrenia than now seems credible. Laing's *The Divided Self*
     (1960) was issued in paperback in 1965 and was much in vogue when
     Wilden's commentary was published.

34   Martin Heidegger, *Being and Time* (1927), trans. J. Macquarrie and E.
     Robinson (London: SCM Press, 1962), 373.

35   Lacan's famous aphorism, "The unconscious is structured like a
     language," is anticipated here although it does not in fact appear until
     The Four Fundamental Concepts of Psycho-analysis (1973), trans. Alan
     Sheridan (Harmondsworth: Penguin, 1979), 20.

36   Indeed, before the publication of Malcolm Bowie's *Freud, Proust and
     Lacan*, Stanley Edgar Hyman's *The Tangled Bank* (New York: Atheneum,
     1962) was one of the few studies of Freud's metaphors available.

37   Wilden at this point offers a detailed discussion of Jakobson on meta-
     phor (244–6), which seems to me an anticipation of Lacan's later
     paper, "Agency of the letter in the unconscious." In 1968, however,
     Wilden was practically alone in offering commentary on Lacan in
     English. Roudinesco's perceptive comments on Lacan's two readings
     of Jakobson and Saussure are relevant here. She argues that he had
     read both linguists by 1953, when he was also very obviously in-
     fluenced by both Lévi-Strauss and Heidegger, but she thinks that he
     reread the linguists sometime after 1953 and gave their theories greater
     prominence (297–8).

38 Jean Laplanche and J.-B. Pontalis, *The Language of Psycho-analysis*, trans. Donald Nicholson-Smith (London: Hogarth Press and Institute of Psycho-Analysis, 1973), 121.

39 Ferdinand de Saussure, *Course in General Linguistics* (1916), ed. Charles Bally and Albert Sechehaye and trans. Roy Harris (La Salle, IL: Open Court, 1986), 65; following extracts from 67, 68, 14, 69. Roudinesco states that Lacan read Saussure "with Lévi-Strauss on the one side and Heidegger on the other" (297).

40 Jonathan Culler attributes this view to Saussure, explaining that "both signifier and signified are purely relational or differential entities": *Saussure* (London: Fontana Press, 1986), 23. This seems to me to go beyond Saussure to anticipate the use that has been made of his work. The uncertain condition of the text of the *Course,* none of which was actually written by Saussure, and the important relationship of his notebooks to what is in the *Course* make such judgments necessarily very tentative, however. Culler makes the excellent point that Saussure's text should be read in such a way as "to grasp a thought which is not yet fully born" (10).

41 This passage, perhaps more than any other in *Écrits*, marks the distance between the thought of Lacan and Derrida. Although they share the Saussurean-Freudian point of departure, Lacan's commitments to speech, origin, the centrality of the word, and what he sees as the symbolic essence of human beings ("Man speaks, then, but it is because the symbol has made him man" (65)) will take his theories in a direction Derrida is unable to accept. Derrida writes about the *Fort! Da!* game in *The Post Card: From Socrates to Freud and Beyond*, trans. Alan Bass (Chicago: University of Chicago Press, 1987), 41ff. Lacan's subsequent discussion of Lévi-Strauss (70–6) anticipates Derrida's in "Structure, Sign and Play," and his "historical era of the 'ego'" (71) parallels Derrida's history of the age of Rousseau in *Grammatology*. The issues in these parallels are matters not of intellectual priority but of theoretical difference, in my view.

42 For a stimulating discussion of this topic throughout Lacan's work but with particular attention to the "Rome Discourse", see Anthony Wilden's "Lacan and the Discourse of the Other" in *Speech and Language in Psychoanalysis*, 159–311.

43 Lacan's reference to the *Theaetetus* would appear to be to the critique in that dialogue of the simplistic view that knowledge is perception (151–86e) and to its exploration of three possible meanings of *logos* (206c–210b). The argument that *logos* is an essential ingredient of knowledge (210c–10b) seems to suit Lacan's argument here.

44 5.1 begins, *Om!*

> The yon is fullness; fullness, this.
> From fullness, fullness doth proceed.

> Withdrawing fullness's fullness off,
> E'en fullness then itself remains.

The Thirteen Principal Upanishads, trans. Robert Ernest Hume (London: Oxford University Press, 1921), 149; following quotation from 150. The yoni is origin, the womb, and the emblem of the Ultimate. Eliot perversely cites a German text, but this is more likely the one he used.

45   Kanti Chandra Pandey, *Indian Aesthetics* (1950), *The Chowkhamba Sanskrit Series*, Studies II (Varanasi, 1959), 258–9, following quotation from 263 and 272.

46   Here Lacan is very close to the concept of deconstruction, which Derrida will elucidate in *Of Grammatology* (esp. 14–15). Both Lacan and Derrida are heavily influenced by Heidegger's hermeneutics, but Lacan wants to insist that what he needs from Heidegger is already there in Freud. See, for example, "The agency of the letter in the unconscious," 175. Roudinesco gives a full account of Lacan's meetings with Heidegger in 1950 (298–9).

47   See Bowie's observation that in Lacan "The future perfect . . . emerges as the tense *par excellence* of desire and the prospective human imagination": *Lacan*, 185.

48   Roudinesco has an important discussion of Lacan's "short sessions" (229–31), which contributed to his problems with his colleagues in the IPA and SPP.

49   Of the many recent attempts to reassess Viennese culture in Freud's time, the most useful here is Carl E. Schorske's *Fin-de-Siècle Vienna* (New York, Knopf, 1979). See especially his superb account of Freud's "A Revolutionary Dream" (193–8), which situates Freud's famous dream of 1898 in the context of then contemporary Austrian politics. Although Lacan does not refer explicitly to Freud's account of the dream (SE, IV: 209–19), he seems to assume it as a subtext.

50   See especially *Thoughts for the Times on War and Death* (1915), SE, XIV: 275–300.

51   Here Lacan would seem to be anticipating a point of dispute – or of difference – with Derrida's later theory of *différance*. Lacan's "difference" and Derrida's *différance* both imply a theory of history that may allude to Hegel's discussion of a different or differentiating relation [*differente Beziehung*] in the thought of the present. Manfred Frank has prepared the way for a detailed comparative examination of Hegel's influence on Derrida and Lacan concerning this matter in *What Is Neostructuralism?*, trans. Sabine Wilke and Richard Gray (Minneapolis: University of Minnesota Press, 1989 (1984)), esp. 271–5.

52   *Poetry, Language, Thought*, trans. Albert Hofstadter (New York: Harper & Row, 1971), 168, 127.

53 *The Will to Power in The Complete Works of Friedrich Nietzsche*, trans. O. Levy (London: J. N. Foules, 1909–13), XV: 20.

54 Cf. Philip Rieff, *Freud: The Mind of the Moralist* (Garden City: Anchor Books, 1961). Rieff welcomes those ego psychologists who depart from Freud in order to strengthen his "weakling conception of the ego" (66).

55 The emblematic attributes of Vérité summarized in E. Droulers, *Iconologie: dictionnaire des attributs, allégories, emblèmes et symboles* (Turnhout: Établissements Brapols, n.d.), 225, illus. 254. See also Guy de Tervaruet, *Attributs et symboles dans l'art profane, 1450–1600* (Genève: Librairie E. Droz, 1958), esp. 165–7.

56 Lacan later (174) mentions Erasmus by name. Bowie comments perceptively that Lacan's argument levitates "towards the threshold of madness" as the monologue reaches its climax (*Lacan*, 111), and he also comments on Lacan's text in terms of Erasmus's. Both Erasmus and Lacan, however, may also be alluding to Proverbs 8, where wisdom speaks of herself in an extended monologue.

57 Erasmus, *The Praise of Folly*, trans. John Wilson (1668) (Ann Arbor: The University of Michigan Press, 1958), p. 26.

58 In this connection, see Freud's discussion of the rebus in SE, IV: 277–8.

59 I am grateful to Greg May for pointing out to me that Lacan's allusion to Cleopatra's nose refers to Pascal's *Pensées*, no. 162.

60 *Of Grammatology*, 14. This image does not appear in his French text, however.

61 For an excellent discussion of epistomophilia in Freud, see Toril Moi, "Patriarchal thought and the drive for knowledge," in *Feminism and Psychoanalysis*, ed. Teresa Brennan (London: Routledge, 1989), 198–203. Moi quotes the following passage from Lacan's Kanzer seminar: "[Freud] spent a lot of time listening, and while he was listening, there resulted something paradoxical, a reading. It was while listening to hysterics that he read that there was an unconscious. That is, something he could only construct, and in which he himself was implicated; he was implicated in it in the sense that, to his great astonishment, he noticed that he could not avoid participating in what the hysteric was telling him, and that he felt affected by it" (197–80).

62 See the excellent commentary by Frances Yates, *Giordano Bruno and the Hermetic Tradition* (Chicago: University of Chicago Press, 1964), esp. 278–84. I am also indebted to Malcolm Bowie's discussion of Lacan's Actaeon in *Freud, Proust and Lacan*, 168–73, although my reading differs from his. Bowie points out that a complete French translation of Bruno's text appeared two years before the composition of "The Freudian thing." In *The Four Fundamental Concepts of Psychoanalysis* Lacan alters the myth again by identifying himself with Actaeon: "The

truth, in this sense, is that which runs after truth — and that is where I am running, where I am taking you, like Actaeon's hounds, after me. When I find the goddess's hiding place, I will no doubt be changed into a stag, and you can devour me, but we still have a little way to go yet" (188).

63   *Yale French Studies*, 63 *The Pedagogical Imperative: Teaching as a Literary Genre* (1982), 3–20.

64   See Sherry Turkle's useful account of the differing receptions of psychoanalysis in America and in France: (*Psychoanalytic Politics: Freud's French Revolution* (New York: Basic Books, 1978), 4–23. Lacan actively participated in her research (ix). Roudinesco's much more detailed history of the French reception has superseded that part of Turkle's narrative.

65   J. Hillis Miller, *Hawthorne and History: Defacing It* (Oxford: Basil Blackwell, 1991), 95–6. This book is an extended investigation into the ways of prosopopoeia, as its subtitle suggests.

66   See especially "The Thing," in *Poetry, Language, Thought*, 179–81.

67   Miller, 99.

68   A rare instance of both these functions of prosopopoeia operating simultaneously is Chomsky's theory of a "linguistic-acquisition-device" that can be abbreviated LAD. The theory objectifies a human process of language learning in theoretical language that in its abbreviated form recalls the human child (lad), who was at first objectified. See *Aspects of a Theory of Syntax* (Cambridge: MIT Press, 1965), 30–7. The term "chosification," as used for example by Aimé Césaire, signifies the de-humanizing consequences of racial and social oppression. Like Sartre's *objectité*, it is a form of negitivity. Lacan's concern here is less with these consequences of social manipulation than with the ego's potential to thingify the human subject by projecting its destiny as identity or individualism.

69   Kristeva's *Black Sun*, trans. Leon S. Roudiez (New York: Columbia University Press, 1989), takes *chosisme* even beyond language in her study of melancholia. Her image of the black sun is an oxymoronic figure for the melancholic's unrepresentable "thing:" "an insistence without presence, a light without representation" (13). Here, it would seem, the melancholic is either beyond metaphor or has come to live in a world of vehicles without tenors.

70   Joseph H. Smith's *Arguing with Lacan* ignores these textual ambiguities in his efforts to Americanize Lacan.

71   For example, by Bice Benvenuto and Roger Kennedy, *The Works of Jacques Lacan: An Introduction* (London: Free Association Books, 1986), 107.

72   See Philippe Lacoue-Labarthe and Jean-Luc Nancy, *Le Titre de la lettre: une lecture de Lacan,* (Paris: Éditions Galilée, 1973), 19. Theirs is the best and most detailed commentary on this text.

73 Lacan delivered a lecture on Chomsky on December 2, 1964, but it remains unpublished. See Roudinesco's comments on it, 401–2.

74 Heidegger, *Early Greek Thinking*, trans. David Krell and Frank A. Capuzzi (New York: Harper and Row, 1975 (1954)), 64.

75 Ibid., 61.

76 On this topic, see, for example, Samuel Weber, *Return to Freud*, trans. Michael Levine (Cambridge: Cambridge University Press, 1991), 176–82.

77 Saussure, *Course in General Linguistics*, 31.

78 Ibid., 66–7.

79 Roman Jakobson and Morris Halle, *Fundamentals of Language* (The Hague: Mouton, 1956), 60.

80 Jean Starobinski, *Words upon Words: The Anagrams of Ferdinand de Saussure* (New Haven: Yale University Press, 1979.) A preliminary version of Starobinski's work appeared in 1964, in time for Lacan to take note of it (177n.).

81 See especially *Cahiers*, XXVIII, 763 and XXIV, 816. Other relevant passages from the unedited notes can be found in Jeannine Jallat, "Valéry and the mathematical language of identity and difference," *Yale French Studies*, 44 (1970), 51–64. Valéry's fascination with mathematical models was also not lost on Lacan.

82 Jakobson and Halle, 81.

83 Ibid., 81.

84 Macey points out the uncertainty of Lacan's classifications too: "in 'Fonction et champ' both metaphor and metonymy were 'semantic condensations', but in the Seminar of May 9, 1956 condensation, displacement and representation are all said to belong to an order of metonymic articulation which allows metaphor to function" (157). What little Freud writes explicitly about metaphor can be found in SE, VIII: 213–14. Whether Lacan favors metaphor or metonymy remains a matter of dispute. Lacoue-Labarthe and Nancy see a bias toward metaphor (145), while Weber takes the opposite view (66–7).

85 *The Four Fundamental Concepts of Psycho-analysis*, 20.

86 Macey is particularly good on Lacan's mathematical models (esp. 164–71).

87 See Weber, 64.

88 No one has described the linguistics of Lacanian desire better than Malcolm Bowie: "Metonymy keeps desire on the rails, and always pressing ahead to the next destination, but metaphor supplies a limitless profusion of junctions, loops, and branch-lines. This is a network that goes everywhere, and those who travel have no choice but to use it, however little it can be relied upon to take them where they want to go": *Lacan*, 132.

89 See Harold Bloom, *The Anxiety of Influence* (New York: Oxford University Press, 1975). Bloom's brilliant series of subsequent books

flows from this idea, which may be understood as emerging from Freud's theories of defence.

90   *Brief über den Humanismus* (Frankfurt am Main: V. Klostermann, 1947), 64.

91   The *OED* lists the first printed use of the term "phallocentrism" as appearing in that debate. See *International Journal of Psychoanalysis*, VIII (1927), 459. Lacan's only footnote in this paper is his citation of Jones's article (291), although he also refers, without citation, on 283 to Jones's "The Phallic Phase," which was first presented in 1932. For a review of the Jones–Freud controversy, see Juliet Mitchell, *Psychoanalysis and Feminism* (New York: Vintage, 1975), 121–31. Jane Gallop reviews and renews the charge of phallocentrism against Lacan in *Reading Lacan* (Ithaca: Cornell University Press, 1985), 133–56, and *Feminism and Psychoanalysis: The Daughter's Seduction* (London: Macmillan, 1982), 15–32.

92   For Freud's discussion of "the phallic mother," see SE, XXII: 126–7.

93   Lacan also alludes to Longus's tale in "Remarque sur le rapport de Daniel Lagache" (*É*, 669).

94   There are excellent color photographs of the frieze in Richard Seaford's *Pompeii* (New York: Thames and Hudson, 1978), 63–75. I am indebted to his commentary also.

95   The most detailed assessments of Lacan's theory in the context of feminism are Juliet Mitchell's and Jacqueline Rose's introductions to *Feminine Sexuality. Jacques Lacan and the "Ecole freudienne"* (London: Macmillan, 1982) and Elizabeth Grosz, *Jacques Lacan. A Feminist Introduction* (London: Routledge, 1990).

96   I borrow this term from Northrop Frye's *Anatomy of Criticism* (Princeton: Princeton University Press, 1957), 121.

97   Thomas Gilby, O.P., points out that Aquinas's dialectic of love amounts to a critique of reductive forms of faculty psychology: Thomas Aquinas, *Summa Theologiae*, ed. Thomas Gilby, OP (New York: Image Books, 1969), vol. I, 246–7.

98   *Phenomenology of Spirit*, 493.

99   Ibid., 212.

100 I find this another indication that Lacan is reading Hegel closely. Section CC of the *Phenomenology* places consciousness, self-consciousness, reason, and spirit in the context of a critique of religion.

101 Paul de Man, *Blindness and Insight: Essays in the Rhetoric of Contemporary Criticism* (New York: Oxford University Press, 1971) and Frank Kermode, *The Uses of Error* (Cambridge, MA: Harvard University Press, 1991).

102 Plato, *The Symposium*, trans. Walter Hamilton (Harmondsworth: Penguin, 1951), 83.

103 Ibid., 100.

104 Lacan's recently published *Le Transfert (Le Séminaire, VIII)* (Paris: Seuil, 1991) includes a much more detailed reading of the *Symposium* (see chapters II–XI). This text is a culmination of Lacan's speculations about a Socratic model for psychoanalysis. Chapter XI, "Entre Socrate et Alcibiade," purposes a different reading of the Alcibiades scene from the one offered in *Écrits*.

3

Of Grammatology

Just as no other psychoanalyst has brought to Freud's texts as intellectually and imaginatively powerful a reading as Lacan's, so in the Heideggerian tradition of theories of writing and textuality no one has made a contribution equal to Jacques Derrida's.[1] Even though his *Grammatology* is a comparatively early work (1967), it offers a classic statement of deconstructive processes and a detailed formulation of Derrida's theories of written language. Parts of the text were composed in 1965 as reviews of books on writing by Madeleine V.-David and André Leroi-Gourhan and of a collection of papers from a colloquium entitled *L'Écriture et la psychologie des peuples*. These reviews in substantially their original form appear in part I, chapter 3. Similarly, much of Derrida's discussion of Lévi-Strauss, first published in 1966 in the Lévi-Strauss issue of *Cahiers pour l'analyse*, reappears in part II, chapter 1. The complete text of *De la grammatologie*, which Derrida calls a two-part essay, was translated into English by Gayatri Chakravorty Spivak and published in 1976. While her own accomplishment in this translation is superb, it is apparent from her detailed translator's preface that Derrida served, however modestly, as the translator's collaborator.[2]

Derrida sometimes takes textual and compositional sequences quite seriously, writing at length about the problems of dating Rousseau's *Essay on the Origin of Languages* in *Grammatology* (192–4) and adding a passionate footnote to *Positions* on the priority of his publications dealing with problems of language and interpretation in Freud to Lacan's treatment of the same subjects.[3] The structures of texts – including certainly his own – are for Derrida by no means static. Indeed, many of his metaphors for and about texts emphasize the temporal processes of writing and reading: event, birth, deconstruction, trace, dissemination, desire, deferring, supplement, absence, appropriation, reappropriation, play, forgetfulness, closure, end. But Derrida is also suspicious of any simplistic sense of linear time. He thus proposes two possible relationships between *Of Grammatology* and *Writing and Difference*:

> One can take *Of Grammatology* as a long essay articulated in two parts (whose juncture is not empirical, but theoretical, systematic) *into the middle* of which one could staple *Writing and Difference*. *Grammatology* often calls upon it. In this case the interpretation of Rousseau would also be the twelfth "table" of the collection. Inversely, one could insert *Of Grammatology into the middle of Writing and Difference*, since six of the texts in that work preceded – *de facto* and *de jure* – the publication in *Critique* (two years ago [i.e. 1965]) of the articles that announced *Of Grammatology*; the last five texts, beginning with "Freud and the Scene of Writing," are engaged in the grammatological opening. But things cannot be reconstituted so easily, as you may well imagine.[4]

For Derrida no less than Freud, time in its various and discontinuous ways both shapes and disrupts texts.

Since Derrida meditates with such concentration on what transpires in the reading of a text, the reader of *Grammatology* cannot for long postpone meditating as well on the complex textual ways of Derrida's essay. Indeed, Derrida has conducted wonderfully inventive experiments with the printed page – especially in his multi-intertextual *Glas* and in his recently published *Cinders* – challenging even the stylistic and typographical virtuosity of Sterne, Blake, and John Cage. Although *Of Grammatology* is more traditional in typography, it is nonetheless radical and highly inventive in its strategies of allusion and metaphorical argumentation.

I

Preface and Exergue

Grammatology opens with a preface and an exergue. The preface outlines the structure of the text: part I offers "a theoretical matrix," which is then tested in part II by a reading of the "age" of Rousseau. Already, after only a few words of what appears to be a straightforward description of the book's organization, the reader is hit by several surprises. The privileged attention given here to Rousseau runs counter to the usual modern assessment of his place in the history of philosophy. Bertrand Russell is more generous to Rousseau than is typical of historians of philosophy:

> Jean-Jacques Rousseau (1712–78), though a *philosophe* in the eighteenth-century French sense, was not what would now be called a "philosopher." Nevertheless he had a powerful influence on philosophy . . . Whatever may be our opinion on his merits as a thinker, we must recognize his immense importance as a social force. This importance came mainly from his appeal to the heart . . . At the present time [i.e. 1945], Hitler is an outcome of Rousseau.[5]

Even here, where Russell gives Rousseau a chapter in the history of Western philosophy, in contrast to Wildeband's and Randall's quick, embarrassed dismissals, Russell, nevertheless, will not call Rousseau a philosopher; instead he implies Rousseau's deficiency as a thinker and sees him in his irrationalism as a precursor of Nazism. Copleston is similarly ambivalent and concludes his two chapters on Rousseau by lifting him out of history entirely, insisting that he is *sui generis*: "He is and remains Jean-Jacques Rousseau."[6] Jean Starobinski, one of the most admired Rousseau scholars, on whose work Derrida heavily relies, has written informatively and at length about the bipolarity of Rousseau's views on reflection, which is both the destroyer of mankind's original goodness and the only means available for overcoming the vices of reason itself.[7] For Derrida, Rousseau's example and influence extend undiminished from the eighteenth century to our own time. To read the age of Rousseau is to assess the structures of thought that reach from the years Rousseau wrote to the present. Saussure, Lévi-Strauss, and Derrida himself are in this sense Rousseauists. Not only, however, is this *philosophe* who has been marginalized by historians of philosophy allowed to give his name to the chronological expanse that includes Kant, Nietzsche, and Heidegger, but also Derrida has the audacity to select the little-known text of the *Essay on the Origin of Languages* in order to read the age of Rousseau and to test the theoretical work of part I of *Grammatology*. A neglected text by a writer denied the name of philosopher will be used to recover writing in an age that has marginalized the written word in favor of speech.[8]

As he proceeds with his fundamental project "to produce [*produire* (G, 7)] . . . the problems of critical reading," Derrida, while having "no ambition to illustrate a new method," demonstrates the necessity that reading free itself "from the classical categories of history . . . and perhaps above all, from the categories of the history of philosophy" (lxxxix). Already Derrida anticipates ways in which *Grammatology* will be misread. Its methods are not new; rather, they have been overridden, not by history, but by a mode of historical writing that neglects (or refuses) to view the past "in every respect as a *text*" (lxxxix). Although it continues to be claimed that grammatology's (or deconstruction's) project is anti-historical and apolitical,[9] Derrida's argument, forcefully announced on the first page of his text, refutes this claim in advance. *Grammatology* "reads" the age of Rousseau by recovering the textual remains of its past, texts that intervening historians have systematically left unread, justifying their neglect by invoking such unexamined categories as *philosophy* and *literature* and by assigning Rousseau to the latter in the interests of purifying the history of philosophy. Even Derrida's need to turn to the 1817 Bélin edition of the *Essai* underscores the sense that Rousseau has been repressed by philosophical historiography. *Grammatology*'s preface concludes by forecasting a fundamental contradiction in the age of Rousseau: on the one hand, it values documentation and the protocols of historiography – "legibility and the efficacy of a model" (xc) – but even as it sets about the recovery of the past, it necessarily disrupts it, as will be seen in Derrida's later critique of Lévi-Strauss, the as yet unnamed modern anthropologist of the preface's final sentence.

Despite the surprises of the preface, its tone is quiet and restrained, especially in contrast to the messianic call of the exergue. Derrida does not set himself above or apart from the age he is about to read, nor is he claiming himself immune to the contradictions and disruptions of previous Rousseauist historians. Indeed, all of the texts he reads – Hegel, Nietzsche, Freud, Saussure, Heidegger, Lévi-Strauss – he reads with compassionate respect and with a recognition of his own susceptibility to the errors he identifies in others.

In this vein the exergue outlines grammatology as a field of thought by focusing on unexamined metaphysical assumptions concerning phonetic writing in historical linguistics and on the first movements toward the dislocation of those assumptions. Like the preface, the exergue illuminates what has previously been kept hidden or obscure. An exergue, though part of the text, claims to remain outside the work (*ex + ergon* [work]), or more technically, it is the small space on the reverse side of a coin beneath the principal device where an inscription may be found.[10] The sort of writing that is not part of the main inscription on the reverse side of a coin becomes a

trope for the simultaneous dislocation of writing as a concept; that
is, its disparagement in preference to speech, which is erroneously
assumed to be one step nearer than writing to truth. This particular
piece of writing – the portion of *Grammatology* entitled "Exergue" –
is both outside of and part of the text. Clearly Derrida is acclimating
his reader to multiple alterities, directing attention especially to the
refusal of the debased term in a polarized set to be banished, or, more
precisely, the necessity of the debased term for the process of its own
debasement and the privileging of its assumed opposite. Even when
writers who privilege speech are not actively debasing writing in
favor of speech, they cannot avoid writing about speech by using
metaphors of inscription. The exergue, like the uncanny elements
in dream experience or the terms in Freudian discourse, refuses to
remain in its assigned marginal space.

The exergue begins with three numbered quotations. The first, by
way of metaphor, identifies a grammatologist with the sun and the
Babylonian sun-god (Samas) with the light that illuminates the earth,
making the land appear a piece of writing (cuneiform signs), in striking similarity to the grammatological metaphors of the biblical Psalm
19. The second quotation (from Rousseau's *Essay*) identifies the practice of three forms of writing with three progressive stages in the
history of civilization. The final quotation (from Hegel), by an exercise in metonymy, makes the ethnocentrism of Rousseau's history
explicit in its claim for the superior intelligence of alphabetic script
(and by implication, those peoples who use it). The first sentence
of Derrida's own exergue, following these quotations, identifies the
quotations themselves as a "triple exergue," the writing outside the
writing that is outside the text. The witty claim here is that writing
as a concept has been controlled by the kind of ethnocentricism
manifested in the three quotations: religion, social history, and philosophy disguise ethnocentrism as logocentrism. The Word encumbered
by the weight of unexamined metaphysical assumptions becomes the
defining essence of god, civilization, and philosophy.

Derrida proceeds to enumerate three ways by which logocentrism
as the agent of ethnocentrism imposes itself on the world. As "the
concept of writing" (here distinguished from the physical process of
producing signs with pen or keyboard), logocentrism generates a
dissimulated history of phonetic writing even as it proceeds to in-
scribe its own history; as "the history of . . . metaphysics" from the
pre-Socratics to Heidegger, it both identifies the origin of truth with
the logos and the history of truth with the repression of writing;

as "the concept of science" (3), it both assigns language and logic central importance for the project of science and announces its dissatisfaction with phonetic writing. Although this discontent on the part of science with phonetic writing is contained within a logocentric ethos, it nevertheless initiates the dislocation (from within) of the logocentric epoch that is otherwise named the age of Rousseau. At this point the exergue begins to take on a rhetorical resonance reminiscent of Rousseau's "Man was born free, and he is everywhere in chains."

Grammatology is a fecund, liberating force that for the moment is bound in by traditional notions of metaphor, metaphysics, and theology. It nonetheless asserts itself in multiple and interdisciplinary ways, although it can never claim its own essentiality or the unity of its project, given its basic distrust of all essentialisms and all easy claims of reconciling unities. It must instead run the risk of always having its project named for it. Not to run this risk – by assertively defining itself and by reclaiming a centrality occupied by unselfreflective historiography, linguistics, or philosophy – would be to sacrifice its oppositional character and to lose the reflexivity necessary to sustain critique. As a liberating moment within the age of Rousseau, grammatology must work as an underground or marginal science, taking shape within, yet working against, the historical and metaphysical epoch of which it is a part. From the reflective angle of grammatology, the full shape of the age that encloses it (that is to say, its "closure') can be glimpsed, but that is not the same as seeing its end in view. Still, the grounds for optimism – the "signs of [grammatology's] liberation all over the world" (4) – are that science and writing presuppose a privileged concept of the sign whose establishment makes its dislocation possible.

Science's dream of language projects a direct and exact correspondence between sign and phenomenon or object. Such a dream would invest the sign with the power to make present such a phenomenon or object. But the collapse of that dream, especially in the discovery of the arbitrariness and distance between the sign and what it signifies, begins a process of dislocating the Word (language with its historical, metaphysical, and theological freight) from its selfproclaimed centrality. The self-assertion of the centrism (or "privilege') of the logos is the first stage in its dislocation. Therefore, grammatology must be "patient" and "painstaking" (Derrida here echoes Nietzsche's celebration of "slow reading" in *Daybreak*) so that the smug "positivity" of the sign may develop itself to its limit.

Just as Derrida does not name Lévi-Strauss at the end of the preface, so here he does not yet name Saussure, who is extensively alluded to in the exergue's last two paragraphs, especially in the designation of grammatology's future. Just as grammatology (and deconstruction) work oppositionally within established structures in order fully to exhaust those structures' own potential for dislocating themselves, so Derrida works within the language of structural linguistics, adopting Saussure's concept of the sign and his startling characterization of writing as a "monstrosity."[11] The future, which grammatology works to bring about by exploiting the stresses and cracks in the structure of the present historical-metaphysical age, can only be proclaimed or presented – the French text emphasizes a proclaiming and presenting by grammatology itself [*s'annoncer, se presenter* (*G*, 14)] – as "a sort of monstrosity" because that future puts "into question the values of sign, word, and writing" (5). For the representation of that future, there is no exergue, nothing legitimately outside the inscription or text of the moment. Given the impossibility of grammatology's describing itself for itself, except in what may seem grotesquely evasive ways, that it has inspired misrepresentation and caricature would seem almost to confirm the prophetic utterances in the preliminary sections of *Grammatology*.

II

"The End of the Book"

Even in its title, "The End of the Book and the Beginning of Writing," chapter 1 sustains the prophetic tone of the exergue. This chapter offers a classic statement of the ways of deconstruction conceived both as a dynamic process at work in texts and as a theory designed to illuminate such a process. The title announces a necessary change in how texts are to be perceived if they are to be fully read. To consider a text – such as *Of Grammatology* itself – as *a book* presupposes a unified structure and authorial control of meaning that become clear as one reads. Whatever tensions or conflicts are generated by the structure of the book, these are ultimately resolved once the overall design and intention are fully perceived. Unity is the basic structural principle of the book. To consider a text *as writing*, however, liberates it from presuppositions of static, objectified, authorial structure and recovers the sense of signifying and reading as complementary processes. Writing and reading are human activities occurring within the context of history (itself an activity of writing and reading); furthermore, they are activities that have freed themselves from the unconscious tropes of theology. The metaphor linking authorial composition to God's creation of the universe and the related organistic metonymy of the book as a fragment of the deity made present in the word are here suspended. It is not, however, Derrida who suspends them. Rather, he shows that texts which would seem to lend the strongest support to the logocentrism of the book do not themselves submit to such an ideology. "Plurivocity" (7) is the basic structural principle of writing.[12]

But even to claim that texts are multi-voiced is to succumb to the phonocentric metaphor that has helped sustain logocentrism. To write about writing as though it were a secondary and inferior form of speech has been a common strategy in the historico-metaphysical epoch that grammatology sets out to dislodge. Indeed, the age of Rousseau has sustained itself by a mode of writing that self-deprecatingly calls itself a supplementary form of speech. In this age the book is assumed to imprison meaning as the body is assumed to imprison the spirit. When the body dies, the spirit is free; but for now everywhere the voice of spirit is in chains to writing, the bodily prison house of language. Grammatology, however, is suspicious of such spiritual readings that are contemptuous of the textual body. Yet grammatology can offer a critique of the logocentric epoch only from within it, which means that it cannot suddenly disengage itself from the ruling metaphors of its time, becoming a free spirit or a truth somehow immune to the ways of language. Instead, it recognizes that thinking grammatologically about texts begins with a full awareness of the structures of those metaphors designed to suppress writing. Such an awareness constitutes a closure or a virtually claustrophobic sense of the containing metaphysical structure of the age; it does not constitute an end to it.

Following the title to chapter 1, Derrida inserts as an epigraph a phrase from Nietzsche's "Aus dem Gedankenkreise der Geburt der Tragödie": "Socrates, he who does not write" (6). This would seem to identify Socrates as one of the great antitheses to Derrida's grammatological project; Christ, another notorious non-writer, being another. In this sense, Socrates is for Derrida here as he is for Nietzsche in the quoted passage, the antagonist or suppressor both of writing and of tragedy, that written genre of the spoken word. For anyone, however, who has seen the post card that is the ostensible occasion for Derrida's *La Carte postale* (1980), or without its aid thought its intolerable thought, reading Socrates as writing's antagonist is far too simple.

In that book Derrida describes his finding a post card in the Bodleian Library, Oxford, which reproduces the frontispiece of a thirteenth-century fortune-telling book. The future-orientation of the book not only seems to anticipate Derrida's discovery of the illustration but also forecasts grammatology's prophetic mission. As he describes the illustration, Derrida rewrites the passage from Nietzsche while retaining its first simplistic but necessary reading:

> Socrates writing, writing in front of Plato, I always knew it, it had remained like the negative of a photograph to be developed for twenty-five centuries – in me of course. Sufficient to write it in broad daylight. The revelation is there, unless I can't yet decipher anything in this picture, which is what is most probable in effect. Socrates, the one who writes – seated, bent over, a scribe or docile copyist, Plato's secretary, no? He is in front of Plato, no, Plato is *behind* him, smaller (why smaller?) but standing up. With his out-stretched finger he looks like he is indicating something, designating, showing the way or giving an order – or dictating, authoritarian, masterly, imperious.[13]

Suddenly, the historico-metaphysical epoch founded on the centrality of speech and its proximity to truth, together with the suppression of writing, is given a dislodging jolt by a process of historical rewriting. The Bodleian post card, apparently discovered ten years after the publication of *Grammatology*, visually embodies the argument of chapter 1 and its celebration of reversibility.

That argument begins with the claim that the problem of language has never before affected so profoundly research in a multiplicity of disciplines. But the more language is considered "a problem," the less it is valued. There is, however, no escape from language. Even in the loose play of language, it is brought back to itself, while simultaneously losing its self-assurance in the very face of its apparent capacity for infinite signification. Even this debasing inflation of "language" – the ubiquitous articulating of its problematics – must present itself as language. In the midst of this general linguistic anxiety a momentous shift, though barely perceptible, is taking place, transferring what had previously been invoked as "language" to "writing." Writing as a concept [*l'écriture*] is no longer thought derivative, auxiliary, exterior, insubstantial. No longer merely "the signifier of the signifier," one step further removed from truth than speech, writing is that which comprehends [*comprendrait* (*G*, 16)] language. Writing's previous designation, "the signifier of the signifier," is now properly the designation of language, even though the phrase could have been understood that way all along. It is as though even the language previously used to dismiss writing or to keep it in its (secondary) place concealed a truth about writing as an index to language: "The secondarity that it seemed possible to ascribe to writing alone affects all signifieds in general" (7). Writing was never simply a supplement in the sense of that which is simply tacked on; rather it has always required a new understanding of supplement, in the sense also of that which complements. This new understanding can serve as a guide to reading Rousseau.

The privileging of speech over writing, for example in Rousseau's *Essay on the Origin of Languages*, Saussure's *Course in General Linguistics*, or Lévi-Strauss's *Tristes Tropiques*, is exemplary of a wide range of binary oppositions that have shaped thought in the past. To understand writing's disparagement of itself in favor of speech is to gain a foothold in understanding how such oppositions have shaped thought. As a first step toward such an understanding, Derrida writes a paragraph that is mind-bogglingly packed with self-reflective markers, beginning "It is therefore as if" ["Tout se passe donc comme si" (*G*, 18)]. Like Darwin's imaginary examples in *The Origin of Species*, Derrida's "as if" sequence constructs an imaginary history of how writing has been assigned the role of "technics in the service of language" (8). Derrida's reader is called upon to imagine the possibility that in both its origin and end language were only a moment, mode, phenomenon, aspect, or species of writing. Furthermore, the reader is asked to imagine that language somehow has succeeded in making us forget this about itself. Then for three millenia this "adventure" of language merges with that history which amalgamates technics (as distinct from theory) with logocentrism (as distinct from grammatology). But now that adventure and history have reached a point of exhaustion, which can be called the "death of the civilization of the book," even though it is no more than "a death of speech," "a new mutation in the history of writing," or a mutation "in history as writing" (8). This history of language – from its origin as writing to its willful forgetting through its three millennia of logocentrism to the present exhaustion of the perverted history that has been substituted for the one written here – like all histories, is written under

the sign "as if." Or, more exactly, all writing occurs under this hypothetical sign. Such phrases as "death of speech" are therefore quite
obviously metaphors, and Derrida marks them clearly as such. A
major function of this paragraph is then to bring fully to the surface
the "as if" character of Derrida's own discourse, along with the
provisional character of its subject – "what we call language" – and
the ways that subject has been thought about: as *metonymy* (thus, the
words "moment," "modes," "phenomenon," "aspect," "species")
and as *metaphor* ("adventure," "history," "exhaustion," "death,"
"mutation," "archon" (8)).

Derrida's essay has already taken upon itself a multi-layered or
contrapuntal project. First, it sets out to write the history of the age
of Rousseau in all its ethno-logo-phono-phallo-centrism. In this age
language has become a matter of universal concern, but at the cost of
an unreflective metonymy: a part of language (speech) has been elevated to the position of archon in the major *written* texts of the era. But
now the first stirrings toward a grammatological revolution can be
felt. Second, the essay sketches some of the preliminary manifestations of that revolution: it works within the existing structure of
language, metaphysics, and history by searching out the stresses and
disruptions already present within that structure. Furthermore, it
rewrites the history of language in order to recover the adventure of
logocentrism's misleading self-representation. Third, the essay
experiments itself with a style of writing that appropriates all of the
tropological resources of language in the age of Rousseau but then
pushes the narrative of this age to the point of its exhaustion in the
interest of attempting to go beyond it. As one looks from this third
layer of Derrida's project back to the previous two, the compound
adverb "always already" [*toujours déjà*] comes usefully to serve as a
mnemonic recollection and condensation of this multiple project.
Grammatology, that is, explores what is *always* at work in language,
once *language* has expanded itself "to designate not only the physical
gestures of literal pictographic or ideographic inscription, but also the
totality of what makes it possible" (9). Yet what grammatology
explores is *already* at work both in the texts being examined (such as
those examples from Aristotle, Heidegger, and Hegel that Derrida is
about to explicate) and in the text of the explication as well.

What, precisely, is it that is always already at work in the texts
explicated and in the texts of explication? What, precisely, is the
disruption in language that constitutes grammatology's subject?
Again, three levels of answer. First, what is at work is "plurivocity"

(7). All texts say more than one thing, say more than they want to say, say both what they want to say and by doing so undermine what they want to say. Second, what is at work is a desire for presence and a frustration of the possibility of its gratification (which means a continuation of the desire by its lack of fulfillment.) Language promises to make present its subject (or object):

> In the beginning was the Word [Logos], and the Word was with God, and the Word was God . . . And the Word became flesh, and dwelt among us. (John 1: 1, 14).

Derrida will both recall and rewrite these words in *The Post Card*:

> In the beginning the post, John will say, or Shaun or Tristan, and it begins with a destination without address, the direction cannot be situated in the end. There is no destination . . . within every sign already, every mark or every trait, there is distancing, the post.[14]

Third, what is at work is both a distance (or arbitrary relationship) between the word and what it wants to signify and also a rebounding or overflowing of signification. Rather than controlling meaning, defining it, making it present, words are inundated by signification. Words mean both not enough and too much. Finally, such questions as the ones that begin this paragraph ("What, precisely, is . . . ?") manifest the impossible desire of language to limit (define) the unlimited and to make present the permanently elusive. *Deconstruction* is the name given simultaneously to the stress created by these gaps in texts (between what they want to say and what they do say) and to the detection of such gaps. A deconstructive reading attends to the deconstructive processes *always* occurring in texts and *already* there waiting to be read.

The enlarged sense of writing as a concept [*l'écriture*] that arises from Derrida's hypothetical history of language puts in jeopardy a sense of truth dependent on the logos. Here is the moment in *Grammatology* when *deconstruction* as both a term and a concept slowly rises to the surface of the text, disrupting the absolute identification of truth with its signifier:

> A writing thus enlarged and radicalized, no longer issues from a logos. Further, it inaugurates the destruction, not the demolition but the de-sedimentation, the de-construction, of all the significations that have their source in that of the logos. Particularly the signification of *truth*. (10).

Here the search for the apt metaphor is reminiscent of Freud's meticulous, self-reflective textual experimentation in such texts as *Civilization and Its Discontents*, where he experiments with archaeological metaphors as a way of representing the history and structure of the unconscious. As he launches the concept of deconstruction, Derrida looks back to Aristotle's and Hegel's fusing of truth with the spoken logos. For Aristotle, in *De interpretatione*, the spoken word is the "primary symbol" of mental experience, while the written signifier is merely derivative from "what would wed the voice indissolubly to the mind or to the thought of the signified sense, indeed to the thing itself" (11). Whereas Aristotle traces the generation of the spoken word, Hegel, in *The Philosophy of Fine Art*, describes the phenomenological reception of meaningful sound by the ravished ear: "The ear ... perceives the result of that interior vibration of material substance without placing itself in a practical relation toward the objects, a result by means of which it is no longer the material form in its repose, but the first, more ideal activity of the soul itself which is manifested" (12). Here the distinctions between cognition and signification and between signification and reception melt away in the interest of indissoluble presence.

Before he proceeds to deconstruct (or to perceive the self-deconstruction of) logocentrism, Derrida carefully cautions his reader against any temptation to postmodernist smugness in reading the principal texts of logocentrism: "one does not leave the epoch whose closure one can outline" (12). From Aristotle through Hegel to Heidegger, "appurtenance" is the distinguishing feature of logocentric conceptuality. *Appurtenance* is an important entry in Derrida's uncanny vocabulary of alterity. Signifying both "belonging" and "accessory," *appurtenance* (like *supplement*) condenses into a single word, first, the need on the part of Aristotle and Hegel to distinguish the signified and the signifier while working to assert their identity; and, second, the recognition on the part of Derrida that he needs and must respect the oscillation of Aristotle and Hegel if he is to provide a critique of "the great epoch covered by the history of metaphysics" (13). This same affectionate respect is held out to medieval theology, in which "the intelligible face of the sign remains turned toward the word and the face of God" (13). Such figurations cannot, Derrida insists, be summarily rejected: "nothing is conceivable for us without them" (13). They provide the ground for deconstruction's necessary work.

The rest of chapter 1 patiently and carefully describes the style and method of deconstruction (14–18) and offers brief and illustrative deconstructive readings of Heidegger (18–24) and of Hegel (25–6). At the risk of violating the elegant structure of Derrida's argument, it may be useful at this point to range rather freely over the entire chapter in order to gather together exemplary formulations of what deconstruction does and does not do.

Deconstruction does not constitute "a new method" of reading (lxxxix). Although it works to free itself from "classical historical categories," it does not discount history but rather considers it "as a text" (lxxxix). (Indeed, as a key deconstructive text, *Of Grammatology* offers itself as a history of the age of Rousseau.) Deconstruction contributes to the movement to dislocate logocentrism, a movement always already begun (4), even in such texts as *De interpretatione* or the Gospel of John. Nevertheless, deconstruction works toward the dislocation, liberation, de-familiarization of texts in an underground, marginal, oppositional way (4). Deconstruction and grammatology, the science of writing that studies and celebrates deconstruction's ways, take shape within, yet work against "the historicometaphysical epoch" of which the closure rather than the end is visible (4). Deconstruction, therefore, presupposes a privileged concept of the sign, which it works to undermine (4). Allied with the future to break with "constituted normality," it is accordingly proclaimed – indeed, it proclaims itself – a "monstrosity" (5). It repeatedly focuses upon the "as if," the metaphorical, and the metonymic features of discourse, which are usually neglected or despised by professional philosophers (8). This, however, does not constitute an abandonment of traditional philosophical problems and texts for literary ones. (Derrida will later write in *The Post Card*, "literature has always appeared unacceptable to me, a scandal, the moral fault *par excellence*."[15]) Deconstruction questions the dream of logocentrism, which is to make truth present in spoken discourse (10). Instead, deconstruction "inaugurates . . . the de-sedimentation" of truth dependent on the logos (10). Working within a given structure of a text or of the epoch named for Rousseau, deconstruction carefully examines and then looks beyond that structure, designating "the crevice through which the yet un-nameable glimmer beyond the closure can be glimpsed" (14). Thus, it works to free "the text . . . as a fabric of signs" from its con-finement in secondariness (14). Relentlessly, deconstruction challenges the question, "What is . . . ?" (18–19), as a move against essentialism, a logocentric fiction of presence. Deconstruction explores the ways of *différance*, "the production of differing/deferring" (23). In sum, deconstruction does not destroy textual structures from the outside but takes account of those structures by inhabiting them and by borrowing all of their subversive resources, until deconstruction falls prey in turn to its own work (24). In this sense, deconstruction works between structuralism and poststructuralism by establishing its critique of a text on the foundation supplied by that text itself.

Derrida moves toward his illustrative deconstructive readings by first observing that Western tradition continues to exist on the reassurance of a transcendent order of meaning whose discrepant aspects are reflected in an order of signs that forges a unity out of the discrepancies that constitute it. This reassurance requires the sustaining force from answers to such questions as "What is . . . ?," questions that manifest a longing for the present of the always absent. Heidegger is the master of such questions, as the titles of several of his books would suggest: *What Is Called Thinking?, What is Philosophy?, What is a Thing?* [*Die Frage nach dem Ding*]. Challenging the question, "What is . . . ?," however, is fundamental to Derrida's project. (Indeed, his challenge undermines the possibility of deriving any comfort or satisfaction from saying, as here, what is fundamental to his project or of enumerating the distinguishing features of deconstruction, as I have just done.)

Heidegger is important for Derrida, then, for several closely related reasons. Heidegger asks the what of the what and the why of the why. In *An Introduction to Metaphysics* (1953), Heidegger pursues the question, "Why are there essents [*seiendes*] rather than nothing?"[16] This question, Heidegger argues, is *the* broadest, deepest, and most fundamental of questions. It is *the essential* question which lies at the heart of metaphysics and, in turn, of philosophy. It is *the essentialist* question. It can be seen in the original meaning of the Greek word *physis* and in the fate of that meaning when *physis* is translated into the Latin *natura*. *Physis*, Heidegger argues, denotes "self-blossoming emergence . . . opening up, unfolding, inward-jutting-beyond-itself [*in-sich-aus-sich-hinausstehen*]." In this essay in poetic etymology, Heidegger invokes the blossoming of a rose, the rising of the sun, the rolling of the sea, and "the coming forth of man and animal from the womb" as instances of *physis*. The word itself is of great importance to him because "words and language are not wrappings in which things are packed for the commerce of those who write and speak. It is in words and language that things first come into being and are." Furthermore, he insists, it was not from the experience of natural phenomena that the Greeks learned about *physis*, but rather from their "fundamental poetic and intellectual experience of being."[17] The modern reduction of *physis* to the phenomena studied by physics is a pitiful narrowing of the original concept, in Heidegger's view. To ask the fundamental question of philosophy – "Why are there essents rather than nothing?" – is to ask at once the fundamental "What is . . . ?" question and the all-encompassing, self-reflective "Why . . . ?" question: "Why is what is, what is?" Finally, both in the fate of the Greek word *physis* and in the contortions Heidegger puts language through to ask what he wants to ask, the question of language ("How, why, and what do words mean?") arises as well.

Deconstruction works to destabilize the logocentrism of this philosophy of presence not at all by advancing what would appear to be the antithetical argument that it might be possible "to dispose of the sign." Instead, Derrida argues that within the age of Rousseau "reading and writing, the production of signs, the text in general as fabric of signs, allow themselves to be confined within secondariness" (14). Although Derrida does not do so explicitly or so crudely, one might object that Heidegger's interpretation of Greek words and Greek thought uproots individual words from their textual ground. When he does examine specific texts in detail – the two fragments of Heraclitus, the first chorus of *Antigone*, the maxim of Parmenides – the translations he offers are highly inventive.[18] Ralph Manheim, Heidegger's English translator, therefore, finds it necessary to translate from Heidegger's German versions of these texts rather than from the Greek originals. Yet in examining these texts, Heidegger warns his reader, in an elegant evasion, "We must attempt to hear only what is said."[19] Although Derrida does not call attention to this seemingly innocuous sentence, it nevertheless reveals two features of Heidegger's practice that Derrida will scrutinize in some detail: first, Heidegger refers to texts as though they are spoken rather than written; second, he substitutes his voice for the texts even before the text is "heard." The logocentric fiction of truth's presence in the word requires the obscuring of these processes of mediation. Even as he examines the importance of poetic intelligence, thus foregrounding his own distinctively metaphorical language, Heidegger distracts attention from the mediating function of metaphor, which maintains its underground existence in the metaphysical epoch of which Heidegger is a part. Derrida describes that function as "a sign signifying a signifier itself signifying an eternal verity, eternally thought and spoken in the proximity of a present logos" (15). Differing, deferring, distancing are the ways of metaphor; when the presence of truth is claimed for the word, metaphor is denied, forced back underground, repressed.

Metaphor has been the torment of philosophy because of its power continuously to recall the instability of the sign and the sign's escape from "the instituting question of philosophy: 'What is . . . ?'" (19). Unlike Heidegger, however, Nietzsche, in his radical concepts of interpretation, perspective, evaluation, and difference refuses (in Derrida's view) to remain "*simply . . . within* metaphysics." In his work to liberate the signifier from the metaphysics of logocentric presence and to affirm reading, writing, and textuality, Nietzsche is a precursor of grammatology:

> Nietzsche has *written what* he has written. He has written that writing – and first of all his own – is not originarily subordinate to the logos and to truth. And that this subordination has *come into being* during an epoch whose meaning we must deconstruct. (19)

Heidegger's study of Nietzsche, then, in Derrida's view, attempts to contain and control Nietzsche's refusal to assign writing to second-ariness, to a position subordinate to the logos and to truth. Heidegger's *Nietzsche* functions as a massive construction designed to defuse a major threat to Heidegger's sense of philosophy.[20] Although Derrida claims that "the virulence of Nietzschean thought could not be more completely misunderstood" than in the kind of reading Heidegger offers, Derrida nonetheless recommends "underwriting that interpretation" unreservedly, trusting that the "absolute strange-ness" of Nietzsche's discourse will eventually reassert itself, implying that "the Nietzschean demolition" (19) will do its work on Heidegger's text. Derrida then proceeds to read Heidegger as though in the tradition of Nietzsche, finding in Nietzsche's place in Heidegger's thought the deconstructive wedge that Heidegger, in the very attempt to conceal it, makes available to his reader.

In a later work, *De l'esprit (Of Spirit: Heidegger and the Question*, 1987), Derrida examines the recurring theme of spirit [*Geist*] in Heidegger, showing that it has a central place in Heidegger's thought even though – or perhaps especially because – Heidegger assiduously works to avoid it. Derrida finds in what Heidegger wishes to over-whelm – Nietzsche on writing – or to avoid – the theme of spirit – material of major importance for reading Heidegger. The final pages of *Grammatology*'s first chapter offer a preliminary version of such a reading, which serves both to demonstrate Heidegger's recurring interest in redeeming logocentrism – especially in the face of Nietzsche's refusal to be bound by it – and to demonstrate the protocols of deconstructive reading. Derrida's argument proceeds through the following steps. First, Heidegger's project, unlike Nietzsche's, is to "reinstate rather than destroy . . . the logos and the truth of being as . . . the 'transcendental' signified" (20). Heidegger's ambition is to speak the truth of being and by doing so to make such truth present in his very words. The structure of his thought would therefore be all-encompassing. The transcendental signified to which Heidegger would give voice embraces nothing less than that

> implied by all categories or all determined significations, by all lexicons and all syntax, and therefore by all linguistic signifiers, though not to be identified simply with any one of those signifiers, allowing itself to be precomprehended through each of them, remaining irreducible to all the epochal determinations that it nonetheless makes possible, thus opening the history of the logos, yet itself being only through the logos; that is, *being nothing* before the logos and outside of it. (20)

Second, the Heideggerian illusion is an extreme form of solipsism, hearing the voice that is "closest to the self as the absolute effacement of the signifier: pure auto-affection . . . which does not borrow from outside of itself" (20). This unique and spontaneous experience of the signified, is then considered "the experience of 'being.'" Third, However, Heidegger's thought ("the question of being") is enclosed within "an old linguistics" (21). Unknowingly, Heidegger's ontology sustains itself on the assumed indissoluble unity of "the question of being" with "the precomprehension of the *word being*" (21). Once the question of being is posed (that is, once it is put into words), the linguistics that works for its deconstruction (that is, a post-Saussurean linguistics) immediately comes into play. (In an important aside (21), Derrida anticipates his later discussion of Freud by observing that the deconstruction of Heidegger's ontology has major implications for psychoanalytic research no longer dominated by transcendental phenomenology.) Rather than invoking Saussure to dislocate Heidegger's articulation of the unity of being (as Lacan has done), Derrida finds in the text of Heidegger's own meditation the necessary materials for deconstructing the metaphysics of presence and logocentrism.

What is at stake in Derrida's reading is not a matter of attempting to know more than Heidegger knew about what he knew, of suggesting in any way that Heidegger should not be read, or of being for Heidegger or against him. Derrida reads Heidegger with consummate respect and intellectual admiration, which is to say that he does indeed *read* him. While reading Derrida's 1967 reading of Heidegger, it is important to recall that the full extent of Heidegger's involvement with Nazism – his commitment to it in 1933, the limited and unsatisfactory character of his explanations after the fact, and his silence about the Holocaust – has only in the 1980s and 1990s been clearly and inescapably focused upon his philosophical writings. (Heidegger's ten months' public activity in National Socialism has never been a secret.) Derrida, an Algerian Jew, has nevertheless consistently read Heidegger with a compassion all the more remarkable because of its refusal to ignore or to excuse Heidegger's wrong. In *Of Spirit*, which serves as a recent supplement to the reading of Heidegger in *Grammatology*, Derrida writes,

> Nazism was not born in the desert. We all know this, but it has to be constantly recalled. And even if, far from any desert, it had grown like a mushroom in the silence of a European forest, it would have done so in the shadow of big trees, in the shelter of their silence or their indifference but in the same soil. I will not list these trees which in Europe people an immense black forest.[21]

Derrida's language here is heavily allusive with Heideggerian metaphor. But in *Grammatology* Derrida stresses the changing character of Heidegger's writing. Up to 1935 Heidegger worked within what he called the ontic sciences, which chiefly concern themselves with how existence manifests itself in individual objects. Derrida concentrates his critique on *The Introduction to Metaphysics* (1935) because he sees it as Heidegger's renunciation of "the project of and the word ontology" (22).

The following passage, in all its baroque complexity, may be read as the climax of chapter 1, for here Derrida manages to sustain uncertainty and suspend the judgment of his reader with remarkable dexterity:

> The necessary, originary, and irreducible dissimulation of the meaning of being, its occultation within the very blossoming forth of presence, that retreat without which there would be no history of being which was completely *history* and history of *being*, Heidegger's insistence on noting that being is produced as history only through the logos, and is nothing outside of it, the difference between being and the entity – all this clearly indicates that fundamentally nothing escapes the movement of the signifier and that, in the last instance, the difference between signified and signifier *is nothing*. This proposition of transgression, not

yet integrated into a careful discourse, runs the risk of formulating regression itself. One must therefore *go by way of* the question of being as it is directed by Heidegger and by him alone, at and beyond onto-theology, in order to reach the rigorous thought of that strange non-difference and in order to determine it correctly. (22–3)

"What, precisely, is being said here?," one is tempted to ask, violating at a stroke the ban against both essentialist questions and phono-centric metaphors. Is this statement Derrida's own affirmation in opposition to Heidegger's? Is it Derrida's articulation of Heidegger's position as he moved away from ontic science in 1935? Is it Derrida's statement of a necessary Heideggerian position that one must think *through* (or *go by way of*) in order to move to a position *beyond* it? It may be productive to give affirmative answers to all of these questions. *The Introduction to Metaphysics* is important for Derrida because it displays Heidegger's thought on the move; because it manifests Heidegger's and Derrida's own discontent with an "old linguistics" that could not cope with Heidegger's double claim that thought obeys the Voice of Being (20) and that the voice of being is silent and wordless (22); and because it manifests to the full Heidegger's logocentrism in its discontent with itself. Derrida does not allow Heidegger's text to repress that discontent, even though it is not yet prepared to integrate it "into a careful discourse" (23). Derrida, then, retraces the path of Heidegger's thought, going "*by way of* the question of being" (23) in order to determine correctly where that thought is headed. By this means, Derrida projects the trajectory of that thought beyond the path Heidegger has traced for it in his text; he, thus, comes to recognize not only what is within but also what is "on the horizon of the Heideggerian paths" (23). Not only is all "*not to be thought at one go*" (23) (*why* the *what is* the *what is*), but also what can be written about what can be thought both *differs* from the thought and *defers* it, despite the intense desire to bring it nearer, to make it present. The horizon perpetually recedes as one moves forward on thought's path. To arrive at what was previously the horizon is to arrive at a different point than what was previously seen, not least because "now" that point has become a place from which a previously unseen horizon can be seen. Such simultaneous arrival and postponement, approaches and displacements, Derrida here names *différance*.[22]

Although Derrida focuses his initial exposition of deconstruction on *An Introduction to Metaphysics*, his procedure for reading Heidegger is derived from Heidegger's own account of "the task of destroying the history of ontology" in *Being and Time* (para. 6).[23] There Heidegger confronts the problem of how the traditional Western transmission of Being has ironically made Being inaccessible. In order to uncover the question of Being, its "hardened tradition must be loosened up." Although this is a "task of destruction," it is not so in a negative sense. Rather than seeking to bury Being's past "in nullity," this destruction stakes out "the positive possibilities of that tradition." Heidegger is even close to suggesting that this is a problem of writing: "The destruction of the history of ontology is essentially bound up with the way the question of Being is formulated, and it is possible only within such a formulation."[24] Derrida has clearly discovered here an opening in the structure of Heidegger's thought that invites a movement beyond it. Even as Heidegger insists on remaining finally within the "limits" of tradition in order to discover how the history of ontology has "bound up" the question of Being, he wants to be free of the darkness of the past so that the question of Being can be reawakened. However close he comes to setting the program for deconstruction, Heidegger remains, in Derrida's view, bound up in the tradition of ontology while "making explicit its principles."[25]

For Derrida writing and reading are characterized by "the necessity of passing through that erased determination" (24) from which each moment of arrival is also a moment of departure, where the anticipated gratification unleashes new desires. Even before Heidegger, Hegel "was already caught up in this game" (24). The passage on Hegel that concludes chapter 1 offers another example of deconstruction at work in a text that sets out to forestall deconstruction. Like Heidegger's voice of being that cannot speak, Hegel's alphabetic writing ("the best writing, the mind's writing" (24)) participates in the grounding "of interiority within the subject" only when it is effaced by the voice, only when it ceases to be writing and becomes speech. This leads Hegel to conclude, "intelligence expresses itself immediately and unconditionally through speech" (25). Here Hegel's key term is *Aufhebung*, which means not only "raising" and "elevation" but also "cessation" and "suspension." In this sense, *Aufhebung* is a textual process by which a term is simultaneously suspended or annulled and elevated or reaffirmed on a higher level. But since writing for Hegel involves both dilation and contraction, tumescence and detumescence, it betrays life. Yet because Hegel both manifests the ethnocentrism of logocentrism at its fullest and also the onset of the grammatological dislocation of the logos, Derrida celebrates him as "the last philosopher of the book and the first thinker of writing" (26).[26]

III

Linguistics and Grammatology

Following the polemical opening sections of *Grammatology*, its remaining chapters consist of four principal movements, each of which is an extended investigation of an episode in the history of the age of Rousseau. Part I, chapters 2 and 3 offer a reading of Saussure's *Course in General Linguistics* by considering the implications of that text and its legacy for an affirmative science of grammatology; part II, chapter 1 places Lévi-Strauss's "A Writing Lesson" from *Tristes Tropiques* in the tradition of Rousseau; chapters 2 and 3 conduct a microscopic critique of Rousseau's *Essay on the Origin of Languages* through the glass of Jean Starobinski's magisterial scholarship on Rousseau; and chapter 4 is largely devoted to a reading of Vico, Condillac, and Warburton, as all three are refracted through Rousseau, Starobinski, and M. V.-David. Here the archaeological movement of Derrida's text is back from the twentieth to the eighteenth century in order to provide a retracing of the history of the repression or marginalization of writing in the West. Although Plato's *Phaedrus* and Aristotle's *De interpretatione* are texts that can be said to "inaugurate" this history, the eighteenth century, for Derrida, is the time of the "combat and crisis" of the problem of writing (98).[27]

Implicit in each of the sections of his text is a sense of the capacity of critical reading to "produce" a signifying structure. Rather than specifying precisely what the task of reading entails, Derrida enumerates his principles of reading in a negative way. Reading that produces a signifying structure does not take the form of an "effaced and respectful doubling of commentary" in order to recover the "conscious, voluntary, intentional" activities of a writer (158). Far from being contemptuous of the procedures of classical commentary, however, Derrida sees them as forming theory's necessary "guardrail," which serves to keep "critical production . . . [from] developing in any direction at all" and from saying "almost anything." But

commentary finally only protects texts; it does not open them, as
critical reading can. Just as reading for Derrida is not a doubling of
the text, neither is it a transgression of the text "toward something
other than it." Critical reading does not hastily move toward a referent outside the text. Indeed, as Derrida announces in one of his
most famous and most misrepresented proclamations: "*There is nothing outside of the text*" ["*Il n'y a pas de hors-texte*" (*G*, 227)]. Here
Derrida's example is the temptation to turn to people in Rousseau's
life in the interest of understanding his writings. Such a move implies
the erroneous assumption that "real life" somehow determines the
text. This conviction is naïve in at least two respects. First, and less
important, is the fact that the reader of Rousseau has access to
Rousseau's life only through texts. Second, and more radically
important, is the observation that such a move to go beyond and
behind the text in order to escape "supplements, substitutive significations, [and] . . . differential references" is not possible. "There has
never been anything but writing" in the sense that every invocation of the real takes its meaning from the trace and the supplement. Therefore, Derrida concludes, "our reading must be intrinsic
and remain within the text" (159). Rather than confining deconstruction and grammatology to a conventional and limited sense of
discourse, this theory of critical reading discovers supplements,
substitutive significations, and differential references writ large in the
world.

Indeed, these are precisely the discoveries Derrida makes in his
reading of Saussure's *Course in General Linguistics*. In an important
final footnote to chapter 2 Derrida explains that he has given privileged attention to Saussure not only because of Saussure's continuing
importance in contemporary linguistics and semiology, but also because Saussure holds himself at the limit of the structure of thought
that he initiates. Like Heidegger, he remains within the limits of the
metaphysics that calls out for the kind of deconstructive reading to
which Derrida subjects it; but also, again like Heidegger, Saussure
himself has "scruples" and hesitations concerning those limits.
Saussure, then, is important for Derrida, first, because his explicitly
limited view of writing calls out for a grammatological critique; and,
second, because his own text provides the means for that critique,
which Derrida describes this way:

Unless my project has been fundamentally misunderstood, it should be
clear by now that, caring very little about Ferdinand de Saussure's *very*

thought *itself*, I have interested myself in a *text* whose literality has played a well-known role since 1915, operating within a system of readings, influences, misunderstandings, borrowings, refutations, etc. What I could read – and equally what I could not read – under the title of *A Course in General Linguistics* seemed important to the point of excluding all hidden and "true" intentions of Ferdinand de Saussure. (329n.)

This reading of Saussure is simultaneously a demonstration of deconstructive processes always at work everywhere, an exposition of how close Saussure himself came to understanding those processes, and a critique of Saussure's moral and metaphysical denunciation of writing, which keeps him confined by the very limitations he was able to see.

It is ironically fitting, because of its favorable attention to speech at the expense of writing, that Saussure's *Course* survives as a posthumous and disputed reconstruction of his lectures. In 1907, 1908–9, and 1910–11, Saussure taught a course on general linguistics at the University of Geneva. Because he kept few written notes from the course, it has had to be reconstructed from notes taken by his students. After his death in 1913, two of Saussure's colleagues, Charles Bally and Albert Sechehaye, who had not attended the lectures, decided to produce a text based chiefly on notes from 1910–11, but incorporating earlier material as well. Although Saussure's influence was made possible by Bally and Sechehaye's work, it is now apparent that they misrepresented Saussure's thought in a number of key respects, including misunderstanding his concept of the phoneme and giving inadequate consideration to his argument for the arbitrariness of the sign. A recent critical edition of the *Course* has at last made available all of the student notes from which the text was constructed.[28] The arguments in the *Course* that are most important for Derrida are these:

1 Language is a system of signs.
2 The sign has two components: the form that signifies (the signifier) and what it signifies (the signified).
3 The link between these two components is arbitrary, which "is the organising principle for the whole of linguistics, considered as a science of language structure."
4 The signifier and the signified are relational or differential entities.
5 Language, then, is not simply a nomenclature; there are no fixed universal concepts or signifiers.

6   Each language is a distinctive and arbitrary way of organizing and
     conceptualizing the world.[29]

These concepts become part of Derrida's positive science of
grammatology.

What is most problematic for Derrida is chapter VI of the *Course*,
"Representation of a Language by Writing." Like Rousseau, Saussure
values most what is original and natural. In language that is speech,
whereas writing sets out to usurp what is primary and to promote
a forgetfulness about origins. Although it pretends to be an aid to
memory, writing in fact opposes or displaces living memory with its
own artificiality, secondariness, and supplementarity. Here, Derrida
points out, Saussure has made the same discovery that Plato came
upon in the *Phaedrus*: writing signifies forgetfulness,

> because it is a mediation and the departure of the logos from itself.
> Without writing, the [logos] would remain in itself. Writing is the dis-
> simulation of the natural, primary, and immediate presence of sense
> to the soul within the logos. Its violence befalls the soul as uncon-
> sciousness. (37)

Like others before him who have denounced it, Saussure invokes a
series of extreme metaphors for writing: contamination, forced entry,
archetypal violence, eruption of the outside within the inside, sin,
body, clothing, disguise, trap, the pathological, monstrosity.[30] From
his analysis of these metaphors it appears to Derrida that Saussure has
set out simultaneously to show how writing has corrupted speech, to
denounce the harm that writing has done, and to assert, nonetheless,
the inalterable and recoverable nature of language (41). Saussure's
project is important for Derrida's own because Saussure was on the
verge of understanding language as logocentric metaphysics. He saw
without fully understanding a point of convergence of the new
science of linguistics with philosophy of language. Semiotics and
glossematics have given sustained attention to that convergence; and
as Derrida proceeds to examine the contributions of these fields, his
own text manifests the strains produced by concurrently opening
philosophical discourse up to the contributions of linguistics and
alerting linguistics to the metaphysical implications of its most recent
discoveries.[31]

Derrida credits the American philosopher C. S. Peirce, the founder
of semiotics, with having gone "very far in the direction that I have

called the de-construction of the transcendental signified" (49). Although Peirce died in 1914, the year before the publication of Saussure's *Course*, Derrida sees in his semiology an advance over Saussurean linguistics. In his disarming assertion, "We think only in signs,"[32] Peirce had come to see logic as the science of signs. In his view, a sign (or *representamen*) is that "which stands to somebody for something in some respect or capacity" and is, therefore, "anything which determines something else (its *interpretant*) to refer to an object to which itself refers (its *object*)."[33] For Peirce, grammar, logic, and rhetoric are but three branches of the science of semiotics. Although semiology, as proposed by Peirce, is more comprehensive than linguistics, the tenacity of the linguistic sign is such that its operations remain the model for semiology. Thus, Roland Barthes claims that "linguistics is not a part, even if privileged, of the general science of signs, it is semiology that is a part of linguistics."[34] This reversal, which submits semiology to linguistics, is for Derrida exemplary of logocentric metaphysics (51). If read in light of Derrida's argument, Barthes' text can be seen as a fortification of Saussurean linguistics against Peirce and Hjelmslev.

Whereas Peirce's semiotics differs from Saussurean theory by incorporating language into a more comprehensive science of signs, Louis Hjelmslev's glossematics modifies Saussurean linguistics from within its own theory. While largely accepting Saussure's principle that language is, above all, form rather than substance, Hjelmslev departs from Saussure's view that the sign is the basic unit of language.[35] Even before Hjelmslev, linguists had investigated units of language smaller than the sign, such as the phoneme and the seme, which are the distinctive phonetic and semantic units. The prior discovery of these elements made it possible for Hjelmslev to study the combination and interplay of linguistic units, rather than concentrating solely on their distinctive features. Once the authentic form of language that constitutes these combinations emerges, it became possible for Hjelmslev to investigate the form of content. He was careful, however, to remind his readers that the combinatorial units (glossemes) in no way dispense with the distinctive features of language as studied by phonologists, nor did he find it possible to say positively what these units of combination are. For Derrida, Hjelmslev succeeded in finding not only a certain amount of play within Saussurean theory but also in finding that language is more like a game of chess than like the principles of economics. Derrida quotes – apparently with approval – Hjelmslev's declaration that

"The scheme of language is in the last analysis a *game* and nothing more" (57).

This sense of the game of language and the recognition of the specificity of writing made it possible for glossematics to reach the literary element of language and to arrive at "what in literature passes through an irreducibly graphic text, tying the *play of form* to a determined substance of expression." By isolating the bond that links this play of form to the substance of writing, glossematics recaptured, Derrida claims, what in literature is not reducible to voice, epos, or poetry; and it, thus, has made it possible "to study the purely graphic stratum within the structure of the literary text" (59). In his brief passage on the importance of the work of the Copenhagen School of linguistics for literary study, Derrida merely hints at the importance of literature within his own grammatological project.[36] Later (in 1980) he claimed that his "most constant interest, coming even before my philosophical interest I should say, if this is possible, has been directed towards literature, towards that writing which is called literary."[37] In one sense, the literary category for Derrida is broadly inclusive and is an institution or "authorization to say everything," which depends on democracy as its political or ideological place. But on the other hand, literature is distinguishable (though not entirely) from poetry and belles-lettres and from non-European discursive works. The literary texts to which Derrida repeatedly turns – texts by Mallarmé Joyce, Celan, Bataille, Artaud, Blanchot, Rousseau, Flaubert – are texts that are themselves "inscribed in a *critical* experience of literature."[38] They make problematic their own status as literary texts even as they critically reflect upon literature as an institution. Literature's critical self-reflexivity constitutes the play of form [*le jeu de la forme*] within which deconstructive processes occur.[39]

Having celebrated the achievements of the Copenhagen School of linguistics – especially Hjelmslev's isolation of the linguistic system from metaphysical speculation – Derrida proceeds to inquire into the transcendental origin of the linguistic system itself and of the theory that studies it. Is the formalism or scientific objectivity of glossematics simply a concealed metaphysics? In order to pursue this question, Derrida invokes a number of conceptual terms that serve to explore territory beyond or "short-of" the terrain of transcendental criticism or classical reason. These terms are parts of a metaphorical network derived from the physical processes of writing: "trace," "archewriting," "erasure." Although it is difficult to resist the temptation to ask, "What does Derrida *mean* by these terms?," the terms themselves participate in his effort to investigate critically the need to ask "what is" and to answer any such question with a definition that forgets the differential and deferring processes of signification, which Derrida insists is the only way words and concepts receive meaning (70). These particular terms mark Derrida's determination "to see to it that the beyond does not return to the within" (61), which at least is an effort to resist forgetting Saussure's challenge to remain aware of how processes of signification cannot even be thought about without the first move of recognizing the sign as pointing beyond itself, rather than making what it points to present in itself. If that first move is too easily forgotten, it is not surprising, therefore, that such comprehensive and transcendental concepts as Plato's *eidos*, St John's *logos*, or Heidegger's *Dasein* can too easily be conceived as available – and, above all, present – in those italicized words.

If the reader starts, however, with the recognition that the opposition to such transcendental concepts is productive – that, in Blake's terms, "without contraries is no progression," or in Paul de Man's, that insight can come out of blindness – then it should be possible to uncover the pathway [*parcours*] that such concepts leave behind as and when they are opposed. If they leave a track or trace in the text – a footprint for the grammatological detective to follow – then following the track should not be expected to lead back to the source or forward to its presence. Instead, "trace" signifies the minimal element of structure that makes any sense of difference possible. (It may, therefore, be thought of as both inside and outside – before and after – the possibility of definition.) It is like the sign, the glosseme, the seme, the phoneme, and the grapheme in that it is another entry in the lexicon of linguistics that seeks an understanding of the atomic elements of structure that make language possible. The trace is the concept hidden beneath those other entries and simultaneously marks the point in Heideggerian discourse where "the meaning of being as presence and the meaning of language as the full continuity of speech" begins to undermine itself. The trace also marks Derrida's intention in writing *Of Grammatology*, which he describes with uncharacteristic directness: "To make enigmatic what one thinks one understands by the words 'proximity,' 'immediacy,' 'presence' (the proximate [*proche*], the own [*propre*], and the pre- of presence), is my final intention in this book" (70). The trace must be thought through before such oppositions as nature and culture, speech and writing, painting and music, upon which the thought of Rousseau rests, can be critically examined.

As that minimal element of structure that makes possible differentiation, the trace gives rise to such distinctions as primary and secondary, interior and exterior. "Arche-writing" moves back and forth between these distinctions. The judgment that writing is secondary and exterior to speech requires the signifying movements these distinctions make possible. As the origin of writing, arche-writing may be thought to be the spoken word. But if speech is natural, then it would seem to require a sense already of what is not natural, which in this context must be writing. This particular trace – arche-writing – is, then, "the opening of the first exteriority in general, the enigmatic relationship of the living to its other and of an inside to an outside" (70). Such a non-presence of the other and the simultaneous possibility of thinking of the other as though present gives rise to metaphor. Further, the presence-absence of the trace underlies the play that makes metaphorical ambiguity possible, since ambiguity presupposes the logic of presence, which it proceeds to disobey.

As a development from the trace and arche-writing, the graphological technique of putting a word under erasure [*sous rature*] makes possible the visualizing of these traces; thus, Derrida introduces this phrase, derived from Heidegger, before proceeding to theorize the trace (60). Again and again in thinking and writing about Derrida the temptation arises to use such words as "is," "means," "identifies," "says," as though those words retain something of their pre-Derridean innocence. Because these words have been subjected to Derridean critique – because their metaphysical freight has been weighed – they are crossed out; but being unavoidable – indeed, because they make the critique possible – they remain legible. In *The Question of Being* (*Zur Seinsfrage*) Heidegger explores the philosophical problems of definition as he attempts to define nihilism. He thus crosses out the word "Being," while keeping it legible. Derrida's "trace" and the particular trace that he designates "arche-writing" are extensions of Heidegger's textual practice in *The Question of Being*, just as most of Derrida's thought has critical reference points in Heidegger's texts. Indeed, crossing out while keeping legible is not a misleading metaphor for deconstruction.

IV

Of Grammatology as a Positive Science

"On what conditions is a grammatology possible?" Derrida asks in chapter 3. His search for an answer is guided by the work of Madeleine V.-David, whose *Le Débat sur les écritures et l'hieroglyphe aux xvii et xviii siècles* (1965) provided Derrida with the occasion for the first formulation of this chapter, which appeared as a review in *Critique*. In her book and in several journal articles Madeleine V.-David began to carry out a philosophical investigation into the history of writing, which William Warburton had called for in 1742. In his appropriation of her historical research, Derrida makes his way back to Warburton's monumental work, *The Divine Legation of Moses*, a portion of which was published in Paris in 1744 as *Essai sur les hieroglyphes des Egyptiens*. This translation inspired at least the conclusion of Condillac's discussion of language in his *Essay on the Origin of Human Knowledge* and in turn influenced Rousseau.[40] As in natural science, the first efforts to carry out a history of writing in the eighteenth century had to cope with "speculative prejudice and ideological presumption" (75). Grammatology, however, even more than natural science, was hampered by ideology and theological prejudice because of the powerful link between Judaeo-Christian theology and biblical assumptions about writing. The belief that Hebrew script was first written by the finger of God and that biblical Hebrew was the first of the world's languages became eventually linked with the belief that Jesus Christ was the incarnation of God's word and the means by which God makes himself present in the world. Seventeenth- and eighteenth-century historical linguists and grammatologists had to contend with a theological opposition to what threatened theology's fundamental ideological investment: the transcendent word, by which God becomes present in history. "In all its forms, overt or covert, this theologism . . . constituted the major obstacle to all grammatology" (76).

In an effort to overcome this obstacle, Descartes, Leibniz, and others seized upon Chinese script as a model for philosophical language because it was thought to be free of voice and liberated from history. The "Chinese prejudice" thus arises to fill a European philosophical need. That this language of the other is created to fill what the European mind experiences as its lack is best conveyed by a sentence from Leibniz's *Opuscules et fragments*: "Meanwhile [this language of undifferentiated presence] will be a great help – for using what we know, for finding out what we lack, for inventing ways of redeeming the lack, but especially for settling controversies in matters that depend on reasoning" (78). Rather than being considered a distinctive language in itself, Chinese was imagined as a whole and complete metaphysical presence. The other side of this hallucination was the total disparagement of what was thought distinctively European. Thus, the non-European other served only to fill what was designated as the European *lack*, and this ethnocentrism manifested itself specifically as a logocentrism. Here Derrida begins to make good on his claim, in the opening pages of his text, to provide a critique of the ethnocentric underpinnings of logocentrism. There are, then, wide implications of this hallucination of a non-existent Chinese language that solves the problem of all other language. Ethnocentrism can work in more subtle ways than the assumption of unique power and authority in European culture. Derrida sees in the projection of the longing for presence, completeness, and identity *onto* the non-European culture, and the corresponding disparagement of what is Western by the Western mind, an equally insidious form of ethnocentrism. Both forms deny the otherness of the other. The "European hallucination" (80) of a language that lacks any lack is a strategy both to challenge the previously assumed priority of the biblical languages – here, ironically, thought of as entirely Western – and to avoid the full consequences of that challenge.[41] In such an arithmetical ideology, the European is a zero and the other is an undifferentiated totality. The problem, for Derrida, is less the European lack than the European invention of a plentitude in the Other, which denies the Other its linguistic and psychoanalytic (divided) subjectivity.[42] The cost of being the European object of hallucination is nothing less than the non-European's human subjectivity.

Grammatology, therefore, resists being encompassed by the "sciences of man" because it thoroughly suspects – as Lacan had done – the assumption of human identity or unity. Identity assumes sameness always and everywhere. André Leroi-Gourhan's work, which Derrida reviews in this chapter, also emphasizes the productive disruption of this unitary assumption about "man" that is effected by writing: "To free unity from the concept of man is undoubtedly to renounce the old notion of peoples said to be 'without writing' and 'without history'" (83). But once the assumption of viable unity is disrupted, so is the medium by which it is asserted: the book. Derrida, in this carefully structured book, repeatedly announces "the end of the book" (86). Here it would seem that he is haunted by the voice of Koheleth in Ecclesiastes – "of making many books there is no end" – and that his making of many books is an effort to end the era of the book and to initiate the era of writing. At this point in his argument, appropriately, Derrida invokes, with carefully sustained ambiguity, Melanie Klein's "The Role of the School in the Libidinal Development of the Child," which had been translated into French by Marguerite Derrida.[43] In a footnote of his own, Derrida reprints Klein's footnote (p. 75 in her original text, pp. 333–4 in his) on then current (1923) work on Chinese script and its interpretation by psychoanalysis:[44]

> At a meeting of the Berlin P. A. Society, Herr Rohr dealt in some detail with the Chinese script and its interpretation on a psychoanalytic basis. In the subsequent discussion I pointed out that the earlier picture-script, which underlies our script too, is still active in the phantasies of every individual child, so that the various strokes, dots, etc., of our present script would only be simplifications, achieved as a result of condensation, displacement and other mechanisms familiar to us from dreams and neuroses, of the earlier pictures whose traces, however, would be demonstrable in the individual. (334n.)

Derrida is warning that the European hallucination is also invading psychoanalytic theory undetected. He concludes part I with the dire prediction that grammatology, like psychoanalytic theory, will remain walled-in by the metaphysical-theological linguistics of presence. But within the walls of that metaphysics there is thought, which Derrida describes as "the blank part of the text, the necessarily indeterminate index of a future epoch of differance" (93). The play within the structure of the text gives thought room to work and a profoundly serious job to do.

V

The Violence of the Letter

As he prepares to put to the test the critical concepts outlined in part I of *Grammatology*, Derrida carefully explains his focus on Rousseau.

First, Rousseau's work occupies a unique position in the history of metaphysics as presence, as logocentrism, and as an effort to obliterate the trace. But while repeating this history, which was inaugurated by Plato and Aristotle, Rousseau also offers "a new model of presence," which he locates within "*consciousness* or *feeling*" (98). Second, unlike Descartes or Hegel, Rousseau tackles the problem of writing, in which he had seen the consequences of the successful efforts to decipher non-European script.[45] Unlike Descartes and Leibniz, Rousseau had begun to resist the European hallucination. In this respect – and because, like Mallarmé and Pound, he recognized the greater possibility of a logocentric breakthrough in literature than in philosophy – he began to effect a powerful challenge to transcendental authority, which Nietzsche would continue and intensify (92). Third, Rousseau's sustained influence can also be seen in the work of Lévi-Strauss, where the ethnocentric function of logocentrism is clearly manifest even as it is actively resisted.

Part II, chapter 1, "The Violence of the Letter," is largely devoted to Derrida's reading of two episodes in Lévi-Strauss's *Tristes Tropiques*. This reading makes possible both a focusing of Derrida's argument and an expansion of it at the same time. Unlike Saussure, Lévi-Strauss contributes little to Derrida's theory of textual processes; but like Rousseau, he conceives of writing in broad historical and ideological terms that seem to invite Derrida's deconstructive reading. Derrida begins by making a distinction between discourse and text. "Discourse" signifies "the present, living, conscious *representation* of a *text* within the experience of the person who writes or reads it," whereas the "text" not only exceeds such representation but does so "by the entire system of its resources and its own laws" (101), as though guided by an internal avoidance mechanism that keeps it from being totally captured by a single act of reading. Deconstruction might then be seen as operating in this problematic zone between text and discourse. In his chapter entitled "The Writing Lesson," Lévi-Strauss works within this difficult zone. The title of his book suggests much of its tone and point of view. Part autobiography and part retrospective on his field work in Brazil, it is an extended and sweetly melancholy farewell to a world which ceased to exist between the 1930s, when Lévi-Strauss was there, and 1955, when his book was published. In one sense, this beautifully written book provides the tropics with an afterlife even as it sadly records their passing. It is not just Derrida who opportunistically seizes upon the chapter "The Writing Lesson" as a focus for his critique; it rather seems that

Lévi-Strauss has structured his entire text in such a way as to invite this focus.

"The Writing Lesson" begins with a stark reflection on the gradual extinction of the Nambikwara population, which declined from approximately 20,000 in 1915 to no more than 2,000 when Lévi-Strauss visited with them in 1938. It is not only their exemplary vulnerability that makes the Nambikwara important; they also constitute the goal of the ethnographer's professional quest: "I had been looking for a society reduced to its simplest expression. That of the Nambikwara was so truly simple that all I could find in it was individual human beings."[46] As the subject of Lévi-Strauss's dissertation, *La Vie familiale et sociale des Indiens Nambikwara*, published in 1948, they become intimately associated with his reflections on his own writing practices.[47] In this tribe, Lévi-Strauss is convinced, he succeeded in finding not only the most elementary of cultures, but also the equivalent of the natural origin of human life that Rousseau had sought but was unable to find:

> I had gone to the ends of the earth to look for what Rousseau calls "the almost imperceptible stages of man's beginnings" . . . I had continued my search for a state which – as Rousseau also says – "no longer exists, has perhaps never existed, and probably will never exist, and of which it is nevertheless essential to form a correct notion in order rightly to judge our present state." I believed that, having been luckier than Rousseau, I had discovered such a state in a moribund society, about which there was no point in wondering whether or not it was vestigial. Whether traditional or degenerate, this society offered one of the most rudimentary forms of social and political organization that could possibly be imagined.[48]

The incident of "The Writing Lesson" reveals this elemental state as well as Lévi-Strauss's own professional ambition and ambiguous success as an ethnographer.

It had been Lévi-Strauss's practice to distribute pencils and paper among the non-literate tribes he visited. When he observes the Nambikwara drawing wavy lines, he recognizes that they are simply mimicking what they see him do with writing implements. The chief of the tribe, however, had further ambitions, since "he was the only one who had grasped the purpose of writing." What the chief understands is that writing is a matter of power and that if he convinces his companions that he has mastered the white man's writing and has become an intermediary agent for the exchange of goods, then his power will be enhanced. But it is only after the fact that Lévi-Strauss realizes that the chief had seized on writing not to acquire knowledge, to remember, or to understand, but rather to increase his prestige and authority at the expense of others. This realization in turn leads Lévi-Strauss to reconsider the common view that writing has increased the ability of humans to preserve know-ledge, that it is a form of artificial memory, that it makes possible a clearer view of the past and an enhanced ability to organize the pres-ent and the future, and that it marks the distinction between barbar-ism and civilization. This view he rejects because one of the most creative phases of human history occurred before writing, in the early neolithic age; because there clearly was tradition before writing; because writing, invented between 4,000 and 3,000 BC, was itself a result of the "neolithic revolution"; because for 5,000 years, from the birth of writing, "knowledge fluctuated more than it increased;" and because life for a Greek and Roman citizen was not vastly different from that of an eighteenth-century middle-class European such as Rousseau. These reflections lead Lévi-Strauss to the conclusion that writing seems to have favoured the exploitation rather than the devel-opment of human beings.[49]

Indeed, it finally seems, as Lévi-Strauss reflects back on this episode, that the Nambikwara knew this before he did, since they withdrew their allegiance to their chief because of his blatant attempt to exploit a feature of civilization in order to assert his power over them. But even this is in accordance with a principle of Rousseau's. As he becomes corrupted by the uncertain power of writing, the chief refuses to renounce his independence in the interest of the general will. Writing – even as mime – blinds him to the basis of social life, which consists of contract and consent.

Derrida finds his opening for a critique of Lévi-Strauss in an earlier chapter of *Tristes Tropiques* entitled "On the Line." Here the question becomes, whose violence is displayed in Lévi-Strauss's text? This episode opens with Lévi-Strauss's unconvincing assurance that "the Nambikwara were easy-going, and unperturbed by the presence of the anthropologist with his notebook and camera."[50] He proceeds to describe playing with a group of children when a little girl, after being hit by a playmate, tried to whisper something in his ear. He soon realizes that as an act of revenge against her enemy, she is violating the taboo against revealing proper names. Indeed, it had become a practice of the anthropologists to assign Portuguese names to the Indians because they could not learn their proper names.

Lévi-Strauss seizes upon the opportunity supplied by the quarrel between the two girls "to incite the children against each other and get to know all their names."[51] As in "The Writing Lesson," Lévi-Strauss, aware as he is of the devastating consequences of the contamination by Western culture on the disappearing world of the Nambikwara, yet eager as he is to believe that they were "unperturbed by the presence of the anthropologist," proceeds to violate the virgin space of the girls' play, to exploit unscrupulously – as he himself admits – their childish quarrels, to encourage the tribe to mimic literacy, and to tempt their chief to exploit the power of Western literacy in a way that leads eventually to his deposition and exile. Here the ultimate violence is not that of the children against each other or of the chief against his tribe; rather it is the violence of the ethnographer himself, who violates the virginal space of the Nambikwara first with his foreign spectator's presence (113) and then with his political ideology (131).

Derrida recalls that Lévi-Strauss had himself referred to the "Marxist hypothesis on the origins of writing" (119) to be found in *Tristes Tropiques*. That hypothesis – more accurately a blend of Saussurean phonocentrism and Lévi-Strauss's Marxism – combines the two constituents of the European hallucination: (1) "man's exploitation by man is the fact of writing cultures of the Western type," and (2) "communities of innocent and unoppressive speech are free from this accusation" (121). In his critique of Lévi-Strauss's political ideology, Derrida observes that Lévi-Strauss does not distinguish either between hierarchization and domination or between authority and exploitation. As a result of this failure, he "confounds law and oppression" in a way that is totally alien to Rousseau, while nonetheless offered under the name of Rousseau. Lévi-Strauss argues a necessary coincidence of compulsory education, military service, and proletarization, which leads him to conclude that the struggle in the nineteenth century against illiteracy is "indistinguishable from the increased powers exerted over the individual citizen by the central authority" and that it is in the interest of the state for everyone to be able to read so that "Authority can decree that 'ignorance of law is no defence'" (131–2). Derrida warns against the temptation simply to reverse Lévi-Strauss's judgment. Indeed, in Europe in the nineteenth century, Derrida concedes, the progress of education and formal legality might well have had the effect of consolidating power in a given class or in the state. But it cannot be "rigorously deduced" that liberty, illiteracy, and the absence of public instruction go hand in hand. Lévi-Strauss has been driven by the unexamined metaphysical and ethical weight of his suspicion of writing to adopt a univocal conception of law and the state, which substitutes anarchy for Rousseau's contract and consent. In this sense, Lévi-Strauss made his long journey into the jungles of Brazil only to deny the other, which was the object of his search. Without *différance*, which is the recognition of writing in speech, and without the "presence *of the other*," Derrida concludes, there is no ethics (139–40), only ethnocentrism replicated in the name of anti-ethnocentrism.

VI

Introduction to the "Age of Rousseau"

The rest of *Grammatology* (141–316) is devoted to Derrida's reading of Rousseau.[52] Part II, chapter 2, concerns the problematical relationship between Rousseau's experience of writing and his theory of writing. Derrida refers to the first as Jean-Jacques and the second as Rousseau (144). Chapter 3 comprises a detailed reading of the *Essay on the Origin of Languages*, which in turn is divided into three sections. The first section locates the *Essay* in the structure of Rousseau's oeuvre. Here Derrida takes issue with Starobinski, who argues that the *Essay* is distinguishable in its thought from Rousseau's second *Discourse* and from *Emile* in that the concept of natural pity is absent from it. The second section considers the structure of the *Essay*.[53] Its first eleven chapters are devoted to problems of language: its genesis and degeneration, the movement from speech to writing, the formation of language in northern and in southern locales. Its chapters 12 to 19 concern music, arguing that there is no music before language, that music is at first song, that it is born of passion, and that it comes into being at the same time as human society. Art, according to this argument, "operates through the sign and is effective through imitation"; furthermore, "it can only take place within the system of a culture, and the theory of art [consequently] is a theory of mores" (206). Section three elaborates on the problem of articulation, or how it is possible for a child to speak before knowing how. This problem manifests the tension, running through the entire *Essay*, between what Rousseau would like to say and what he is constrained to say. He would like to say that development or "progress" – for example, the movement from the natural to the social or from speech to writing – is either for better or for worse. What he is constrained to say is that "progress" is for the worse and the better and that "the space of writing operates at the origin of language" (229). In such arguments as this, Derrida concludes, eschatology and teleology are annulled by Rousseau. Derrida's final chapter places Rousseau in the context of seventeenth- and eighteenth-century debates about writing and considers the view, most starkly expressed by Condillac, that philosophers write prose because of their inability to bend to the rules of poetry (287).[54]

A major difficulty facing the reader of these chapters is the problem of determining which text Derrida is focusing upon at any given moment. Although this is too schematic a description of the problem, it may help to distinguish three lenses through which Derrida's reader is being invited to read Rousseau's *Essay*. Sometimes Derrida holds up one lens, then another; sometimes all three at once. First, there is Derrida's grammatological theory; second there is Starobinski's theoretical criticism; and third, there is Rousseau's own self-reflective theory of writing. The reader may look through these lenses at Rousseau's text, examine the lenses themselves, or discover that the *Essay* has partially anticipated the sorts of theories being brought to bear upon it. What is unusual here is the importance Derrida attaches to Starobinski's lens. It seems that Derrida wants to dispense with it but cannot see Rousseau clearly without it. For example, in the context of his negative account of the task of reading, where he distinguishes critical reading, which he wishes to promote, from commentary, which he finds suspiciously necessary, he writes: *"The security with which the commentary considers the self-identity of the text, the confidence with which it carves out its contour, goes hand in hand with the tranquil assurance that leaps over the text toward its presumed content, in the direction of the pure signified"* (159, italics in the original). Derrida does not here name Starobinski as the author of such commentary, but his reference at the end of the paragraph to a work on Rousseau with an appendix that details his medical case-history no doubt alludes to Starobinski's *Jean-Jacques Rousseau: Transparency and Obstruction*.[55]

It seems, however, that Starobinski's essay "Rousseau and the Peril of Reflection," which is reprinted in *The Living Eye*, has had a greater impact on Derrida.[56] Although it is not Starobinski's purpose in that essay to deal with this problem explicitly, he nevertheless brilliantly illuminates Rousseau's ambiguous relationship to philosophy, which is startlingly similar to Derrida's. Reflection is for Rousseau the scene of multiple conflicts. It gives the thinker "access to being" and "confers 'a meaning on the word is;' " but also, by making us anxious about the instability of appearances, it "causes us to forget our true being." Reflection is, thus, dual in respect to its interpretation – since it constitutes both progress and fall – and dual, as well, in its cause, since "it results from the combination of an *internal* disposition with an *external* obstacle." The inwardness of reflection "takes shape and becomes aware of itself only in contact with the resistance of the external world." It is, however, in the doubleness of the effects of reflection that Rousseau's view, as mediated by Starobinski, becomes virtually indistinguishable from Derrida's:

> Reflection is double in its effects as well as its causes. An "active principle," it unifies the external world by introducing into it a network of ratios and relations. It takes scattered, isolated sensations and creates unified objects. But it also makes us aware of difference. It destroys the alliance of sympathy that previously united man with nature, animals, and his fellow man. The price to be paid for the unity it brings to the objective world is the condemnation of consciousness to the misery of separation.[57]

This reading of Rousseau anticipates Derrida's repeated emphasis on grammatology's mission to expose the logocentric metaphysics of unified presence, to discover – indeed, to celebrate – the deconstructive resources within that structure, but soberly to recognize how inescapably contained the celebrant is by that logocentric metaphysical structure of which he is a part. That mission is inscribed within the history of the age of Rousseau.

Although all three sections of chapter 3 propose to carry out this mission by a meticulous reading of Rousseau's *Essay*, section I is the most theoretically ambitious; and were it not for Derrida's many warnings about centers, it would be tempting to propose this section as the center of Derrida's text. The topics considered include writing and reading as auto-eroticism, natural pity, the strategies of femininity, the moral imagination, and death. In Rousseau's treatment of each of these topics, Derrida finds an invitation to deconstructive reading. Picking up on Rousseau's comparison in *The Confessions* of "silent and ill-chosen reading" to his first discoveries of auto-eroticism (340n.), Derrida comments on the difficulty of separating writing from masturbation. What links these two activities is the experience of "touching-touched" [*touchant-touché* (*G*, 235)], or the double sensations of two exposed surfaces of the body at once. Not only, he argues, are all living things capable of auto-affection, but also "auto-affection is the condition of an experience in general" (165) because sensory exteriority "submits itself to my power of repetition" (166). Derrida also wants to employ the metaphorical sense of onanism as the expending or ejaculation of seed into the world. Speech does not fall into the exteriority of space. While suppressing *différance*, speech nevertheless requires the listener as present other. Writing, on the other hand, arises from absence. It is what is added to "living self-present speech" (167) as supplement, much as masturbation presupposes (or supplements) the concept of sexual activity with a partner.

As a transition to the concept of pity, Derrida cites a passage from *Émile* in which Rousseau argues against the teaching of foreign languages because each language transmits a culture over which the teacher has no control. Rousseau understands the operation of difference in language, Derrida implies, but in such passages as this he reveals that he does not value it: "Every language has its own form, a difference which may be partly cause and partly effect of difference in national character" (170). Against this background of Rousseau's unstable treatment of difference, Derrida proceeds to consider Rousseau's use of the word "pity" or "compassion" [*pitié*], especially in the second *Discourse* and in the *Essay*. This passage (173ff.) is a good example of Derrida's practice of taking up something that seems at first marginal, but by examining it carefully – especially as it is cast into metaphor – he reveals its radiating significance in Rousseau's thought. What is at stake here is more than a controversy with Starobinski and other scholars over the dating of the *Essay*. Indeed, Rousseau's concept of pity is inextricably bound up in his theory of writing. Natural pity is exemplified in the relation between mother and child. Pity's soft, maternal voice is nature, which makes it possible for the order of pity to supplement the order of the law. Whereas pity is a voice, writing "is *without pity*" (173). Unlike amorous passion, which is its perversion, natural pity is the root of the love for others and is clearly distinguishable from self-love, as it is from amorous passion, both of which limit attachment to a single person.

What is cultural in love serves femininity, which is "made to enslave man to woman" (176). Femininity is not in this sense the prerogative of women but rather the sexual equivalent of Hegel's dialectic of master and slave. Working either among women or among men, therefore, the feminine principle writes the history of love as a history of denaturalization and initiates a move away from pity. In this context, the moral is but a mask for boundless desire, which requires the supplement of reason. Rousseau, thus, finds it necessary to argue that reason is both in nature and a supplement to it. Bound to reason, "moral love," in its lack of biological foundation, "is born of the power of imagination" (177) and degrades whatever it touches, even writing, just as it enervates man. Natural pity is, as a result, in danger of being strangled, as writing – especially "literary" writing – conspires with "moral love" (181). These reflections enable Derrida to arrive at two concluding observations concerning Rousseau's theory of language and the basic structure of *différance* in his *Essay*. First, he announces the immediate consequence of the argument so far:

> Reason, a function of interest and need, the technical and calculating faculty, is not the origin of language, which is also a human property and without which there would be no perfectibility. Language is born of the imagination which arouses or at any rate excites sentiment or passion.

Second, he enumerates two series of terms or concepts in Rousseau's text that "relate to each other according to the structure of supplementarity:"

> We thus see two series working themselves out: (1) animality, need, interest, gesture, sensibility, understanding, reason, etc. (2) humanity, passion, imagination, speech, liberty, perfectibility, etc.

The second set of terms relate to the first as supplementary metaphysical determinations. As supplements, they desire to complete the terms in the first set in order to achieve an integrated metaphysical coherence. While setting up this structure of concepts as though to allow such appropriation by the second set to take place, Rousseau will not allow it to happen. Imagination, for example, is hardly an unambiguously affirmative supplement if it gives birth to "moral love," the depravity of culture, the degradation of writing, and the enervation of man. Out of the supplementary *différance* of these sets comes death, the "dangerous *différance*" (183).

Derrida is not simply dismissing death as a grammatological figure. It is neither dying nor being dead, but rather "the anguished anticipation of death," which underlies supplementarity. This anticipation is "the abyss from which all menaces announce themselves" and of which all supplementarities are but metonymic substitutions. In so far as death, in this sense, is an image generated by the imagination, the imagination for Rousseau – and for Derrida – "is the power that allows life to affect itself with its own representation." Or, more simply, "Imagination is at bottom the relationship with death" (184) in that it is the means by which life refers to the other than itself. As the "faculty of signs and appearances," the imagination both awakens and transgresses what Rousseau calls human perfectibility and Derrida human potentiality. That is, it energizes a power (of pity, for example) previously held back; but because it foresees a potentiality beyond that power in a seemingly endless string of supersessions, it perverts itself and renders itself powerless. The assertion of the imagination's energizing capacity is captured, Derrida argues, by the thesis of Rousseau's *Essay*: "Although pity is native to the human heart, it would remain eternally quiescent unless it were activated by imagination" (185). In opposition to Starobinski, Derrida points out that Rousseau says this invariably in his work and not just in this text. But having once said that the energizing power of the imagination is inescapable in Rousseau, Derrida proceeds to show that it also exemplifies deconstructive alterity, which is clearly manifest in this sentence from Rousseau's *Dialogues*: "Such is the empire of the imagination among us and such is its influence, that from it are born not only the virtues and the vices, but also good and evil." The desire that is beyond satisfaction – as well as the "origin of that surplus and of that difference" – is named the imagination.

VII

From/Of the Supplement to the Source
(Warburton, Vico, Condillac)

Of Grammatology concludes by placing this reading of Rousseau's *Essay* within the context of three other eighteenth-century texts that deal with similar topics: William Warburton's *The Divine Legation of Moses Demonstrated* (1741), Giambattista Vico's *The New Science* (1744), and Etienne Bonnot de Condillac's *An Essay on the Origin of Human Knowledge* (1746). Throughout part II of his text, Derrida uses Vico in his footnotes as a counterpoint to his exposition of Rousseau's argument in the *Essay*, even though Rousseau himself both borrowed

from and argued against Vico. Derrida attributes to Vico the rare, if
not unique, distinction of having advocated the contemporaneous
origin of writing and speech (335n.). In the introduction to *The New
Science* he wrote, "letters and languages were born twins and
proceeded apace through all their three stages." Those stages are
simultaneously the three ages of the world, the three kinds of nature
and government, and the three kinds of language, all of which are
epitomized in the three languages of the Egyptians. These corres-
pondences may be diagrammed as follows:

Historical age	*Kind of language*	*Egyptian version*
1 The Age of Gods: divine government by oracles	1 Mute language of signs and physical objects, which have natural relation to ideas expressed	1 Hieroglyphic or secret
2 The Age of Heroes: aristocratic common-wealth based on the assumption of superior nature	2 Heroic emblems, images, metaphors, natural descriptions	2 Symbolic
3 The Age of Men: popular common-wealths and monarchies based on the assumptions of equality in human nature	3 Human language using commonly agreed upon words by which the people fix the meaning of laws that nobles and priests had kept secret	3 Epistolary or vulgar

Vico anticipates that by using his theory of the stages of history and
language, scholars of any language, ancient or modern, should be able
to advance philological knowledge beyond any previous expectation.
Furthermore, he declares, it is now possible to claim with confidence
that early peoples were poets "who spoke in poetic characters." This
discovery is "the master key" to the new science of man.[58]

Despite his immense learning, Vico appears to be unaware of
William Warburton's monumental defense of Moses against the
Deists.[59] In book IV, section 4, Warburton offers a history of writing
in order to show that Egyptian hieroglyphics constitute an important

proof of the antiquity of Egypt. His thesis is a lucid and succinct statement of the opposite position from Vico's:

> There are two ways of communicating the conceptions of ourminds to others; the first by sounds, and the second by figures.For there being frequent occasion to have our conceptions perpetuated, and known at a distance, and sounds being momentary and confined, the way of figures or characters was, soon after that of sounds, thought upon to make those conceptions lasting and extensive. The first and most natural way of communicating our conceptions by marks or figures, was by tracing out the images of things. To express, for instance, the idea of a man or horse, the informer delineated the form of each of those animals. Thus the first essay towards writing was a mere picture.

As picture writing evolved, Warburton claims, metonymy and metaphor came into being.[60] Although it would have better served his theological interests to argue, as Vico had, that the metaphorical character of primitive languages had a divine origin, Warburton is sufficiently committed to his belief in the representational origin of writing – a picture of a horse representing a horse, for example – that he takes the opposite view from Vico's.

When Condillac appropriated Warburton's history, he kept much of Warburton's language but silently altered his view of the origins of metaphor:

> When mankind had once acquired the art of communicating their conceptions by sounds, they began to feel the necessity of inventing new signs proper for perpetuating them, and for making them known at a distance. Their imaginations then represented nothing more to them than those same images, which they had already expressed by gestures and words, and which from the very beginning had rendered language figurative and metaphorical. The most natural way therefore was to delineate the images of things. To express the idea of a man or of a horse, they represented the form of each of these animals; so that the first essay towards writing was a mere picture.[61]

By locating metaphor at the point of the origin of language, Condillac, like Vico, is able to conceive of the original style of language as poetical, "because it began with depicting the most sensible images of our ideas."[62] By inheriting this debate on original language as mediated by Condillac, Rousseau was able to overcome his pre-Saussurean position in history. Condillac provided him with a sense of the arbitrariness of the sign and with a rudimentary conception of deconstruction.

This legacy of Condillac is more fully sketched in Derrida's *The Archeology of the Frivolous: Reading Condillac* (1973), which elaborates on the allusions to Condillac at the end of *Grammatology*. In this later book, Derrida quotes with obvious approval from one of Condillac's letters to Gabriel Cramer:

> You want me to explain the prerogative of arbitrary signs over natural ones and why the arbitrary signs set free the operations of the soul that the natural ones leave necessary. That is the most delicate point of my system on the absolute necessity of signs. The difficulty has all its force and is so much better founded since I did not anticipate it. That is what causes me to be a little tangled on this whole matter. I even notice that I have said more than I wanted to, than I meant.[63]

An even more striking anticipation of Derrida's formulation of deconstruction is a passage from Condillac's *Essay*, to which he seems to allude without directly citing it:

> Sometimes after having distinguished several ideas, we consider them as forming only a single notion; at other times we prescind from a notion some of the ideas of which it is composed. This is what we call to *compound* and *decompound* our ideas. By means of these operations we are capable of comparing them under all sorts of relations, and of daily making new combinations of them.[64]

This would seem to be the text that informs the account on the final pages of *The Archeology of the Frivolous* concerning what makes construction and deconstruction possible. The frivolous is that elaboration and extension of an idea that leaves it without "the thing," or the elaboration and extension of the sign that leaves it without the idea, "which lets the term's identity fall far from its object."[65] This fragile structure of the frivolous is where cracks or lines of disintegration form in the space of ontology. Even on its own, without the contamination of literature, philosophy is most affected by the frivolous, which it works to conceal but inadvertently reveals, making it at once internally and externally vulnerable. This alone, Derrida claims, makes deconstruction possible.[66]

Condillac also appears to have anticipated the perversion of grammatology both by its Derridean disciples and by those who would make war on what is ultimately a feature of language. First,

Condillac describes the strategies of such a writer as Rousseau or Heidegger or Derrida, who finds that "every style analogous to the character of the language, and to his own, has been already used by preceding writers," leaving him no option but to "deviate from analogy." But "in order to be an original, he is obliged to contribute to the ruin of a language," which in earlier generations he would have worked to improve. Although "such writers may be criticized, their superior abilities must still command success." But because their defects are easy to copy, soon "men of indifferent capacities" rush to acquire what reputation they can, even by imitating those defects. "Then begins the reign of subtil and strained conceits, of affected antitheses, of specious paradoxes, of frivolous turns, of far-fetched expressions, of new-fangled words, and in short of the jargon of persons whose understandings have been debauched by bad metaphysics."[67] These phrases, quoted from Condillac by Derrida himself, indicate how well he knows the perils of his own project and influence. That his work against logocentric metaphysics – from which he is unable to extricate himself – can be turned by his imitators and detractors into empty jargon and a perversion of critical thought is a danger he seems always to have faced. By refusing to gird himself with the defenses of self-definition – by allowing others to name the deconstructive project – he allows grammatology purposefully to make itself vulnerable to sustained attack from all sides. That such perversions and attacks have come and will continue to come – seems the predictable consequence of a theory that celebrates the play in otherwise static structure, points to crevices and openings in conceptualizations that aspire to be definitive, and locates the frivolous that lies waiting to be excavated by archaeologists of knowledge. And Derrida does these things while making himself continuously susceptible to his own critique, which is more ruthless than anyone else's.

NOTES

1   The most useful bibliography of the writings of Derrida, compiled by Albert Leventure and Thomas Keenas, can be found in *Derrida: A Critical Reader*, ed. David Wood (Oxford: Basil Blackwell, 1992), 247–89. Unfortunately there is not yet an edition of Heidegger's works comparable to the *Gesammelte Werke* or the Standard Edition of Freud. George Steiner estimates that only one-third of Heidegger's writing is so far available in a definitive form: *Heidegger* (London: Fontana Press, 1989), 9. The closest approximation to James Strachey's scholarly

apparatus on Freud is William J. Richardson, SJ, *Heidegger: Through Phenomenology to Thought*, 3rd ed (The Hague: Martinus Nijhoff, 1974), which includes a comprehensive list of Heidegger's courses, seminars, and lectures; a bibliography of his publications; and an English–German and German–English glossary of Heideggerian terms. J. L. Mehta, *The Philosophy of Martin Heidegger* (New York: Harper & Row, 1971) is an excellent guide along the path of Heidegger's thought.

2   Spivak's preface is a brilliant and appropriately playful introduction to Derrida's text. Her six-part preface takes up the following topics: (I) the question of a preface and the atmosphere of Derrida's thought; (II) Derrida's precursors – Nietzsche, Freud, Heidegger, Husserl; (III) Derrida and structuralism; (IV) Derrida's vocabulary and practice; (V) the structure of *Of Grammatology* and a note on translation; (VI) the signature of the translator. For some of Derrida's views on translation, see especially "Letter to a Japanese Friend" in *A Derrida Reader*, ed. Peggy Kamuf (New York: Columbia University Press, 1991), 270–6, which includes important reflections on Derrida's translation and appropriation of Heidegger's terms *Destruktion* and *Abbau* in his term "deconstruction." There is a more general roundtable discussion of translation in *The Ear of the Other*, trans. Peggy Kamuf (Lincoln: University of Nebraska Press, 1988), 93–161.

3   *Positions*, trans. Alan Bass (Chicago: Chicago University Press, 1981), 107–13. See Spivak's tactful comment on the relationship of Derrida's thought to Lacan's (lxii–lxv). Derrida's deep indebtedness to Lacan has yet to be fully assessed.

4   *Positions*, 4.

5   *History of Western Philosophy* (London: Allen and Unwin, 1961 [1946], 660.

6   Frederick Copleston, SJ, *A History of Philosophy*, vol. VI (London: Allen and Unwin, 1960), 100.

7   *The Living Eye*, trans. Arthur Goldhammer (Cambridge: Harvard University Press, 1989), 60–1. Starobinski's "Rousseau and the Peril of Reflection" first appeared in *L'Oeil vivant* (Paris: Gallimard, 1961).

8   Derrida's thinking about Rousseau is most influenced by Starobinski's *J.-J. Rousseau: la transparence et l'obstacle* (Paris: Gallimard, 1957.) The second edition of this work (1970) includes a detailed study of the *Essay on the Origin of Languages* that was previously published in 1966, possibly too late for Derrida to have seen it. Starobinski further refined his text as the English edition was prepared: *Jean-Jacques Rousseau: Transparency and Obstruction*, trans. Arthur Goldhammer (Chicago: University of Chicago Press, 1988).

9   By Frank Lentricchia, for example, in *Criticism and Social Change* (Chicago: University of Chicago Press, 1983), who writes, "Politically, deconstruction translates into that passive kind of conservatism called quietism" (51).

10   Cf. the exergue to "White Mythology: Metaphor in the Text of Philos-
     ophy," in *Margins of Philosophy*, trans. Alan Bass (Brighton: Harvester
     Press, 1982), together with Bass's useful note on 209.

11   *Course in General Linguistics*, trans. Roy Harris (La Salle, IL: Open Court,
     1986), 31.

12   Mikhail Bakhtin's principle of dialogism, which Kristeva represents
     under the term "intertextuality," makes similar claims for plurivocity,
     insisting that it is fundamental to the human sciences. He argues, for
     example, that "the novel must represent all the social and ideological
     voices of its era, that is, all the era's languages that have any claim to
     being significant; the novel must be a microcosm of heteroglossia":
     'Discourse in the Novel" (1934–5), in *The Dialogic Imagination: Four
     Essays*, trans. Caryl Emerson and Michael Holquist (Austin: University
     of Texas Press, 1981), 411.

13   *The Post Card: From Socrates to Freud and Beyond*, trans. Alan Bass
     (Chicago: University of Chicago Press, 1987), 9–10.

14   Ibid., 29.

15   Ibid., 38.

16   *An Introduction to Metaphysics*, trans. Ralph Manheim (New Haven: Yale
     University Press, 1959), 1.

17   Ibid., 13–14.

18   Ibid., respectively on 127ff., 146ff., and 166ff.

19   Ibid., 146.

20   See Michael Haar's important essay, "The Play of Nietzsche in Derrida,"
     trans. Will McNeill, in *Derrida: A Critical Reader*, 52–71.

21   *Of Spirit: Heidegger and the Question*, trans. Geoffrey Bennington and
     Rachel Bowlby (Chicago: University of Chicago Press, 1989), 109.

22   See also the essay on *différance* in *Margins of Philosophy*, 1–27.

23   An earlier (1746) and more explicit formulation of deconstruction can
     be found in Condillac, *Essai sur l'origine des connaissances humaines*, section
     59, in *Oeuvres Philosophiques de Condillac*, ed. Georges Le Roy (Paris:
     Presses Universitaires de France, 1947), vol. I, 24.

24   *Being and Time*, trans. John Macquarrie and Edward Robinson (New
     York: Harper & Row, 1962), 44.

25   *Margins of Philosophy*, 48.

26   See Derrida's fuller discussion of Hegel's semiology in ibid., 71–108.

27   Derrida offers a detailed reading of the *Phaedrus* in "Plato's Pharmacy,"
     reprinted in *Dissemination*, trans. Barbara Johnson (Chicago: University
     of Chicago Press, 1981), 65–172.

28   *Cours de linguistique générale*, ed. Rudolf Engler (Wiesbaden: O.
     Harrassowitz, 1967–74). The standard French edition is *Cours de
     linguistique générale*, ed. Tullio de Mauro (Paris: Payot, 1973.) The best
     English edition is now *Course in General Linguistics*, trans. Roy Harris (La
     Salle, IL: Open Court, 1983). John Ellis, in his irresponsible caricature
     of Derrida, ignores the complexities of Saussure's text in his attempt to

show that Derrida does not understand it: *Against Deconstruction* (Princeton: Princeton University Press, 1989), esp. 46–50.

29 These principles appear on the following pages of the standard French edition, which are preserved as marginal indicators in Harris's edition: 97ff., 144ff., 244, 100ff.

30 A recent example of phonocentric metaphysics is Florian Coulmas's claim that "Writing is a cultural achievement rather than a universal property and as such is much less important than speech for our self-understanding": *The Writing Systems of the World (Oxford: Basil Blackwell, 1989), 3.*

31 See Oswald Ducrot and Tzvetan Todorov, *Encyclopedic Dictionary of the Sciences of Language*, trans. Catherine Porter (Baltimore: Johns Hopkins University Press, 1979) for reliable guidance in the schools, fields, and methodological and descriptive concepts of the sciences of language.

32 *Elements of Logic*, book II, section 302, in *Collected Papers*, ed. Charles Hartshorne and Paul Weiss (Cambridge, MA: Harvard University Press, 1931–58), vol. II, 169.

33 Ibid., sections 228 and 303.

34 *Elements of Semiology*, trans. Annette Lavers and Colin Smith (New York: Hill and Wang, 1973), 11.

35 See Louis Hjelmslev, *Prologomena to a Theory of Language* (Madison: University of Wisconsin Press, 1961) and the important commentary by A. Martinet, "Au sujet des fondements de la théorie linguistique de L. Hjelmslev," *Bulletin de la société de linguistique*, 43 (1946), 19–42.

36 The recent anthology *Acts of Literature*, ed. Derek Attridge (London: Routledge, 1992) makes it possible to assess that importance more fully than previously.

37 "The Time of a Thesis: Punctuations," in *Philosophy in France Today*, ed. Alan Montefiore (Cambridge: Cambridge University Press, 1982), 37.

38 "This Strange Institution Called Literature," in *Acts of Literature*, 37, 40–1. See also "Passions," trans. David Wood in *Derrida: A Critical Reader*, 22–4.

39 Rodolfe Gasché makes the important point that if Derrida's work is to be useful for literary criticism, his continuing controversy with phenomenology must not be forgotten: *The Tain of the Mirror: Derrida and the Philosophy of Reflection* (Cambridge, MA: Harvard University Press, 1986), 270. It should also be kept in mind that Derrida's conception of literature operates on the principle of defamiliarization; he does, after all, distinguish literature from poetry, which much of post-Romantic criticism sees as what literature wants to be. The extreme form of this view is Heidegger's assertion that "art is in essence poetry": (*The Origin of the Work of Art*, in *Poetry, Language, Thought*, trans. Albert Hofstadter (New York: Harper & Row, 1971), 73. Christopher Norris usefully warns readers of Derrida against equating Derrida's "play of form" with "a kind of hermeneutic free-for-all": *Derrida* (London:

Fontana Press, 1987), 139. This "American" misreading has been turned against Derrida by John Ellis *Against Deconstruction*, 52–6, who does not want to see any ambiguity in Derrida's *le jeu*. Indeed, he needs to misread Derrida's "play" in order strategically to misread Saussure's word "arbitrary."

40 Hans Aarsleff usefully contextualizes these debates in "Eighteenth-Century Doctrines Concerning Language and Mind," in *The Study of Language in England, 1780–1860* (Minneapolis: University of Minnesota Press, 1983), 3–43.

41 The work of Edward Said is specifically relevant here, especially his *Orientalism* (New York: Pantheon Books, 1978). If there were any evidence needed that an intellectual initiative is productively under way to deal with the cultural pathology of this "European hallucination," it is the work of Said and Noam Chomsky, whose importance for "European" linguistics – not to say, the cause of Palestinians – may be more clearly understood in England and France than currently in the United States. This was particularly clear during the recent Gulf War, when Chomsky's and Said's voices of dissent were more clearly heard than those of any other American intellectuals in Europe.

42 The annoying use in theoretical discourse of parentheses – to which I have just resorted – is but one consequence of the attempt to make language assert its simultaneity, which is also but one aspect of the concept/term "erasure."

43 Klein's original paper appears in her *Contributions to Psycho-analysis, 1921–1945* (London: Hogarth Press, 1948), 68–86. The paper concerns libidinal sublimation effected by school experience.

44 The relevant pages in the French text are *G*, 132–3. I am uncertain of my own reading of the entire footnote. Although I have followed the punctuation as it appears in the text, it is possible that Klein, Madame Derrida, or J. Derrida has introduced new material that cannot be attributed to a definite source.

45 The climax of this process in the eighteenth century was the discovery of the Rosetta Stone in 1799 by Napoleon's soldiers. Coulmas offers an excellent account of some key episodes in the history of deciphering in *Writing Systems*, (205–24), but he makes the curious judgment that "Much more than reading, deciphering is a genuinely linguistic task, and it is quite surprising, therefore, that linguists have taken practically no interest at all in this most challenging activity" (207).

46 *Tristes Tropiques*, trans. John and Doreen Weightman (London: Jonathan Cape, 1973), 416.

47 All that Lévi-Strauss wrote about the Nambikwara seems to have been based on a single expedition conducted from June to December 1938. Edmund Leech confirms the impression that the professional details of the expedition are virtually impossible to determine from what

Lévi-Strauss writes about it: *Claude Lévi-Strauss* (New York: Viking Press, 1970), x.

48 *Tristes Tropiques*, 416.

49 Ibid., 388–92.

50 Ibid., 364.

51 Ibid., 365.

52 See Paul de Man's "The Rhetoric of Blindness: Jacques Derrida's Reading of Rousseau," in *Blindness and Insight: Essays in the Rhetoric of Contemporary Criticism* (New York: Oxford University Press, 1971). This is one of the earliest – and still one of the best – commentaries on *Grammatology*, even though it totally ignores the theoretical, and more important, first part of Derrida's text. Robert Bernasconi offers a detailed critique of de Man's reading of Derrida in "No More Stories, Good or Bad: de Man's Criticisms of Derrida on Rousseau," in *Derrida: A Critical Reader*, 137–66.

53 The Essay is now conveniently available in *On the Origin of Language*, trans. John H. Moran (Chicago: University of Chicago Press, 1986).

54 This judgment might explain Derrida's readiness, as cited above, to exclude poetry from the category of literature.

55 Especially 365–77.

56 The essay was originally published in *L'Oeil vivant* in 1961. Paul de Man (in *Blindness and Insight*, 112–13) misreads Starobinski, not realizing that the portion of Starobinski's text to which he objects (184) is Starobinski's presentation of Rousseau's ideas rather than Starobinski's own. In his gentle correction of de Man, Starobinski (in *The Living Eye*, viii–ix) identifies his own style as largely what stylisticians have called *style indirect libre*. Derrida is himself a master of that style, especially in his reading of Rousseau and Starobinski – simultaneously, so to speak. That such an otherwise careful reader as de Man would not have detected this stylistic mode is but one indication of its uncertainty of success and its assumption of a willingness to read carefully. My own text is largely a rudimentary exercise in this mode, especially rudimentary when considered in light of the three masters of it whose work I am here attempting to describe. Perhaps it is worth considering that the scandalous extent of the misreading and destructive – not, of course in Heidegger's sense – mis-representation of theoretical texts in several recent popular polemical books may in part be the result of a failure to recognize this stylistic mode. A case in point is David Lehman, *Signs of the Times: Deconstruction and the Fall of Paul de Man* (New York: Poseidon Press, 1991), who seems to have succeeded in writing an entire book on deconstruction without managing to read the texts of Derrida or de Man with critical attention. Needless to say, he does not attempt the style of which Derrida, de Man, and Starobinski are masters, which presupposes a necessarily scholarly care and a generous inclination – or at least, a willingness – to read the relevant texts.

57   *The Living Eye*, 59.
58   *The New Science of Giambattista Vico*, trans. Thomas Goddard Bergin and Max Harold Fisch (Ithaca: Cornell University Press, 1970), 3–5.
59   *The Divine Legation of Moses Demonstrated*, ed. René Wellek (New York: Garland, 1978), 4 vols.
60   Ibid., vol. II, 67, 71–2.
61   *An Essay on the Origin of Human Knowledge*, trans. Thomas Nugent (1756) (New York: AMS Press, 1974), 273–4.
62   Ibid., 228–9.
63   *The Archeology of the Frivolous: Reading Condillac*, trans. John P. Leavey, Jr. (Lincoln: University of Nebraska Press, 1987), 110–11.
64   *An Essay on the Origin of Human Knowledge*, 66–7. The French text better suggests how close this formulation is to Derrida's: "Quelquefois, aprés avoir distingué plusieurs idées, nous les considérons comme ne faisant qu'une seule notion: d'autres fois nous retranchons d'une notion quelques-unes des idées qui la composent. C'est ce qu'on nomme *composer* et *décomposer* ses idées. Par le moyen de ces opérations nous pouvons les comparer sous toutes sortes de rapports, et en faire tous les jours de nouvelles combinaisons." *Oeuvres Philosophiques de Condillac*, vol. I, 24.
65   *The Archeology of the Frivolous*, 132–3.
66   Ibid., 132.
67   *Essay on the Origin of Human Knowledge*, 296–7, quoted by Derrida in *The Archeology of the Frivolous*, 68n.

4

Revolution in Poetic Language

Although Julia Kristeva has published several important books since *Revolution in Poetic Language* appeared in 1974, it remains her most far-reaching theoretical text, as well as the one that links her work most directly to Lacan's *Écrits* and Derrida's *Of Grammatology*.[1] It would be a mistake, however, to read any of her writing as simply an uncritical synthesis or opportunistic appropriation of previous theory. Just as Noam Chomsky has always insisted on being prepared to mesh his work with developments in neighboring disciplines that contribute to his project, so Kristeva has a scientific sense of the necessarily communal effort required to advance knowledge about the speaking subject. This affirmation of intellectual community should be seen not, in any sense, as an act of professional submission on her part, but rather as a confident assertion of an engagement with the most productive thinking and writing in linguistics, psychoanalysis, philosophy, and literary studies that advance her enterprise. During the two decades since its first publication, *Revolution in Poetic Language* has provided its readers with a convincing theory of the speaking subject, as well as a productive means of critically reading texts by Husserl, Hjelmslev, Frege, Hegel, Freud, Marx, Mallarmé, Lautréamont – in addition to Lacan and Derrida – all of which require a bridging of the divide that usually separates linguistics from psychoanalysis, philosophy, and literary studies.[2]

Only the first part of *La Révolution du langage poétique: l'avant-garde á la fin du XIXe siècle: Lautréamont et Mallarmé*, which Kristeva entitled "Préliminaires théoriques," has so far been completely translated.[3] The massive three-part text was submitted in 1973 as Kristeva's thesis for the *doctorat d'état* in Paris. Her thesis defense, for which Roland Barthes served as an examiner, was itself a major intellectual event that was vividly described in *Le Monde*.[4] Kristeva's thesis led to her prompt appointment to a chair in linguistics at the University of Paris VII, a position she still holds. Although the French text was published in 1974, the excellent English translation by Margaret Waller did not appear until 1984. The dates are important because Kristeva's French text is more closely contemporaneous with the work of Lacan and Derrida than the date of the English translation suggests. Indeed, soon after Kristeva's arrival in Paris in 1966, she began to publish preliminary studies in *Critique, Tel Quel*, and other distinguished journals, which laid the foundation for her monumental thesis.[5] This early work was appearing in the same journals, and at about the same time, as Derrida's first publications. Furthermore, Kristeva's education as a linguist in Bulgaria (before coming to Paris) and her Russian fluency made it possible for her and Tzvétan Todorov to introduce not only the work of the Russian Formalists but also the brilliant theoretical writings of Mikhail Bakhtin, whose thought was virtually unknown at the time outside the Soviet Union.[6] These various strands of her intellectual life are woven into the argument of her thesis, which in parts B and C also provides detailed readings of the poetic texts of Lautréamont and Mallarmé. *Revolution in Poetic Language* is at once a major study in semiotics, psychoanalysis, philosophy, and literary criticism, while leaving none of these disciplines undisturbed. As Barthes put it in 1970, Kristeva persists in disturbing the *already-said*.[7]

The first part of *Revolution in Poetic Language* is divided into four sections, prefaced by a prolegomenon that forecasts the argument to come. Kristeva begins with a startling sentence that recalls the messianic arguments of the opening pages of Lacan's "Rome Discourse" and of Derrida's *Grammatology*, while simultaneously diminishing the significance of its antagonist: "Our philosophies of language, embodiments of the Idea [*avatars de l'Idée*, (R, 11)], are nothing more than the thoughts of archivists, archaeologists, and necrophiliacs" (13). This intellectual poverty of philosophy of language is the result, in Kristeva's view, of its isolation from historical and social thought, which leaves its utterances to "hang in midair." Yet, unwittingly, this abstract thinking about language points a way out of the repression of the body and the subject, which has been encouraged by capitalist society. Even so, the fragmented study of language has failed to develop an understanding of the signifying process. On the one hand, Kristeva is determined to recover the historical and social dimensions of language; but on the other, she is equally committed to resisting repressive and normative social restraints that have divided language into isolated idiolects and that have lost a sense of the subversive power of language as a dynamic process that manifests the variety and shapes the diversity of the human subject. The closed sets of discrete systems posited by philosophy of language need to be de-centered, she argues, in order, first, to reveal the dialectical processes within the always heterogeneous structures of language and, second, in order to ground a theory of signification on the speaking subject, who is no less heterogeneous than the structure of language that forms him. In order to base a theory of signification on the subject, the study of language must continually reach out to Freudian psychoanalysis and to its elaboration in the writings of such theorists as Lacan and Klein. Unlike the archival practices of philosophers of language, psychoanalytic work marks its own position and rejects the totalizing and reductionist inclinations of positivist discourse (15).

The inevitable dilemma confronting anyone who sets out to write or speak about signifying practice is that the theory constructed operates in the same medium as what it proposes to investigate; both are produced in language. But the meshing of linguistic and psychoanalytic theory has the potential of enriching linguistics and psychoanalysis, at the same time that it illuminates both the signifying practice and a type of early modern literature that seems best to reflect the dynamics of that practice. There have often been crises in social, ideological, and other signifying structures – Kristeva cites the unexpected example of the strategic obscurity of Pindar after the clarity of Homer – but in the work of such writers as Lautréamont, Mallarmé, Joyce, and Artaud the crisis of signification becomes a new phenomenon, which promises to reveal the dynamics of signification itself. In these writers, both the subject and his ideological limits are exploded at once. The consequences of Kristeva's detection, in what are now often termed "modernist" writers, of an opening in poetic practice that effects not only a crisis in ideology but also the potential for contact with the fundamental processes of signification, need to be explored in terms of a reassessment of "postmodernist" theory. It may be that recent literary history has created a nineteenth-century "Romanticism" – which exalts the quest for an encompassing image or myth at the expense of social engagement – and a twentieth-century "modernism" – which reflects the pressure upon and the difficulty of maintaining such images – that purposefully ignores what Kristeva sees as already taking place in the writings of Lautréamont and Mallarmé This modernist crisis Kristeva envisions as having a threefold consequence.

First, the shattered discourse of modernism reveals that "linguistic changes constitute changes in the *state of the subject* – his relation to the body, to others, and to objects" (15), while revealing also that language is but one manifestation of the signifying process. Second, the expression in art of this ideological explosion reveals the foundation, in what is called either the primitive "sacred" or the modern "schizophrenic," of the signifying processes that shape the subject and ideology. Third, this crisis, explosion, or shattering reveals processes of signification – especially in poetic language and in the "prose" of such writers as Joyce and Artaud – that are usually repressed by socially useful discourse. By erupting from its repressed or marginalized place and by thus displacing established signifying practices, poetic discourse corresponds in its effects, in terms of the subject, to revolution in the socioeconomic order. Poetic language (or, in this sense, "literature") – but perhaps better termed "the *text*" – becomes an instrument of productive violence because it involves "the sum of unconscious, subjective, and social relations" (16).[8] Far from being a unified, aestheticized object or well-wrought urn, the text is in this sense a *practice*; that is, it becomes a means of transforming "natural and social resistances, limitations, and stagnation" (17), once these enter any of the various codes of signification. Kristeva calls this heterogeneous practice *signifiance*, a limitless and unceasing "operation of the drives toward, in, and through language," which is studied, therefore, by a meshing of psychoanalysis and linguistics. In the course of its operation, the signifying practice structures and de-structures as it moves toward and against the previously conceived, defining limits of the subject and society.

I

The Semiotic and the Symbolic

After this exhilarating forecast of her argument, Kristeva carefully positions her work in relation to theories of meaning, language, and the subject, which she proceeds critically to assess, modify, and appropriate. What distinguishes modern linguistic theory, as she sees it, is its consideration of language as a structure or an object. This formal conception of language, which dominates linguistics from Saussure to Chomsky, has eclipsed any viable conception of the human subject; or when linguistic theory conceives a subject – as in the writings of Husserl and Benveniste – it is a transcendental ego, which itself is a formal and static objectification of the human subject. Yet even as he offers such a view of the ego, Husserl seems immediately to resist his own formulation:

> The Ego appears to be permanently, even necessarily, there, and this permanence is obviously not that of a stolid unshifting experience, of a "fixed idea." On the contrary, it belongs to every experience that comes and streams past; its "glance" goes "through" every actual *cogito*, and towards the object. This visual ray changes with every *cogito*, shooting forth afresh with each new one as it comes, and disappearing with it. But the Ego remains self-identical.[9]

By accepting Husserl's invitation to read his text against the grain of its main argument, Kristeva discovers in his writing, much as Derrida does in Heidegger's, an opening to that which not only lies beyond its own explicit formulation, but also calls into question its metaphysical foundation.

Benveniste goes further than Husserl in destabilizing the Cartesian inheritance of a synthesizing and unifying *cogito* or consciousness that constitutes Being. For Benveniste, subjectivity is clearly a property of language: "'Ego' is he who says 'ego.'" Or more specific, and ultimately more useful to Kristeva, is his argument that it is in particular the dialogic character of language that constitutes the person:

> I use *I* only when I am speaking to someone who will be a *you* in my address. It is this condition of dialogue that is constitutive of *person*, for whom it implies that reciprocally *I* becomes *you* in the address of the one who in his turn designates himself as *I*. Here we see a principle whose consequences are to spread out in all directions. Language is possible only because each speaker sets himself up as a *subject* by referring to himself as *I* in his discourse. Because of this *I* posits another person, the one who, being as he is completely exterior to "me," becomes my echo to whom I say *you* and who says *you* to me.[10]

Benveniste's understanding of the dialogism of language and its potential relation to Freudian theory is not sufficient for him to abandon the metaphysical foundation of the subject as transcendental ego. Kristeva has the intellectual daring to follow a path that Husserl and Benveniste saw opening up before them but which they were unprepared to explore.

Not only has linguistics failed to consider the subject except as a transcendental ego, it has also failed adequately to consider the externality of the subject (that is, the subject as not contained by or fully reducible to language). This omission has been a particular problem for semiotics, which studies signifying processes not confined to language, such as painting and myth. There have, however, been two significant movements to deal with the externality of the subject in the context of the study of language: first, developments in Freudian psychoanalysis, such as Melanie Klein's *The Psycho-analysis of Children*, which considers the motivated (rather than arbitrary) relationship between signifier and signified;[11] and, second, developments in semiotics, such as the work of Benveniste, that investigate the formal relations between interlocutors in the speech act as operations in the deep structure of language. The effect of this work has been to open linguistics up to the study of "the subject who means" (23) in such a way as to end the isolation of linguistics from philosophy, history, and psychoanalysis.

Kristeva proceeds to describe the two inseparable modes within the signifying process as *the semiotic* and *the symbolic*, which refer to (or manifest) two aspects of the subject. The concept of *the semiotic* Kristeva derives from the Greek term σημεῖον, signifying "mark" or "trace," as in *Antigone* (257). This mode is familiar to Freudian psychoanalytic theory concerned with the structure of drives and with the primary processes of their displacement and condensation (SE, XXIII: 98–9). *The symbolic* Kristeva defines as "a social effect of the relation to the other, established through the objective constraints of biological (including sexual) differences and concrete, historical family structures" (29). In order to account for the dynamic interrelations between the semiotic and the symbolic, Kristeva boldly introduces the concept of *the chora*.[12] In part this concept is derived from her incisive reading of Plato's *Timaeus* (239n.). But as she amplifies and reworks this concept – following, in this way, Plato's own example – *the chora* comes to function both as an image opportunistically employed to fill a conceptual need in Kristeva's theory and as a precise technical term (chorion) from embryology that specifically defines the bodily site of the first signifying processes of the fetus.

In the *Timaeus* (49–52) Plato sets out to describe "the receptacle of being" in words that he admits are extraordinarily "difficult and obscure." In earlier sections of his text he had described two forms of reality – an intelligible and unchanging model and its visible and changing copy – to which he is now ready to add a third form. This he initially sketches as "the receptacle and, as it were, the nurse of all becoming and change." But as he tries out and then discards image after image, Plato becomes more explicit about the metaphorical and experimental character of his own language and thought, as though to suggest that the mercurial quality of his text has been enacting all along the changeable form he wishes to describe.[13] He proceeds to substitute the image of the mother for that of the nurse: "We may indeed use the metaphor of birth and compare the receptacle to the mother, the model to the father, and what they produce between them to their offspring.'[14] But having presented this powerful image of human generation for the receptacle of becoming, Plato proceeds to undermine it, substituting the word "space" or "chora" [χώρα] for "receptacle:"

> Space . . . is eternal and indestructible . . . provides a position for every-
> thing that comes to be, and . . . is apprehended without the senses by
> a sort of spurious reasoning and so is hard to believe in – we look
> at it indeed in a kind of dream and say that everything that exists must
> be somewhere and occupy some space, and that what is nowhere in
> heaven or earth is nothing at all.[15]

Kristeva seems determined to retain both Plato's maternal image and his more abstract formulation. This is a remarkable rhetorical decision because when Kristeva writes about the body, unlike Lacan and Derrida, she gives it a sense of having bone and flesh and hormones. For her the body both is and is not external to language. It would seem to be in the interest of sustaining this ambiguity that she alludes to without actually naming the chorion.

"Chorion" [χοριον] is a term used by Aristotle, in *Historia Animalium* (562a6), to signify the membrane that encloses the fetus in the womb. As it is now understood, this membrane has two physiological properties that make it an apt Kristevan metaphor, even though it was in this sense unknown to Plato but, nevertheless, seems a natural extension of his protean image. First, because the chorion is, in effect, a double structure of tissue, it might be thought a place where simultaneously the structure of the mother's body ends and that of the fetus begins. In this sense, it constitutes the space within which the otherness of the fetus is distinguishable. Kristeva begins her essay "Motherhood According to Giovanni Bellini" with this description of the maternal body: "Cells fuse, split, and proliferate;

volumes grow, tissues stretch and body fluids change rhythm, speeding up or slowing down. Within the body, growing as a graft, indomitable, there is an other."[16] Although Kristeva does not here or elsewhere explicitly refer to the chorion, the processes she describes could only be taking place within its structure. Secondly, the chorion is where one of the earliest processes – perhaps the first – of signification occurs. A standard biological textbook describes it this way: "The implanted embryo sends an important hormonal signal into the blood of the mother. The trophoblast cells secrete human chorionic gonadotrophin (HCG), which stimulates the corpus luteum to continue secreting progesterone and estrogen."[17] This hormonal signal prevents menstruation and the loss of the embryo. The presence of HCG in the mother's urine is also one of the earliest signals of pregnancy. The chorion, thus, defines the semiotic space of the other within the mother, and within its double structure the first communication between the fetus and m(other) occurs.

In the Kristevan chora the linguistic sign has not yet emerged as the absence of the object; thus, the distinction between the real and the symbolic has not yet arisen. The chora is, however, already subject to socio-historical restraints, such as sexual difference and family structure. In this context, then, even before the establishment of the sign, the semiotic functions in the processes of connecting the subject's body to objects and to "protagonists" in family structure, especially in the orientation toward the mother. The fundamental dualism created by the drives "makes the semioticized body a place of permanent scission" (27). Nevertheless, the mother's body is both "the ordering principle of the semiotic chora" and the means of mediation between the symbolic law of social relations and the foetal subject. The chora is, then, the space where "the subject is both generated and negated, the place where his unity succumbs before the process of changes and stases that produce him" (28). Kristeva calls this process of changes and stases "a negativity," a topic to which she returns in the second section of her text.

The imagery of the chora and the sense of the mother's body as both theoretical concept and biological entity recur throughout *Revolution in Poetic Language* and are often recalled by a single word or phrase. The semiotic is "englobed" by the signifying process (41); the mother, occupying the place of alterity, is "the receptacle" of all demands and "the place" of all gratifications (47); because it plumbs the depths of the signifying process, art is an agency of rebirth (70), and poetry (or literature of the kind celebrated by Mallarmé in "The

Mystery of Literature") is generated within a rhythmic feminine space (29). As she works with this image-concept, Kristeva seems determined to avoid the risk of its becoming, as Derrida charged, an ontological essence.[18] This she does in part by retaining and embellishing Plato's ambiguous language. For example, she persists in using the word "receptacle" even though Plato replaces it with the word "space." This receptacle/space is not only mobile and divisible, but also "pre-syllable" and "pre-word" (239n.). It is amorphous, yet necessary; it is the nurse/mother of all becoming, yet it becomes static and "ontologized" once it is named. Perhaps the Platonic chora functions well precisely because of its instability, even as it makes "explicit an insurmountable problem for discourse: once it has been named, the chora, even though pre-symbolic, is brought back into a symbolic position. All discourse can do is differentiate, by means of a 'bastard reasoning,' the receptacle from the motility" (239–40n.). Kristeva's most successful means of resisting the ontologization of the chora is her supplementing of Plato's concept with an anticipation of what she will later call "guiltless maternity." The experience of pregnancy, she argues in "Women's Time," provides the mother with the most immediate apprehension possible of the scission of the subject and the love for an other:

> Pregnancy seems to be experienced as the radical ordeal of the splitting of the subject: redoubling up of the body, separation and coexistence of the self and of an other, of nature and consciousness, of physiology and speech. This fundamental challenge to identity is then accompanied by a fantasy of totality – narcissistic completeness – a sort of instituted, socialized, natural psychosis. The arrival of the child, on the other hand, leads the mother into the labyrinths of an experience that, without the child, she would only rarely encounter: love for another.[19]

The experience, not as here of giving birth, but of either watching it happen – uncertain whether to look or to turn away, as in the concluding image of Derrida's "Structure, Sign, and Play" – or of assisting in the delivery – as in Lacan's recurring image of the psychoanalyst as midwife – is presumably as close to the metaphor of birth as it is possible to come for anyone who is not a mother.

Having introduced the chora as the space or state in which the speaking subject is formed, Kristeva next turns to texts by Husserl, Hjelmslev, Lacan, and Frege in order to assess their contributions to an understanding of signifying processes and to position her theory in relation to theirs. Husserlian phenomenology, according to Kristeva, provided the foundation for twentieth-century theories of signification.[20] Husserl's *Ideas* and *Formal and Transcendental Logic* develop a theory of the structures of consciousness and an account of how the mind works, based on a series of overlapping distinctions, including sensuous *hyletic data* in contrast to intentional *noeses*.[21] Hyletic data are sensory materials passively received by the mind and are without meaning or conceptual articulation. They are thus, literally, the given (*datum*) of experience. Noetic elements, in contrast, are those that, by virtue of their intentionality, bestow sense on the otherwise inert hyletic data. The noetic relies on the assumption of the stable, transcendental ego, a suspect Husserlian assumption to which Kristeva has already registered her objection (21). Husserl's phenomenology, however, seems to assume ego psychology as its base:

> The "object" referred to, is the goal aimed at, set in relation to the Ego only (and by the Ego itself), but is not itself "subjective." An attitude which bears the personal ray in itself is thereby an act of the Ego itself; the Ego does or suffers, is free or conditioned. The Ego, so we also expressed, "lives" in such acts. This life does not signify the being of any "contents" of any kind in a stream of contents, but a variety of describable ways in which the pure Ego in certain intentional experiences, which have the general mode of the *cogito*, lives therein as the "free essence" which it is.[22]

Despite his continued affirmation of the ego, as here in the distinction between the hyletic and the noetic, Husserl approaches but does not mesh his thought with Freud's (*Ideas*, it should be recalled, was first published in 1913).[23] As Kristeva points out (33), the Husserlian hyletic includes what he calls "impulses" [*Triebe*]; but because meaning for Husserl only resides with the noetic or the intentional, he is unable to anticipate or to come to terms with Freudian drives [*Triebe*], which precede the distinction between subject and object.

Kristeva rehearses Husserl's phenomenological categories in order to arrive at his concept of the *thetic*. In his preface to the English edition of *Ideas*, Husserl explains that his purpose in the book is to advance a science of Beginnings, or a "first" philosophy. In order to provide philosophy with such a scientific beginning, he insists that he remain "aloof from all theories" in the sense of "anticipatory" ideas. To this end, he asserts "The General Thesis of the Natural Standpoint:"

I find continually present and standing over against me the one spatio-temporal fact-world to which I myself belong, as do all other men found in it and related in the same way to it. This "fact-world," as the world [*sic*] already tells us, I find to *be out there*, and also *take it just as it gives itself to me as something that exists out there*. All doubting and rejecting of the data of the natural world leaves standing the *general thesis of the natural standpoint*. "The" world is as fact-world always there; at the most it is at odd points "other" than I supposed, this or that under such names as "illusion," "hallucination," and the like, must be struck *out of it*, so to speak; but the "it" remains ever, in the sense of the general thesis, a world that has its being out there.

Husserl's "fact-world" is heavily personified. Not only do all men "belong" to it, but it speaks, gives itself, is inscribed with or defaced by such graffiti as "illusion" and "hallucination." Although Husserl never wants to lose contact with the world that "gives itself" to him, nevertheless, by positing it as "The General Thesis," he has already begun to theorize it or to anticipate not only its place in a dialectic and also its eventual suspension [*Aufhebung*], disconnection, or bracketing:

> The *attempt* to doubt any object of awareness in respect of its *being actually there necessarily conditions a certain suspension* (*Aufhebung*) *of the thesis*; and it is precisely this that interests us. It is not a transformation of the thesis into its antithesis, of positive into negative; it is also not a transformation into presumption, suggestion, indecision, doubt (in one or another sense of the word); such shifting indeed is not at our free pleasure. *Rather is it something quite unique. We do not abandon the thesis we have adopted, we make no change in our conviction* . . . And yet the thesis undergoes a modification – whilst remaining in itself what it is, *we set it as it were "out of action," we "disconnect it," "bracket it."* [24]

Kristeva's conception of theory is quite unlike Husserl's "anticipation," however much she incorporates his bracketing procedure. [25] For her, "theory" or "contemplation" (95–6) is a signifying system composed of instinctual dyads, whose "plus" and "minus" valuations interpenetrate without being synthesized or neutralized. [26] Elaborating on Lacan's image, she compares these dyads to the ends of a magnetized chain, which close to form a ring (rather than a Lacanian necklace) for which there is no outside, even though the ring can be endlessly split, deeper and deeper; the ring is boundless and without origin (like Lacan's Moebius strip); it both eternally returns and is perpetually trapped. Perhaps most importantly, materiality is (or occupies) the hole in the ring, "whose existence it suspects and covets but never reaches" ["La matérialité est, pour cet anneau, un trou, un manque: il se doute de son existence, la convoite, mais ne l'atteint jamais" (R, 91)]. Although she does not mention Husserl by name in this context, her cautious use of his language (enclosed in suspicious quotation marks) suggests that she is constructing her conception of theory on the foundation of a critical reading of Husserl's unsuccessful attempt to distance himself from it: "It is as if," she writes, "once [the signifying ring of theory] posits the real, rejection . . . folds back in upon itself, never to touch the real again, returning instead to attack its (own) corollary – the affirmative, the 'positing' " (96). In Husserlian terminology, "positing" is a nominal act in which the object presented is referred to as existing, which involves an active, rational commitment on the part of the thinker. The thetic, then, is a quality or function of positing, or as Husserl succinctly puts it, "Such are '*thetic*' acts, acts that 'posit' Being."[27]

Kristeva's intellectual investment in Husserl's concept of the thetic manifests a commitment to resist the assimilation of all phenomena to language. However much Husserl projects signifying capabilities onto the thetic, it constitutes for Kristeva "a break in the signifying process, establishing the *identification* of the subject and its object as preconditions of propositionality" (43). It requires a separation of the subject from both its image and its objects. Even the pre-sentence utterances of a child are already thetic in that they are positings, positions, or committed attributions, as in the metonymic association by the child of "woof-woof" with all animals. Any enunciation, by word or sentence, is thetic and requires identification (or perhaps, a resurgence of identification) of speaking subject with object. The thetic phase, therefore, is for Kristeva the "deepest structure" of enunciation, signification, and proposition. Or, more pointedly, it is the "only one signification" (44). Every sign requires the world beyond language that Husserl labored to posit. But Kristeva supplements his position with her conviction that the Lacanian development of the Freudian unconscious can account for the production of the thetic without reducing the subject, as did Husserl's theory of the ego.

Kristeva makes her way from the hyletic to the thetic by way of Hjelmslev's theory of presupposed meaning, which binds glossematics to phenomenology. Hjelmslev amplified Saussure's distinction between the forms of language and the substance it represents, but in the process he failed adequately to distinguish language from other signifying systems (40). Meaning, for Hjelmslev, requires, in Kristeva's view, an "unavowed thetic consciousness" or totalizing rationality. Consequently, his concept of semiological process is not a "heterogeneous production" but an eidos or pure phenomenality, which rests on an assumption of a consciousness or transcendental ego that has not been investigated with Husserl's disarming candor. Whereas Derrida is prepared to applaud Hjelmslev's view of language as a game,[28] Kristeva finds its presuppositions about meaning and the speaking subject impoverished. In her account of Hjelmslev's work in *Language the Unknown*, however, Kristeva credits him with the determination to see linguistics "invade the domain of epistemology," because he sensed the impossibility of elaborating the theory of any science without such an invasion.[29] Hjelmslev was the first structural linguist to recognize fully how linguistic and other scientific discourse constructs the object it sets out to investigate, thus avoiding the unreflective claims of objectivity that dominate much of descriptive linguistics.[30] For him, linguistics is a thetic science.

Having exposed what she takes to be the impoverished conception of the speaking subject in the work of Husserl and Hjelmslev, while at the same time accepting their invitation to go beyond the limits of their own theories, Kristeva turns to Lacan's reading of Freud in order to locate the thetic phase in the development of the subject. Not only does Kristeva here (46–7) offer a brilliant reading of Lacan and a succinct presentation of his theories of the mirror stage and castration, she also weaves her own conception of the chora and her critical assessment of the Husserlian thetic into her exposition. During the mirror stage, the child posits his imagined ego, which in turn leads "to the positing of the object." Thus, the thetic is for him, like his conception of himself, thought to be "separate and signifiable" (46). In a single sentence Kristeva retains Husserl's theory of thetic positing and Lacan's theory of the captation of the child by the fiction of his unified image. But by linking these theories as she does, Kristeva replaces Husserl's "ego" with Lacan's ego-image and supplies Lacan's theory with a phenomenological epistemology derived from Husserl.[31] This is one of her finest demonstrations of the necessary interrelations among philosophy, psychoanalysis, and linguistics.

The second point in the development of the subject at which signification is structured is the moment of the "'discovery' of castration." Here Kristeva turns to Lacan's "The signification of the phallus" to develop the theory that "castration puts the finishing touches on the process of separation that posits the subject as signifiable" (47). As for Lacan, the experience of being under the threat of separation or division, which pushes the early mirror stage into its inevitable future, is for Kristeva the point in the history of the subject when the scission of language and the scission of the subject inform each other. Poetry figures here in the diphasic onset of the thetic in a strange but important way. Kristeva reminds her reader that neurotics and psychotics are defined in terms of their disrupted relationship to the thetic, which partly explains why psychoanalysis deals with these conditions in terms of a disturbance in language. When poetry becomes a hypostasization of semiotic motility, it can also be seen as a refusal of the thetic. But for Kristeva, this deprives poetry of its power to manifest the semiotic chora and threatens to collapse the distinction between a text "as *signifying practice*" and neurotic discourse. Indeed, a great deal of verse may simply be "a substitute for the analyst's couch" (51), while resisting, nevertheless, the discoveries of psychoanalysis and linguistics. For the subject to develop a signifying practice with a socio-historical function, the thetic must not be simply the repression of the semiotic chora but rather its positing; and castration must have been sufficiently problematic and traumatic as to effect a return of the semiotic through the symbolic it generated.

In an effort to answer the question, "What becomes of signification once the signifier has been posited?", Kristeva turns to Frege's notion of reference, which she attempts to accommodate to Husserl's thetic positing. Although Kristeva insists that "Frege's departure from Husserl is only apparent" (52), the differences between them may simply have been lost in the translation of Frege's terminology into French.[32] Here the problem is whether in their theories of meaning, Husserl's "sign," "meaning," and "object" are roughly equivalent to Frege's "expression," "sense," and "reference." Indeed, it seems almost inevitable that the meaning of "meaning" [*Bedeutung*] would be in dispute in any attempt to assess theories of meaning. Husserl repeatedly insists that "Each expression not merely says something, but says it *of* something: it not only has a meaning, but refers to [one or more] objects.'[33] But here it must be recalled that objects for Husserl are functions of positing or thetic acts; "objects" may not exist other than as manifestations of intentionality. Indeed, Husserl seems unequivocal on this point: "To use an expression significantly, and to refer expressively to an object . . . are one and the same . . . It makes no difference whether the object exists."[34] For Frege, on the other hand, the key elements in reference are, first, that an expression refers to an entity that is independent of expression and, second, that an expression has no reference without such an independent entity. For him, reference is a matter of the relation between the expression and the independent object. Kristeva's carrying over of Husserl's term "positing," which served her well in her recollection of Lacanian theory (46), blurs a critical distinction here between Husserl and Frege when she asks: "Doesn't the immense profusion of signs, even before denoting objects, imply the very *precondition of denotation*, which is the *positing of an object*, of the object, of object-ness?" (52). At this point Frege's world of independent objects becomes eclipsed by the Husserlian thetic and by the substitution of Frege's "reference" with the word "denotation."[35] In a brilliant critical reading of the French translation of Frege, Kristeva, nonetheless, restores his concept of meaning, even though she announces it as though it were a correction to his theory: "Judgment produced *Bedeutung* but does not enclose it, referring it instead elsewhere, to a heterogeneous domain, which is to say, within the existing object" (53). By thus restoring Frege, Kristeva is able to rely on him later (119–24) for her theory of negativity.

Having advanced her argument through the treacherous terrain of Husserlian phenomenology, Hjelmslevian glossematics, Lacanian psychoanalysis, and Fregean referentiality, Kristeva arrives at last at a point where she can consider the problem of literary signification. In the first sentence of chapter 8, her problematic rendering of Frege's "reference" remains in the word "denotation," but even that terminological problem is useful as a way in to the critique of mimesis that follows. Here she cuts through the divide that separates Husserl from Frege by arguing that mimesis can best be understood not as a *reference to* or *rendering of*, but rather as a *positing of* an object. Mimesis is, thus, dependent upon a subject who does not suppress but in fact elevates the semiotic chora. This is where the transgression of grammatical rules by the language of early modern poetry becomes most important for her theory. With this transgression, the symbolic is subverted as a "possessor" or syntactic meaning (57). Modern poetic language – the allusion here and later is especially to Mallarmé and Lautréamont – attacks denotation, or reference and meaning [*Bedeutung*], subverting both and eroding verisimilitude. The result of this process is to put the subject on trial, to raise most powerfully and poignantly the question Kristeva has been pressing: how is it that the

formation of language and of the subject – and through them the
social order – occur as a trial [*un procès du sujet*]? Poetic language puts
the subject on trial, and mimesis becomes a transgression of the
thetic. Within this plurality of transgressions and trials, Kristeva
introduces a third process alongside of Freud's displacement and
condensation. "The passage from one sign system to another," which
may be called "intertextuality" or, preferably, "transposition," requires
a revised sense of the thetic in order to capture Kristeva's "semiotic
polyvalence," which cannot help but recall Derrida's "plurivocity."[36]

When Kristeva raises the question of truth in mimesis and poetic
language (60–1), it is more the discreteness of her position, Husserl's,
and Frege's than their similarities that becomes important. Truth for
Frege is in the referentiality of what we say about the world to the
world itself; for Husserl truth requires an intellectual commitment
manifested in a conception or judgment, something that is conceived
or judged, and an adequate correspondence between the committed
conception and the thing; for Kristeva truth is what mimesis and
poetic language can tell about the thetic after having passed through
it.[37] In its passage through the thetic, poetic language exposes the
"unicity" of the thetic, which emerges particularly in ideological and
theological discourse. In this capacity, poetic language and mimesis
expose the pretentions of ideology and theology; they reactivate what
dogma sets out to repress; and they protest against the posturings of
the sacred (61).

As Kristeva's argument begins to move beyond her critical readings of Husserl and Frege – and as the concept of the thetic becomes
thoroughly appropriated to Kristeva's own theoretical discourse – it
may be well to consider the interrelationships among the chora, the
thetic, the semiotic, and the symbolic. The chora is a posited space
within which language and the subject develop. In its Platonic
context it is an imaginative, theoretical necessity: it "answers" the
question, where is the place where the first things come to be? But in
its maternal, physiological context it is a specifically bodily and
distinctively female space within which language and subject come to
be. The thetic might be said to arise as a necessary concept to mediate
between the chora and chorion – the imaginative and the biological
space(s) – by virtue of its introduction of the agency of commitment
into the act of positing. Kristeva retains Husserl's "the thetic," it
seems, mainly to avoid losing this sense of intellectual investment.
But she also merges the thetic with Lacan's mirror stage by locating
its psychoanalytic origin at that point in the development of the

subject. The semiotic "precedes" the thetic; it has already gestated there in the chora/chorion, so to speak, taking precedence over language but also preparing to disrupt the symbolic as it develops later. The Kristevan symbolic travels within the image of the eyelid. Even when it brings together two edges of a fissure, it waits to reopen and to separate what it had previously joined. It is always vulnerable to being breached by the semiotic and the thetic; perpetually unsettled, it is particularly accessible in poetic language, where the influx of the semiotic and the passages through the thetic are registered with exemplary sensitivity. In ideological and theological discourse the symbolic appears more stable, but simply awaits there the arrival of the poetic.

The final chapters of the first section of *Revolution in Poetic Language* advance by stages Kristeva's conception of "the *text*." The trajectory of these chapters rises out of her critical readings of Husserl, Hjelmslev, Lacan, and Frege, reaching its rhetorical height in the final pages of the first section, where, in a manner structurally reminiscent of Vico's theory of the stages of language in *The New Science*, Kristeva distinguishes four signifying practices: narrative, metalanguage, contemplation (or "theory'), and "the text." At the risk of beginning at the end of this sequence of chapters, it may be useful to consider the possibility that Kristeva's *le texte*, like her term *la chora*, implies a carefully controlled ambiguity. Because a certain sort of literary practice – epitomized in the writings of Mallarmé, Lautréamont, Artaud, and Joyce – has managed not only to register the creatively disruptive force of the signifying process but also to transmit that force in ways that have become acceptable, the term "text" sometimes (e.g. 104) signifies the literary realization of the signifying practice in all its psychoanalytic and social power. For Kristeva, however, these are rather momentary – however strategically fortunate – manifestations of the potentially explosive charge that courses through the semiotic chora. There is another, related sense of "text" that does not necessarily depend on any formulation in language, however much such a sense can inform the understanding of language.

Kristeva has already introduced the term "inter-textuality" (59) in order to suggest that no text is just itself, that all are dialogical even when they do not explicitly allude to any others. Primarily this is the consequence of inescapable divisions in the subject, but it is also the result of the birth of the semiotic within the same choric space as the subject. Kristeva's large, social sense of "text" seems to be written back-to-back with (or against) Roland Barthes" book on

Japan, *Empire of Signs*, which was first published in 1970. That book blends Barthes's verbal text with several "illustrations," including photographs, maps, reproductions of Japanese and French hand-writing. Here is a passage from the verbal portion of Barthes's text:

> The dream: to know a foreign (alien) language and yet not to under-stand it: to perceive the difference in it without that difference ever being recuperated by the superficial sociality of discourse, communica-tion or vulgarity; to know, positively refracted in a new language, the impossibilities of our own; to learn the systematics of the inconceiv-able; to undo our own "reality" under the effect of other formula-tions, other syntaxes; to discover certain unsuspected positions of the subject in utterance, to displace the subject's topology; in a word, to descend into the untranslatable, to experience its shock with-out ever muffling it, until everything Occidental in us totters and the rights of the "father tongue" vacillate – that tongue which comes to us from our fathers and which makes us, in our turn, fathers and proprietors of a culture which, precisely, history transforms into "nature."[38]

In the spring of 1974, the year *Revolution in Poetic Language* was published, Kristeva made a journey to China with other members of the *Tel Quel* circle. Later that year, she published *About Chinese Women*, which she confesses is not so much a book as a journal or collection of notes.[39] Just as Barthes was tempted to think of Japan as a country that epitomized the semiotic, so too Kristeva in *Revolution in Poetic Language* is ready to think of China as the place of the text. In an approximation of Derrida's "European hallucination," Kristeva seemed ready, before her visit to China, to think of the East as a cultural space where the rhythmically unsettling dynamics of the semiotic chora had not been rendered static by the rigors of capital-istic society; thus, she thought it a place where the full energy of the signifying process could be realized. In the Asiatic mode of produc-tion – as in the ideograms she reproduces – there is an identity of the word-concept "to be born" with "to produce," both of which derive from the ancient image/ideogram of the growing plant (100). Having borrowed the concept of "a hierarchically fluctuating social system" from Joseph Needham's study, *Science and Civilization in China* (99), Kristeva is ready to conceive of at least "ancient" Chinese society as structured with sufficient dynamism as not to "threaten the code or authority governing the whole, thus ensuring the harmonious dynamic of the social process ... without bringing it into conflict with insurmountable repression" (100). As she reports later, after her visit to China, Kristeva found there something other than what she had previously imagined. Indeed, her principal discovery seemed to be the extent to which her ideas of the East were molded by "universalist humanism, proletarian brotherhood, and (why not?) false colonial civility."[40] The rhetoric of *Revolution in Poetic Language*, however, had not yet been chastened by that journey to China.

Kristeva's unrestrained sense of text is that it is charged by the entire gamut of drives that course through the chora, which "underlies" the text (99). Rather than being reified or repressed, negativity is there introduced into every textual reality. As instinctual rhythms pass through the thetic structure of the text, meaning is no sooner constituted than it is exceeded by what remains outside of meaning: the material discontinuity of "real objects." (Here, it would seem, "the text" has resolved the differences between Husserl and Frege.) Because the human body, too, is caught up in the dynamic of the text, the process and trial of the subject, as it breaches the boundaries of definition and law, are energized there. Whatever written texts a Mallarmé or a Joyce may produce to reflect this sense of the human "in process/on trial," they seem not to (be able to) contain it by the usual laws of rhetoric, such as the imposition of a definable speaker communicating with or to a definable addressee. Indeed, whatever is combined or fitted together, whatever totality or aesthetic unity is formed, is there only briefly to be "dynamited" by a charge of drives that pulverizes signification. The drive processes, however, need a text, which serves them, like a body, as a medium through which they move, into which they seep, and from which they unleash their "violent rhythm . . . by alternating rejection and imposition" (103). The text, therefore, always and everywhere, is a force for social change; refusing to attach itself to established society, it promotes "instinctual and linguistic change" in order to bring about new social relations and the "subversion" of capitalism (105).[41] One manifestation of the text is sheer work, political activity, or – better still – revolutionary practice. "Radical transformation of social structures is, no doubt, one of the most obvious manifestations of this process" (104). Simply because the word "revolution" is juxtaposed with the word "poetic" in the title of Kristeva's book should not, therefore, lead to the assumption that Kristeva has simply aestheticized revolution or adopted it as a chastened metaphor. To unleash the forces of the semiotic chora is to explode, dynamite, pulverize (103; R, 97) the aesthetic, psychic, and social containments or combinations of the divided subject, who is momentarily captivated, like the child during the mirror stage, by its illusion of a unified present and future.

Although the language of theory cannot capture the disruptive potentialities of the text, the stylistics of theory already has begun to reflect its near association with the disruptive and highly charged energy of the semiotic chora, pulsating – or boiling like a crucible (104) – beneath the text. Separated perhaps only by a thin crust from the magma of the chora, the language of contemplative or theoretical discourse is highly unstable. "Strewn with shifts in style," it

> plays on phonic similarities, obsolete turns of phrase, ellipses, parables. Archaic and mannered, borrowed from the textual practices of bygone eras, and following the traces but not the facilitation of previous collapsings of signifiance, the various devices of the signifier's drifting oscillate, depending on the era, between the baroque and the esoteric. (99)

It is not surprising, therefore, that in order to protect itself from such textual threats, theorists – those "specialists of the negative" (97) – have come into being as a class assigned to represent, sublimate, set apart, and finally purge society of negativity and self-questioning. Theory is, then, an escape valve for the accumulating pressure within the semiotic chora that threatens to erupt and to break social structure apart. Although theoretical discourse occupies an uncertain position beyond narrative and metalanguage, it is not quite yet a text, however close it comes. Reading theory is to encounter a displacement from the text's crucible – from the rhythmic chora of the maternal body or the boiling magma beneath the earth's crust – because to experience the crucible itself were to expose the subject to impossible dangers: "relinquishing his identity in rhythm, dissolving the buffer of reality in a mobile discontinuity, leaving the shelter of the family, the state, or religion" (104). However disconcerting theoretical discourse has been to many readers, it remains, for Kristeva, a socially acceptable and serviceable means of releasing semiotic pressure from the chora that otherwise would destroy all constancy.

Kristeva arrives at this apocalyptic vision of the text's seismic activity by way of a series of speculative images of the signifying process, particularly as it operates in poetry and visual art. If these images were combined in what is possibly a misleadingly reductive question, chapters 9 through 13 would seem to ask, "Is poetic language fetish, murder, or sacrifice?" Kristeva's discussion of fetishism (62–7) presupposes Freud's description of it as the replacement of "the normal sexual object . . . by another [such as the foot or hair] which bears some relation to it, but is entirely unsuited to serve the normal sexual aim" (SE, VII: 153). In poetry, as in other metalanguages, the symbolic order is being continually remodelled by the "influx" of the semiotic (62), while fetishism is a compromise with the thetic, an erasure from the symbolic and a displacement onto the drives in such a way as to make it possible for the signifying practice to take place (64). Poetry substitutes an object − the book, the *oeuvre* − for the symbolic order that is under attack by the semiotic, which is in a state of perpetual "revolution." Because, however, the poetic function maintains signification − because it does not relinquish its investment in meaning − poetry is not identical with fetishism, however closely it "converges" (65) with it. Murder may also be entertained as an appropriate image for poetry and all other arts. In *Moses and Monotheism* (SE, XXIII: 7−137), Freud advances the thesis that society is founded on the complicity of its members in a common crime, its foundation a break with the symbolic order in the form of a murder, such as the sacrifice of the first-born or the Crucifixion. Art, similarly (in Kristeva's tentative formulation), takes on, moves through, or assumes murder in its consideration of death as the "inner boundary of the signifying process" (70). The artist's crossing that boundary reintroduces an asocial, unharnessed drive (71) back into the symbolic order in a way that profoundly threatens it without, as in actual murder, destroying it.[42] Finally, in an incisive critique of René Girard's *Violence and the Sacred*, Kristeva contrasts sacrifice with totemism, arguing that "sacrifice reminds us that the symbolic emerges out of material continuity through a violent and unmotivated leap; whereas totemism is already an appropriation of this continuum based on the symbolic that has already been set in place" (78). Rather than constituting an apt metaphor for art, sacrifice presupposes art and is preceded by it. In artistic practice semiotic violence is expended in the process of breaking through the semiotic barrier, which makes it possible for the subject to cross the border of the symbolic and to reach the semiotic chora (79).

Having entertained these images of art and the poetic function, Kristeva arrives at last at the image-concept of revolution. Echoing again Mallarmé's "Le Mystère dans les lettres," she finds in the transformation of literature in France during the nineteenth century an explicit realization of the condition of the signifying subject (82) and a denial of the images of poetry as fetish, murder, or sacrifice. In part this literary revolution was an explicit social revolution, since it manifested a refusal to supply a poetry of linguistic formalism for bourgeois consumption. But this revolt soon took on larger social aims:

> The problem, then, was one of finding practices of expenditure capable of confronting the machine, colonial expansion, banks, science, Parliament – those positions of mastery that conceal their violence and pretend to be mere neutral legality. Recovering the subject's vehemence required a descent into the most archaic stage of his positing, one contemporaneous with the positing of social order; it required a descent into the structural positing of the thetic in language so that violence, surging up through the phonetic, syntactic, and logical orders, could reach the symbolic order and the technocratic ideologies that had been build over this violence to ignore or repress it. (83)

Unlike the images of poetry as fetish, murder, or sacrifice, poetry as revolution has a historical reality, providing it with its metaphorical grounding. But for Lautréamont and Mallarmé, the poetic revolution was also a revolt against a force within poetry itself. For them, the combat against fetishism and madness in poetry was no less important than the release of the social and psychosexual powers that poetic language could tap. But even in their multiple radicalism, as Kristeva points out, Lautréamont and Mallarmé – coming as they did before Freud – were able to unleash a revolution that lasted only until the end of the century, when it was effectively concealed and capped. Only after Freud, in the work of Joyce and Bataille, was its potential released.

II

Negativity: rejection

The two words that give this section its title bring together – or set in opposition – basic concepts in the thought of Hegel and Freud. Kristeva begins her discussion of negativity by announcing that she is taking this concept directly from Hegel, for whose theory of consciousness it is fundamental. Although she does not explicitly refer to it until the end of her section on heterogeneity (184–5), Kristeva is here working with an important passage in the introduction to Hegel's *Phenomenology of Spirit* (Sections 77–80) in which he considers negativity [*Negativität*] in the context of the "history of the education of consciousness."[43] There the dynamically developing consciousness, explicitly characterized by its capacity to reflect upon itself, is continually advancing beyond its own limits. For this reason, one of Hegel's tentative definitions of consciousness is "something that goes beyond itself." The history of the education of consciousness is composed of these breaches of the previously conceived limits of consciousness as it drives toward its goal of reaching "the point where knowledge no longer needs to go beyond itself, where knowledge finds itself, where Notion corresponds to object and object to Notion."[44] Doubt, or scepticism, plays a large part in this history of consciousness, which makes it fitting that Hegel's images for the stages of consciousness are religious metaphors that allude both to the Stations of the Cross and to the successive days and nights in the discipline of religious mysticism.[45] Hegel is less concerned either with shallow doubt – the "shilly-shallying about this or that presumed truth" – or with the zealous pursuit of truth that characterizes scientific enquiry, than he is with a "thoroughgoing skepticism," which is the "conscious insight into the untruth of phenomenal knowledge, for which the supreme reality is what is in truth only the unrealized Notion." Negativity can be discovered at work there, as a fundamental term in the course of the future of consciousness.

As consciousness drives toward its goal, where knowledge no longer need go beyond itself, while driving through previously conceived (false) limits along the way, those instances of untrue consciousness, when exposed as such, are not merely negative, in the sense of being unproductive or of no account. In Hegel's view, a conception of knowledge that adopts *that* sense of the negative, seeing skepticism as "pure nothingness," is itself a pattern of untrue or incomplete consciousness, a limit that waits to be breached. If instead, "the exposition of the untrue consciousness in its untruth" can be conceived as a *determinate* negation, seeing x not merely as *not y*, but as *other than y*, then negativity can be understood as what gives rise to a new era in the history of consciousness: "A new form has thereby immediately arisen, and in the negation the transition is made through which the progress through the complete series of forms comes about of itself."[46] In this passage from *Phenomenology of Spirit*, three distinguishing characteristics of Hegel's "negativity" can be seen: (1) negativity is determinate of what it negates; (2) when a negation (such as "pure nothingness") is negated, we are not simply returned to square one, to some original unnegated stage, but rather the negated negation becomes incorporated into the cumulative developmental history of consciousness; and (3) negativity is not simply a matter of judgment but is fundamentally characteristic of concepts and things.[47]

In her earlier remarks (30–5) concerning Husserl's reliance upon the concept of a transcendental ego, Kristeva anticipated her critique here of Hegel's theory of consciousness. Although negativity introduces a useful and potentially exploitable instability into Hegel's view of the movement of consciousness toward its ultimate unity and stability – that is, the point where "the 'I' is not merely the Self, but the *identity of the Self with itself*"[48] – that instability is merely temporary. Indeed, it is the principal means of propelling consciousness beyond its temporarily perceived limits and on to its eventual identity and individuality, which "absolute knowing" makes possible. Even Hegel's idea of force is insufficient to produce permanent divisions in the ego, despite its "labyrinthian" double movement (114). Such a sense of force [*Kraft*] is distinguishable from power, either in the institutional political sense [*Macht*] or in the irresistible, manipulative sense [*Gewalt*]. *Kraft* for Hegel is principally the intellectual, moral, or physical capacity of a person to affect events, things, or other persons, rather than being a collection of conflicting mental faculties.[49] If, however, Hegel is read through Freud and Lenin, as Kristeva seems to want to read him here, negativity can be seen to register "a *conflictual state* which stresses the heterogeneity of the semiotic function and its determination . . . as instinctual" (118).

Passing first through Frege's critique, in his *Logical Investigations*, of Hegel's inconsistencies concerning negation (119–22), Kristeva proceeds to supplement Hegel's negativity with Freud's concept of negation [*Verneinung*], before playing her own views off both Hegel's and Freud's in order to develop her idea of rejection [*le rejet*] (123–6). Although Kristeva does not at first cite a specific Freudian text, she would appear to be offering a reading of Freud's 1925 paper on "Negation," which quite literally deals with what is involved in answering "No" [*verneinen*]. Although Freud makes no explicit reference here to Hegel,[50] the account he gives of negation reads as though it were a critical reflection on Hegel's theory of consciousness. This is the passage that seems most directly relevant to Kristeva's argument:

> The content of a repressed image or idea can make its way into consciousness, on condition that it is *negated*. Negation is a way of taking cognizance of what is repressed; indeed it is already a lifting of

the repression, though not, of course, an acceptance of what is repressed. We can see how in this the intellectual function is separated from the affective process. With the help of negation only one consequence of the process of repression is undone – in fact, namely, of the ideational content of what is repressed not reaching consciousness. The outcome of this is a kind of intellectual acceptance of the repressed, while at the same time what is essential to the repression persists. In the course of analytic work we often produce a further, very important and somewhat strange variant of this situation. We succeed in conquering the negation as well, and in bringing about a full intellectual acceptance of the repressed; but the repressive process itself is not yet removed by this. (SE, XIX: 235–6)

Kristeva invites the readers of her text to look at Hegel's theory of consciousness, initially, through Freud's theory of negation, which may itself already be a critical reading of Hegel. What, in short, are we to make of that mark of punctuation – the colon – that Kristeva uses to separate (or to join) "negativity" from (or to) "rejection"?[51]

As a sequence of chapters, this second section of *Revolution in Poetic Language* begins with Hegel in chapters 1 and 2 and ends with Freud in chapter 7. In between these chapters are a brief return to Frege (119–22) for his logical critique of negation; a critical examination of Kierkegaard's "kinesis," Heidegger's "cura," and Lacan's "desire," considered in terms of their unacknowledged debts to Hegel's negativity (chapter 4); a discussion of the legacy of the Hegelian concept of desire [*Begierde*] in Feuerbach and Marx (chapter 5); and a critical analysis of Derrida's concept of *différance*," considered in the context of the earlier discussions of negativity and desire (chapter 6). Rather than constituting a movement from Hegel to Freud – or even a reading of Hegel through Freud, as Kristeva claims (118) – this sequence of chapters amounts to a recovery of Hegelian negativity, to a recuperative reading of Hegel after Freud. Just as Alexandre Kojève saw Marx already anticipated in the texts of Hegel,[52] so Kristeva sees an opening for Freud's theory of negation in Hegel's concept of negativity.

Freud's "negation" [*Verneinung*], however, because it is the means of access to consciousness by that which has been repressed, presupposes the unconscious and by doing so reveals a scission that for Kristeva specifies the human subject "as a process, an intersection – an impossible unity" (118). As Freud explains, the content of a previously repressed image or idea, travelling under the disguise of negation, rises into consciousness and initiates a partial lifting of repression. As important as this process is, however, it is only intellectual, leaving the unconscious, affective processes intact. Even when analytic work succeeds in conquering negation itself, the repressive processes continue. Although he does not say so, it would seem that for Freud there is a negativity unconsciously working "beneath" negation (or, at least, a negation that continues even when negation is negated). There is, in short, a "No" in the unconscious that will not be silenced.

Hegel – because he thinks of consciousness as relentlessly moving forward, progressing through the complete series of its forms, breaching each successive limit – sees the certain goal of consciousness as at once a transfiguration, resurrection, and apotheosis of the previously struggling consciousness. When it reaches its goal, the ego, from the depths of its negativity, is externalized as the Self that knows itself totally and absolutely, the Self that thinks (knows?) it need not (cannot?) go beyond itself. It has become the absolute Self that knows absolutely. It is not surprising that the final magnificent sentences of the *Phenomenology* turn to apocalyptic imagery in order to render the Self's final transformation, which can also be read as a rhetorical culmination of Hegel's successive appropriations of the language of biblical and mystical Christianity:

> This revelation is, therefore, the raising-up of its depth, or its *extension*, the negativity of this withdrawn "I," a negativity which is its externalization or its substance: and this revelation is also the Notion's Time, in that this externalization is in its own self externalized, and just as it is in its extension, so it is equally in its depth, in the Self. The *goal*, Absolute Knowing, or Spirit that knows itself as Spirit, has for its path the recollection of the Spirits as they are in themselves and as they accomplish the organization of their realm. Their preservation, regarded from the side of their free existence appearing in the form of contingency, is History; but regarded from the side of their [philosophically] comprehended organization, it is the Science of Knowing in the sphere of appearance: the two together, comprehended History, form alike the inwardizing and the Calvary of absolute Spirit, the actuality, truth, and certainty of his throne, without which he would be lifeless and alone.

Hegel does not quite stop here but moves onto an even higher register of rhetoric by leaving prose for poetry, adapting for his purpose two lines from Schiller's *Die Freundschaft*:

> from the chalice of this realm of spirits
> foams forth for Him his own infinitude.[53]

Here, it would seem, Hegel demonstratively makes good on his conviction that the language of German philosophy descends from German mysticism.[54] Even so, he will not relinquish his idea of the divided subject.

The reader of the final sentences of the *Phenomenology* cannot but mentally trip over the phrase, "the Calvary of absolute Spirit." The moment of the triumph of consciousness would seem to be here the occasion, at least, of the body's death, however much that moment may promise a metaphorical resurrection. It is quite understandable, therefore, that Kristeva makes Hegel run the gauntlet from Frege to Derrida in chapters 3 to 6 before bringing his theory and Freud's together at last in chapter 7.

What Kristeva discovers by this process of textual trial is that "it is possible to read between the lines in Hegel and find the statement of a truth about the subject: *the subject is a paranoid subject constituted by the impulse of Desire that sublimates and unifies the schizoid rupture*" (134). Although Hegel works to transcend all instances of negativity in the dialectically developing consciousness, any sublation [*Aufhebung*] is in fact also a sublimation of negativity.[55] The inwardizing Calvary remains within the absolute Spirit in that previously negated limits of consciousness are precisely what makes it possible for consciousness to advance, incorporating those negated forms of itself into the (human) subject that exceeds but retains them.[56] Hegel's notion of desire [*Begierde*] plays an indispensable role in what Kristeva calls this "superseded" movement of consciousness by which the "amputated object" is introduced into the knowing subject (133). Kristeva's reading of Hegel's account of desire recovers an important passage in the *Phenomenology* (sections 174–6) that has often been ignored or misread:[57]

> Self-consciousness is Desire. Certain of the nothingness of [the] other, it explicitly affirms that this nothingness is *for it* the truth of the other; it destroys the independent object and thereby gives itself the certainty of itself . . . In this satisfaction, however, experience makes it aware that the object has its own independence. Desire and the self-certainty obtained in its gratification are conditioned by the object, for self-certainty comes from superseding this other: in order that this supersession can take place, there must be this other. Thus self-consciousness, by its negative relation to the object, is unable to supersede it; it is really because of that relation that it produces the object

again, and the desire as well. It is in fact something other than self-consciousness that is the essence of Desire; and through this experience self-consciousness has itself realized this truth.[58]

Rather than constituting a self-contradictory argument concerning the function of desire in self-consciousness, this passage mirrors the very process of incorporating negativity into consciousness, which is driven to exceed its own negativity by the desire for the other than itself. That other must be legitimately *other* for any such supersession to take place; but once it does take place, there are, it would seem, two perpetual others for Hegel, (a) the one that/who effected the supersession that has taken place and (b) the former, and now negative, limited definition of the expanding consciousness. Hegel can here be read as straining after the distinction that Lacan will make between the two others in his paper on "The subversion of the subject."[59] Hegel concludes his theory of desire by distinguishing three "moments" in which desire "completes" different forms of self-consciousness: first, "the pure undifferentiated 'I'"; second, the desire for, and the supersession of, an independent object; and third, the "double reflection" in which consciousness has for its object (a) itself – including "its otherness or difference" – and (b) the independent other.[60] Kristeva's argument that the legacy of Hegel's concept of negativity has been squandered or mishandled – with the possible exceptions of its treatment by Lacan and Derrida – seems irrefutable.

Kristeva's critical discussion of grammatology (chapter 6) includes what is still the most astute assessment of Derrida's reading of Hegel; indeed, it is a reading of *Grammatology* as itself a reading of Hegel's *Phenomenology*. Kristeva sees grammatology as "the most radical of all the various procedures that have tried, after Hegel, to push dialectical negativity further and elsewhere" (140). Not only do Derrida's principal concepts – difference, the trace, the grammé, writing – precisely embody this dialectic; they may be thought of "as metaphors for a movement that retreats before the thetic but, sheltered by it, unfolds only within the stases of the semiotic *chora*" (141–2). Indeed, as Derrida, in *Writing and Difference*, seemed about to acknowledge himself, *différance*, constituted as the absence of the other, inscribes negativity.[61] But Derrida does not simply incorporate Hegelian negativity. Rather, he interrogates it in such a way that, first, it becomes "positivized and drained of its potential for producing breaks;" second, "it holds itself back and appears as a delaying [*retardement*];" third, "it defers and thus becomes merely positive and affirmative;"

and fourth, "it inscribes and institutes through retention" (141). Although Kristeva does not put it so bluntly, she implies that Derrida's grammatology succeeds in changing the valence of negativity more completely than did Hegel's apocalyptic rhetoric in the final sentences of the *Phenomenology*.

Kristeva sees among the consequences of Derrida's unprecedented achievement a loss, however. As it inscribes negativity, *différance* sacrifices the dynamics of the subject:

> In its desire to bar the thetic and put (logically or chronologically) previous energy transfers in its place, the grammatological deluge of meaning gives up on the subject, and must remain ignorant not only of his functioning as social practice, but also of his chances for experiencing jouissance or being put to death. Neutral in the face of all positions, theses, and structures, grammatology is, as a consequence, equally restrained when they break, burst, or rupture: demonstrating disinterestedness toward (symbolic and/or social) structure, grammatology remains silent when faced with its destruction or renewal. (142)

By completely textualizing discourse, grammatology has in a sense impoverished it by barring the thetic dimension, which is for Kristeva the "deepest structure" of signification (44) because it contains the complicity between the object and its proposition. Even when read sympathetically, Derrida's announcement that there is nothing outside the text that will serve as a base from which to read it comes at great theoretical cost.[62] Kristeva does not imply, however, that this amounts to any sort of reduction in intellectual energy, but rather a transfer of it. Grammatology unleashes a "deluge of meaning," but it does so by abandoning the social functioning of the subject. Since for Kristeva the forming of the speaking subject in the semiotic chora (or maternal chorion) is *the* shaping social process for the subject – *the* moment when subject and other are most intimate, yet still discrete – thus, to abandon social practice is indeed to give up on the subject. Concerning the social function, the jouissance, or the death of the subject, grammatology is mute. Furthermore, by not engaging social practice, grammatology condemns itself to silent disinterestedness when it witnesses the destruction or renewal of the symbolic or social structures that have nonetheless been profoundly affected by the revolution it has itself facilitated. Here Kristeva's argument is not the now familiar one that deconstruction makes nothing happen (ethically or politically); rather it is that grammatology has nothing to say about the social consequences of its work. Derrida seems to have anticipated this charge when he warned that deconstruction, resisting the temptation to define its own project, risks having that project defined for it.[63]

In an effort to redeem grammatology, however, Kristeva shrewdly folds Derrida's account of *différance* back into Lacan's theory of the mirror stage. In doing so, however, Kristeva signals her own control over these arguments by giving yet another turn to Lacan's play on the ambiguities of the word "stage":

> If in this way the trace dissolves every thesis – material, natural, social, substantial, and logical – in order to free itself from any dependence on the *Logos*, it can do so because it grasps the formation of the symbolic function preceding the mirror stage and believes it can remain there, even while aiming toward that stage. Grammatology would undoubtedly not acknowledge the pertinence of this psychoanalytic staging [*stadialité*], which depends on the categories and entities of beings. (143)

While candidly admitting in advance that Derrida would most likely not accept this claim, Kristeva convincingly argues that psychoanalysis "paves the way" for grammatology. Were grammatology to acknowledge its psychoanalytic legacy, which would not in the least be a retreat from the recognition that it "designates" an insurmountable "enclosure," then grammatology's untenable and (in her view) impoverished sense of the subject would be radically changed.[64] Once such a theoretical *rapprochement* between Lacanian psychoanalysis and Derridean grammatology comes about – or, more immediately, because Kristeva's reading of their texts sees it as necessary and possible that it come about – the creatively disruptive force of writing can be theoretically seen as occurring in that spatio-temporal stage-space that Kristeva has *posited* (in Husserl's sense) as the semiotic chora.[65] Although she has suggested a number of ways in which critical reading can expand one text to what is beyond it – even to which it is determinedly closed – Kristeva is not simply building toward an assimilation of Hegelian negativity to Freudian negation. Her concept of rejection builds on these but is not reducible to them. Freud provided a lens, initially, through which Kristeva reads Hegel. But she also identifies a number of other lenses – from Kierkegaard's "kinesis" to Marx's "desire" – which she finds offering distorted views of negativity and of the human subject. Kristeva, however, generously sees these distortions as forming an instructive sequence of misreadings of Hegel's negativity, from which Derrida's stands apart. His is only a misreading if Hegel's final negation of negativity is considered as occurring unconvincingly at the end of the *Phenomenology* – fascinatingly undermined by his image of an internalized Calvary and awaiting Derrida's redemptive reading, which recovers negativity's irrepressible *différance*.

Kristeva's discussion of rejection (chapter 7) is an extraordinarily difficult portion of her theory of negativity. By this point in the reading of *Revolution in Poetic Language*, a number of Kristeva's textual strategies have become familiar. At key moments in her argument (e.g. 144, 162) she will introduce a series of questions that at first may seem merely rhetorical perching posts, allowing her reader to prepare for the next phase of intellectually strenuous theoretical flight. But these questions also make it possible for Kristeva to be conceptually speculative without being reductively and prematurely definitive, thus enabling her text to be carefully structured – these questions usually appear about two-thirds of the way through a chapter – but at the same time open to her readers' participation, inviting their skepticism. There are also moments when a sentence will enact the point being made, as in the use of interjection in the sentence on anality and interjection (152). Most often, however, Kristeva is putting language under extreme pressure in preparation for moving beyond her readings of other theorists. For example, when she writes about the semiotic chora, the thetic, the text, negativity and rejection, heterogeneity, and poetic language, that sense of pressurized prose – reaching further beyond what already is certainly language under extreme stress (as in the texts of Freud, Husserl, Heidegger, Lacan, Derrida) – seems most acute. Whatever a reader may say about these passages cannot help but cool them down or decompress them, which loses, of course, much of their creatively disturbing and destabilizing effect.

"What does Kristeva mean by 'rejection'?" her readers are entitled to ask, however. Rejection, clearly, is a concept generated by her critical reading of Hegel and Freud. It is not synonymous with Hegel's negativity or Freud's negation, though it is conceptually related to both. Although Kristeva has been reading Hegel "through" Freud, when she turns at last (162–4) to Freud's text on "Negation," she finds him silent concerning rejection [*le rejet*], which would have seemed to offer some hope of bringing Hegel and Freud simultaneously into focus. Whereas Hegelian *negativity* is the retention of a previously conceived definition of consciousness within the developing

subject and Freudian *negation* the incomplete repression (or symbolization) of pleasure and the erotic drives that have come to be
intellectually but not affectively accepted, *rejection* is a semiotic mode
of perpetual aggressivity, of continually renewed disruption that may
be thought of as energizing both negativity and negation (150).[66] In
order to introduce this concept, Kristeva invites her reader to imagine
a physiologically vivid journey of the drives through the body during
the anal phase, when the subject's fundamental experience of separation occurs not as a sense of lack but as a pleasurable discharge:

> Energy surges and discharges erotize the glottic, urethral, and anal
> sphincters as well as the kinetic system. These drives move through
> the sphincters and arouse pleasure at the very moment substances
> belonging to the body are separated and rejected from the body. This
> acute pleasure therefore coincides with a loss, a separation from the
> body, and the isolating of objects outside it. (150–1)

What is being described here with such remarkable tactility is the
positing of "detached alterity" or the founding experience of objective separation. Furthermore, this pleasurable fecal discharge is also
the occasion for the acquisition of language, which will continue to
represent "a capacity for symbolization through the definitive detachment of the rejected object, through its repression under the sign"
(152).

If rejection lies beneath, energizing and disrupting negativity and
negation, then poetic language, which is its medium of expression, is
understandably a "third-degree negativity" (164). By now it should
be clear that Kristeva's phrase "poetic language" does not signify any
and all forms of poetry, much less an indiscriminate sense of an
exalted and unproblematic aesthetic category. The promise of the first
theoretical part of *Revolution in Poetic Language* is that the second and
third untranslated (perhaps untranslatable) parts, which consider in
scrupulous detail the texts of Lautréamont and Mallarmé, will demonstrate how in certain texts by those poets (and in some by Artaud,
Joyce, and a very few others) the survival and affirmation of
rejection has been captured, or perhaps liberated. The two poetic/
semiotic/psychoanalytic modes of that survival are "oralization," or
the reunion with the mother's body, and "homosexual phratry," or
the reunion with the bodies of brothers (153). These modes constitute not just thematic or metaphorical material in the poems of
Lautréamont and Mallarmé but more importantly, they are textually

enacted processes that are manifested in prosody and syntax. By these means, the reiterated death drive – negativity, negation, rejection – finds its place in a language charged by and invested with instinctual drives and erotic energy. Poetic (third-degree) rejection perpetually recalls, therefore, "the dialectical moment of the generating of signifiance" (164). It continually replays the vitally disruptive formation of the speaking subject in the semiotic chora.

III

Heterogeneity

By beginning with Freud (chapter 1) and ending with Hegel (chapter 5) this section of Kristeva's text not only reverses the order of the preceding section but also replays and intensifies its argument. Freud's theory of drives, Kristeva points out, is characterized by both heteronomy and dichotomy. Because they serve as a bridge between the psychic and the somatic and between the biological and social foundations of the signifying function, the drives are heteronomous; but because they also operate in conflicting pairs – life/death, ego/ sexual – they are dichotomous. Indeed, in his opposition to Jung's monistic libido theory, Freud militantly proclaimed his affirmation of dualism (SE, XVIII: 53). Freud, thus, "makes drives the shattered and doubly differentiated site of conflict and rejection"; they are "the repeated scission of matter that generates signifiance, the place where an always absent subject is produced" (167).

Although several attempts have been made by post-Freudian theorists to place greater emphasis on the neurobiological aspect of drives, the consequence of thus mechanizing the drives, in Kristeva's judgment, is a loss of the capacity of Freud's theory to deal with social and signifying practices. Kristeva's review of Constantin von Monakow, Raoul Mourgue, and Lipot Szondi's biological studies (167–9), however, serves to contextualize her own biological metaphors, which retain their neurophysiological specificity and fleshy tacticity in a way that Lacan's do not. Rejection, Kristeva argues, positively activates the drives. Here, it is particularly the sense of rejection as a throwing back [*reicio*] that links it with a number of other processes that defy efforts of elimination: rectivate, re-inscribe, re-present, re-new. Re-jection is constituted by the re-inscription (or "mark") that positively re-turns as a sign what had previously been negated. In its structure of reincorporation of what was negated, rejection is a form of negativity; as a process of saying no, such that the denial can begin to lift repression, it is a form of negation. Because the signifying subject is "positioned" at the point of intersection where semiotic lines arrive and depart, where heteronomous and dichotomous drives move in an intricate network, thetic heterogeneity characterizes all aspects of the subject. Kristeva here (171) puts the word "humanity" in quotation marks to indicate how suspect a term it has become in light of the investigation of the subject that she and others have undertaken. In the French text (R, 155) that suspicion is even clearer. The English translation breaks up Kristeva's sentence, apparently to simplify it, but sacrificing much of her irony in the process. To call into question the adequacy of a particular notion of human beings – that they are essentially unified, stable, and conscious, for example, rather than heterogeneous – is not to be anti-humanistic in the sense of having no interest in or concern for human beings. It is to be anti-humanistic, however, if such a judgment is based on an absolute, foreclosed, and unreflective sense of what human beings are.

There is, however, a "contradiction" within semiotic heterogeneity that multiplies its complexity. Kristeva's description of this contradiction is one of the most staggeringly difficult passages in her text:

> We now arrive at the heart of a contradiction, which is far from formal, between two qualitatively different heterogeneous orders: the second of which (the sign) is produced by the repeated accumulation of the successive rejections (facilitations – stases – facilitations) of the first. What is more, although this double counter-charge (engrammatic and symbolic) depends on material scission, it is by necessity *ultimately* generated by the social apparatus and the social practice in which the subject is led to function. Thus, through the transference-relation and its demonstration of the *lack* [*manque*] that constitutes desire and the symbolic, the psychoanalytic device ends up binding material, heterogeneous rejection through so-called primary processes (metonymies, metaphors) within secondary processes. This device transposes the conflict between them by linking it up within the system of the *representamen* – the system of the signifier, the sign, and, finally, the understanding. (173)

The lure that precedes the reader through this rather murky passage is the possibility of understanding the ways in which the heterogeneity of language and the psychobiological heterogeneity of human beings are all knotted together. The distinction here between "first" and "second" successions of rejection is simply a rhetorical, expository distinction, since Kristeva's argument all along has been that language and the human subject are generated together. While not wanting to neglect the indispensable advances in biological research into the "material scission" of human beings, Kristeva wants to supplement that work with her own investigations – following Freud's lead – of the social practices that determine the subject. Furthermore, this complementarity of the biological and the social is here to be investigated in such a way as not to lose the prominence of language; and it is soon to be shown that a particular sort of modernist poetic text provides the angle of vision that enables the theorist to look through it and to see, as in a kaleidoscope, the multiple heterogeneities of the human subject. What makes this act of seeing difficult in this portion of Kristeva's text is that she will not let her reader forget that what is seen is viewed through a series of theoretical lenses: psychoanalysis, linguistics, biology, philosophy, literary criticism. Because these lenses are human structures in language, they never cease to be implicated in what they theorize about.

As important as these conceptual systems are, it is in art, poetic language, and textual practice that Kristeva finds fundamental rejection most powerfully and positively at work:

> The text's principal characteristic and the one that distinguishes it from other signifying practices, is precisely that it introduces, through binding and through vital and symbolic differentiation, heterogeneous rupture and rejection: jouissance and death. This would seem to be "art"'s function as a signifying practice: under the pleasing exterior of a very socially acceptable differentiation, art reintroduces into society fundamental rejection. (180)

It is not because of its pleasing, aesthetic exterior – and certainly not because it supports or sustains unreflected assumptions of cultural or humanistic totality – that art has the importance she finds in it. Lacan heard in poetry the polyphony of the unconscious, and Derrida found that literature makes it possible to "say anything." Kristeva adds that poetry and art clandestinely continue the revolutionary processes of positive rejection, both within the subject and within the social order(s) of which the subject is a part. In this sense, art's perverse and perennial rejection of aesthetic or formal unity is an eloquent testament to its irrepressible assertion of "human" heterogeneity.

In chapter 5 Kristeva turns directly to the passage in Hegel's *Phenomenology* (sections 77–80) that has haunted her argument for some time. Whereas her earlier reading (109–13) had emphasized the drive of consciousness to exceed its previously conceived limit, incorporating that breached limit into itself as a negativity of what it was, she now considers the consequences that arise from the anxiety generated by this process. Each movement beyond a previous limit of consciousness, which Hegel calls its uprooting [*Hinausgerissenwerden*], is a kind of death. That this is more than an extravagant simile is indicated by Hegel's view that consciousness is the "Notion of it-self."[67] In its anxiety that surpassing itself entails the death of what it was and is, consciousness resists its own progression and opts for unthinking inertia, until thought overcomes (or "troubles") this defensive inaction. Here Hegel candidly, if somewhat inelegantly, struggles to retain his sense of the forward drive of consciousness, its goal of complete unity, the successive deaths of what it was, its anxiety and inertia in the face of possible (or certain) death(s), the disruptive effects of thought on defensive inertia, the incorporation of exceeded versions of itself into consciousness as it relentlessly moves forward, and the apparently untranscendable presence of an inward-ized Calvary that is an immutable negativity.

Kristeva recalls this Hegelian scenario in order to contrast it with nineteenth-century avant-garde experience, particularly in the poetry of Lautréamont and Mallarmé. Their poetic language renders the powerfully disruptive and potentially psychotic (189) processes that Kristeva calls "textual practice," which consist in "accentuating the very movement of negativity", *within* the processes of the speaking subject (183). What distinguishes this notion of textual process from Hegelian phenomenology is that "textual experience introduces death into the signifying device" itself (186). Here Kristeva finds in the texts of Lautréamont and Mallarmé a link with, but a movement be-yond, Hegelian negativity.[68] By relocating death within the signifier, no defensive inertia and no promise of ultimate unity are possible. Indeed, textual practice knows no defenses:

> Textual experience is not . . . immobilized in an unthinking inertia; instead, it shatters conceptual unity into rhythms, logical distortions (Lautréamont), paragrams, and syntactic inventions (Mallarmé), all of which register, within the signifier, the passage beyond its boundary. In these texts, it is no longer a question of mere anxiety, but of a separa-tion, which is so dangerous for the subject's unity that, as Artaud's

text testifies, signifying unity itself vanishes in glossolalia. One might
say, then, that since the late nineteenth century, the avant-garde text's
essential purpose has been to insert within a non-thought and through
the process of language, the violence of rejection, which is viewed as
death by the unary subject and as castration by the analyst. (186)

But as threatening to any defensively stable ego as are these processes
inscribed in the text, there is a more powerful agency yet that awaits
them, ready to accommodate, ignore, or label as "esoteric" what
courses through and energizes the human subject. That agency is
the ideological network of capitalist society, where several factors
conspire to make heterogeneity "inaudible or complicitous with
dominant bourgeois ideology" (190). These include (1) the disruptive
strategies of capitalism itself, which unsettle institutions, subjects, and
discourse as they operate through class struggle; (2) the tactics of
liberal accommodation, which absorb and neutralize challenges to itself, enabling it merely to tolerate or effectively to reject any sustained
critique of its foundations; and (3) the esotericism of avant-garde
discourse, which blunts its social impact and invites its dismissal
as mad or incomprehensible.[69] Kristeva, however, has confidence
in the irrepressibility of heterogeneity, which recalls Hegel's vision
of thought's determination to overcome even the anxiety-ridden
inertia within consciousness. As heterogeneity opens up into the symbolic, putting the speaking subject in process/on trial, it meets there
the social processes of historical materialism that are already under
way. Such a meeting, as Kristeva sees it, generates an energizing
force for revolutionary change.[70]

IV

Practice

This final section of the theoretical prologue to *Revolution in Poetic
Language* puts forward a theory of textual practice, consolidates
Kristeva's exposition of the signifying subject, and provides a transition to her extraordinarily detailed readings of Lautréamont and
Mallarmé that are to follow in parts B and C (R, 209–620). Kristeva's
theory arises out of a critical assessment of Hegelian practice and its
successive revisions by Marx, Lenin, and Mao Tse-tung. The starting point for these revisions that lead to Kristeva's theory is not

surprisingly a passage in Hegel's *Phenomenology of Spirit* (section 86), which meditates on the perennial problem that consciousness can simultaneously know *something* while critically reflecting on the adequacy of what it knows. There are, thus, two objects of consciousness: the "in-itself" and the "being-for consciousness of this in-itself."[71] The dialectical movement from the one to the other, by which consciousness affects both its object and its knowledge, Hegel calls "experience" [*Erfahrung*]. The direction of movement in experience, as Kristeva observes (198), is back from the externality of the object to the reconstituted unity of consciousness in the face of the "new." This movement is counter-balanced, however, according to the argument of Hegel's *Science of Logic*, by the "Practical Idea," which moves out from a preoccupation with self-knowledge toward the externality of the object by a path that does not pass through the dialectic of consciousness, marked as it is by successive accommodations of negativity.[72] By this means, as though "behind the back of consciousness,"[73] a new object is originated; and, in terms of Hegel's theory, the Practical Idea of this new object is arrived at, so to speak, by a discontent with the idea of experience. "Practice" for Hegel is not simply "a subordinate moment of theoretical synthesis, it must also be a test – a confrontation with heterogeneity" (197). As productively far as Hegel is willing to strain his controlling theory of an ultimately unified consciousness – whose backside (like Moses' God) is a rare form of visible metonymy – he does not, however, relinquish his idea of the subject as a "consciousness-present-to-itself."

As Kristeva reads these theorists of practice, Hegel's charting of a path behind the back of consciousness points the way for the materialist dialectic of Marx and Lenin. By positing "human sensuous activity" as the foundation of his epistemology and by encompassing practice in such activity, Marx frees practice from its subordination to consciousness. In turn, this enables Lenin, in his "Conspectus of Hegel's Book on *The Science of Logic*," to elevate practice over theory. The critical point here is that both Marx and Lenin stress "the orientation of *practice* toward *externality, objectivity,* and the *real*" (199). While accepting Hegel's invitation to go beyond him in terms of practice, however, they miss his tantalizing offer to deconstruct his theory of consciousness and by that means to anticipate an adequate conception of the heterogeneous subject. Marx and Lenin fail to recognize the pervasiveness of negativity in Hegelian consciousness, which Kristeva sees as the disabling oversight in dialectical materialism that immobilizes the Marxist view of the subject (133–9, 203).

For Kristeva, Marx and Lenin overturn Hegelian dialectic only once, ignoring a further and more important possibility of critical reading.

In a passage that seems to provide a theoretical grounding for her journey to China in 1974, Kristeva reads Mao as offering an important advance over Marx and Lenin in his understanding of Hegel.[74] In his essay "On Practice," Mao insists that experience and practice must be combined rather than separated, or the one hidden from the other. It is only by engaging in the effort to change a "thing or class of things," he argues, that either is truly and fully known. Rather than leading away from the externality of the object, direct experience in an effort to effect change provides the only true knowledge of the external (200).[75] Kristeva credits Mao with going beyond Marx, even though his notion of subjectivity is "impregnable, impersonal, atomistic" (201). While ready to engage critically the texts of Marx, Lenin, and Mao, Kristeva reads Hegel as closer than they to having articulated a dynamic theory of the divided subject, especially in his concept of negativity. Although she never mentions Louis Althusser by name, his thought seems to haunt her discussion of Marxism and ideology. Even though this can be merely speculation, it is likely that Kristeva might associate Althusser's "ideological apparatuses," which she alludes to only once directly (96), as much with their repressive forms in Bulgaria, as she knew them, as with their capitalist forms in Western Europe. Unlike Michel Foucault, for example, whose membership of the Communist Party resulted in part from the personal influence of Althusser, Kristeva is more confidently critical of Marxist theory, which she has seen in practice.[76]

Practice, for Kristeva, provides yet another means of access to the processes of the signifying subject, which is not to say that they are *merely* textual, in the sense of having no *social* or political dimension. Signifying processes are for her *social* processes from the start, literally *ab ovo*. But because Marx, Lenin, and Mao have manifestly failed to understand the heterogeneity of the subject, Kristeva announces that

> practice encloses and brings to knowledge the *direct experience* of reality – an immediacy Lenin notes only in passing – which incorporates the stage of *Erfahrung* (experience), that of the signifying apprehension of the new heterogeneous object. By implication, direct experience includes the border on which the subject may shatter. (202)

It is, however, by manifesting itself through the text – that is, by making itself available to readers – that practice achieves its effects.

Although Kristeva does not cite Derrida's exposition of critical reading, she shares with him a remarkably specific understanding of
what critical reading and commentary involve. First of all, the most
important, transforming event in reading occurs when a new text
produces "the most intense moment of rupture and renewal" (204).
Such a deconstructive moment opens the present structure (of consciousness or text) to the new that previously was excluded from
it. But its arrival constitutes a rupture or shattering of the earlier
form. Secondly, this new arrival avoids becoming simply a "free-
flow 'escape' [*fluit*] of the signifier" (209) by being kept on track
by the "guardrails" [*des garde-fous*] of critical commentary. Although
Kristeva uses exactly the same image as Derrida,[77] she does not
simply repeat his theory; rather she uses it as a means to return to her
image of the chora, elaborated now by its assimilation of Mallarmé's
metaphor of the text as empty place, seen here as providing the site of
practice:

> Now the situation becomes clearer. As the text constructed itself with
> respect to an empty place . . . it in turn comes to be the empty site of a
> process in which its readers become involved. The text turns out to be
> the analyst and every reader the analysand. But since the *structure and
> function of language take the place of the focus of transference* in the text, this
> opens the way for all linguistic, symbolic, and social structures to be
> put in process/on trial. The text thereby attains its essential dimension:
> it is a *practice* calling into question (symbolic and social) *finitudes* by
> proposing *new signifying devices*. (210)

As texts of practice, in this sense, the poems of Mallarmé and
Lautréamont serve to bring momentarily out of concealment "an
objective truth" that otherwise remains hidden: "the moment of
struggle exploding the subject toward heterogeneous materiality"
(211). They reveal the condition of the speaking subject as in
process/on trial, however quickly the dominant ideology of capitalist
society scrambles to conceal the subject's heterogeneity once again in
order to forestall a critique of bourgeois ideology (212). The second
overturning of Hegelian dialectic that Kristeva advocates amounts to
the recognition that

> The subject never *is*. The *subject* is only the *signifying process* and he
> appears only as a *signifying practice*, that is, only when he is absent *within
> the position* out of which social, historical, and signifying activity
> unfolds. There is no science of the subject. Any thought mastering the

subject is mystical: all that exists is the field of a practice where, through his expenditure, the subject can be anticipated in an always anterior future. (215)

Far from claiming to have achieved this second overturning in her own reading of Hegel, Kristeva sees it as already having occurred in the avant-garde poetry at the end of the nineteenth century.

Reading Kristeva may often seem like a groping search by under-standing for the always elusive and ungraspable certainty that is forever beyond it. Maurice Blanchot describes such a search this way: "Understanding seeks what eludes it; it moves powerfully and constantly forward toward the moment when understanding is no longer possible, when the fact, in its absolutely concrete reality, becomes the obscure and the impenetrable."[78] However, when the reader of *Revolution in Poetic Language* arrives at the chapters on Lautréamont and Mallarmé, which forecast the next two-thirds of Kristeva's text, reading is not at all a plunge into obscurity and impenetrability, even though it offers no certainty or security. But instead of a plunge into the obscure and impenetrable, these chapters offer the reader a display of Kristeva's remarkable skills as a literary critic, which have been kept purposefully in reserve throughout the preceding chapters, awaiting their greatest test in parts B and C of her text.

Her preliminary comments on Lautréamont's *Maldoror and Poems* in chapter 6 provide, if not a moment of rest or sense of arrival, at least an open space of clarity and argumentative condensation. Kristeva credits Lautréamont as the first writer to assert that poetry must orient itself toward "truth-in-practice" [*vérité pratique*] (217)]. Indeed, in his life and work Lautréamont seems to have embodied the princi-pal features of Kristeva's theory of the signifying subject. By the time of his death at age twenty-four, he had produced a surrealistic narra-tive, entitled *Chants de Maldoror* (1868), and the epigrammatic *Poésies* (1870). The first volume appeared under the pseudonym Comte de Lautréamont and the second under his patronymic Isidore Ducasse. The two texts and the two names of its author suggest a "split but indivisible unity" (219). In *Poésies* Ducasse attacks by name a startling number of lyric poets − including Byron and Goethe − for abusing their intelligence and isolating themselves from philosophy:

> Judgements on poetry are worth more than poetry itself. They are the philosophy of poetry. Philosophy, in this sense, includes poetry. Poetry cannot do without philosophy. Philosophy can do without poetry.[79]

Ducasse is particularly contemptuous of "personal poetry . . . with its relative sleights of hand and its contingent contortions." Poetry that has severed its ties to philosophy, abandoned its social responsibility, and uprooted itself from the vital resources of poetic language deserves neglect and scorn. Above all, he insists, the poet is a thinker who can help satisfy the longing for an imaginary life led "in other people's minds." The poet does this by being an absorbent reader who appropriates in a critical way what others have written, eliminating what is false and supplementing it with what is true. Above all, truth is the poet's concern. But to arrive at truth requires the slow and careful processes of deconstructive reading:

> If these sophisms were corrected by their corresponding truths, only the corrections would be true; while the work which had been thus revised would no longer have the right to be called false. The rest would be outside the realm of the true, tainted with falsehood, and would thus necessarily be considered null and void.[80]

This extraordinary manifesto, which recalls Sidney's "Defence of Poetry" more than Shelley's, opens up for Kristeva the distinction between poetry and poetic language, or between verse and textual practice that manifests the heterogeneity of the speaking subject.

There is, of course, a danger inherent in the facility of Kristeva's presentation of Lautréamont, namely, that argumentative clarity and resolution may betray the argument itself: the sense of the subject always in process and on trial. The chapter on Mallarmé, which concludes the first part of *Revolution in Poetic Language* avoids that danger by continuing the process of critical reading begun in the previous chapter in such a way as to challenge its own legitimacy or possibility. Mallarmé's *Igitur* (1869) and *Un coup de dés* (1897) take their readers from logic to madness to chance in a rendering of "the wild panic of reason" (231) that, in Kristeva's judgment, "no psychoanalysis has yet been able to match" (230). Igitur, who may with some reluctance be called the "character" in the poem, has become the "interdependent opposite" of logic. Although his name in Latin means "therefore," he is more a personification of madness than of logic, or perhaps madness as the shadowy backside of logic. What is missing from both sides of Igitur – missing, that is, from logic and from madness – is chance. Although chance defies the possibility of linear representation, *A Throw of the Dice* [*Un coup de dés*], in its fractured poetic lines and experimental typography, becomes its approximate realization in language. Mallarmé calls this movement through madness useful, Kristeva explains,

> because it foils the piracy of a certain logic whose order is dependent upon the social order, which is to say the familial, ancestral, and repro-ductive order handed down through the ages. Madness places the infinity of signifiance within a subject who then imagines he possesses it; as a result, he splits off from his family and its history, which had relegated infinity to the Absolute of religion. In making himself the living representative of infinity, the subject (Igitur) immobilizes it, immobilizes himself, and dies the victim of the logic he had contested. (226)

Mallarmé's brilliant achievement in this frictional pair of poems is to give Igitur a profoundly human texture, not allowing him to slip into mathematical abstraction, yet never letting the reader forget that he personifies signifying infinity.

Mallarmé's poems constitute a practice in ways that are usually closed to theoretical discourse. Elaborating on an observation of Philippe Sollers's, Kristeva insists that "*the only way theoretical discourse itself can be a practice* is to become the historian of [the] practices that streak through historical reasoning" (232). Indeed, that would seem to be the ambition of her text. Both Lautréamont and Mallarmé knew that there is an ethical potential in art that is too often ignored, aban-doned, or betrayed, no less by artists and poets than by critics, sociologists, and aestheticians. For Kristeva, practice – which posits *and* dissolves both meaning and the unity of the subject in itself and for others – necessarily encompasses the ethical, which she defines as "the negativizing of narcissism" (233). Lautréamont's tirade against "personal poetry"[81] can here be read as a warning that great quan-tities of verse fail to achieve the ethical or revolutionary potential of poetic language. For Kristeva, the text carries out its ethical imperative when it assumes "all positivity in order to negativize it and thereby make visible the process underlying it." In fulfilling its ethical and revolutionary function, the text, art, or poetic language "pluralizes" and "pulverizes" truths about the speaking subject-in-process in the interest of developing them and the subject further (233). In the continuation of her book and in her later texts, Kristeva has assiduously heeded her own imperative.

NOTES

1 The standard bibliography of Kristeva's work through 1982 was compiled by Elissa D. Gelfand and Virginia Thorndike Hules, in *French Feminist Criticism: Women, Language, Literature. An Annotated Bibliography* (New York: Garland, 1985).

2 Reliable surveys of Kristeva's work are difficult to find. Toril Moi's introduction to *The Kristeva Reader* (Oxford: Basil Blackwell, 1986), 1–22, and her chapter on Kristeva in *Sexual/Textual Politics: Feminist Literary Theory* (London: Methuen, 1985), 150–73, are among the best guides. See also Philip E. Lewis, "Revolutionary semiotics," *Diacritics*, 4:3 (Fall, 1974), 28–32, which is an important early assessment of *Revolution in Poetic Language*.

3 The other two parts have the following contents: B. Le dispositif sémiotique du texte: 1. Rythmes phoniques et sémantiques, 2. Syntaxe et composition, 3. Instances du discours et altération du sujet, 4. Le contexte présupposé; C. L'état et le mystère: 1. Le texte à l'intérieur d'une formation économique et sociale, 2. Maintien et limitation du pouvoir et de la conscience de classe, 3. L'anarchisme politique ou autre, 4. Le mariage et la fonction paternelle, 5. Le mystère – doublure du code social, 6. L'instance du pouvoir à sujet absent, 7. La traversée des frontiéres, 8. A la recherche d'une souveraineté: le héros, le théâtre, le chant. Part B, section I, chapter 2, "Phonétique, phonologie et bases pulsionnelles," was translated by Caren Greenberg in *Diacritics*, 4:3 (Fall, 1974), 33–7.

4 Francois-René Buleu, "*Tel Quel* à l'amphi," *Le Monde*, July 5, 1973, 15. Barthes' extraordinary praise – "Julia Kristeva changes the order of things" – was published three years before her defense, in "L'étrangère," *La Quinzaine Littéraire*, 94 (May 1–15, 1970), 19–20.

5 She also published two other books before presenting her thesis: *Séméiotiké. Recherches pour une sémanalyse* (Paris: Seuil, 1969) and *Le Texte du roman* (The Hague: Mouton, 1970).

6 See, for example, her paper, "Word, Dialogue and Novel," in *The Kristeva Reader*, 34–61. This paper was written shortly after Kristeva's arrival in Paris in 1966. Here she introduces the concept of "intertextuality" (37).

7 "L'étrangère," 19.

8 No doubt because she is leading up to a discussion of Mallarmé and Lautréamont, Kristeva does not mention here that "the modern" can also be a standard under which battles against crisis are fought and declared too easily won. On this point see Moi, *Sexual/Textual Politics*, 97.

9 Edmund Husserl, *Ideas: General Introduction to Pure Phenomenology*, trans. W. R. Boyce Gibson (London: Collier Macmillan, 1962), 156. Kristeva does not cite this passage, although it seems closer to her argument than

the quotations from Husserl in her important discursive footnote on the transcendental ego (237n.). "Self-identical" would seem to suggest here that the subject is the same under all occasions and circumstances. Kristeva does not seem to credit Husserl's argument that phenomenological reduction splits the ego. On this point, see *The Paris Lectures*, trans. P. Koestenbaum (The Hague: Nijhoff, 1985), esp. 16.

10   "Subjectivity in Language," in *Problems in General Linguistics*, trans. Mary Elizabeth Meek (Coral Gables, FL: University of Miami Press, 1971), 224–5.

11   Trans. Alix Strachey (London: Hogarth Press, 1932).

12   Philip E. Lewis in "Revolutionary semiotics" was perhaps the first commentator to note the importance of this concept: "In its entirety, *La Révolution du langage poétique* is a testimonial to the importance, for the revolutionary avant-garde, of recovering the semiotic *chora*, of deploying its potential for *jouissance* in the symbolic sphere, initially and most immediately by reinforcing the lingual with the release of the instinctual in its artistic activity" (31).

13   There is an excellent but impatient commentary on this passage in W. K. C. Guthrie, *A History of Greek Philosophy* (Cambridge: Cambridge University Press, 1978), vol. V, 62–70.

14   *Timaeus and Critias*, trans. Desmond Lee (London: Penguin, 1977), 69.

15   Ibid., 71–2.

16   *Desire in Language: A Semiotic Approach to Literature and Art*, ed. Leon S. Roudiez (Oxford: Basil Blackwell, 1981), 237.

17   Janet L. Hopson and Norman K. Wessells, *Essentials of Biology* (New York: McGraw-Hill, 1990), 317. There is a sense in both the terms "chora" and "chorion," as Plato and Aristotle use them in the cited texts, that the space referred to is not completely filled, as though there is other even in the space of the other.

18   Kristeva cites this charge, which appeared in *Positions*, trans. Alan Bass (Chicago: University of Chicago Press, 1981), 75 and 106n. The first interview in this volume, which was published in Paris in 1972, was conducted by Kristeva.

19   *The Kristeva Reader*, 206. This important paper was originally published in 1979.

20   Kristeva's most accessible discussion of structuralism's unacknowledged debt to Husserl appears in *Language the Unknown: An Initiation into Linguistics*, trans. Anne M. Menke (London: Harvester Wheatsheaf, 1989), 221–3.

21   An excellent bibliography of Husserl's work can be found in David Bell, *Husserl* (London: Routledge, 1990), 252–5. Bell also provides one of the clearest and most reliable expositions of Husserl's arguments available in English.

22   *Ideas*, 249.

23 Husserl was, nevertheless, attacked for his "psychologism" by Frege. On this, see Bell, 61, 79–80.

24 *Ideas*, 20, 95, 96, 97–88.

25 Bell, 165–6, has an excellent discussion of the importance of bracketing in Husserl and Frege.

26 Here Kristeva cites Pythagoras's Θεωρια, which recalls the Pythagorean allusions in the thought of Plato's *Timaeus*; this connection is briefly discussed by Guthrie, vol. I, 210 and vol. V, 277.

27 *Ideas*, 273.

28 See *Of Grammatology*, 57.

29 Louis Hjelmslev, *Prolegomena to a Theory of Language*, trans. Francis J. Whitfield (Baltimore: Waverly Press, 1953), 8.

30 *Language the Unknown*, 232–7.

31 It is tempting to reflect at this point on the cost to Derrida of his apparently continuing resistance to – or interminable quarrel with – Lacan. Kristeva's linking of Lacan with Husserl can, in this light, be read as an appropriation of Derrida's theoretical starting point. His first two books, published in 1962 and 1967, were a translation and introduction to Husserl's "Origin of Geometry" and a study of the problem of the sign in Husserl's phenomenology. To put the matter much too simply, Kristeva sees a productive relationship between Husserl's thought and Lacan's that Derrida apparently does not. Derrida is an extraordinarily generous reader, but Lacan and Foucault seem to haunt and unsettle him.

32 See Margaret Waller's note on the problem of consistently rendering Kristeva's terminology and that of the French translations of Frege she uses (245n.). David Bell, *Husserl*, 130, notes a similar problem with English translations.

33 *Logical Investigations*, trans. J. N. Findlay (New York: Humanities Press, 1970), 287.

34 Ibid., 293.

35 For a fuller discussion of the differences between Husserl and Frege on meaning, see David Bell, *Husserl*, 128–42, and Michael Dummett, *Frege: Philosophy of Language* (London: Duckworth, 1981), who summarizes Frege's realism with admirable clarity: "For Frege . . . we really do succeed in talking about the real world, a world which exists independently of us, and it is in virtue of how things are in that world that the things we say are true or false objectively, in virtue of how things stand in the real world . . ." (198). See also, Dummett, "The Relative Priority of Thought and Language," in *Frege and Other Philosophers* (Oxford: Clarendon Press, 1991), 315– 24.

36 *Of Grammatology*, 7.

37 Here Kristeva anticipates Derrida's image of truth as *pointure* in *The Truth in Painting*, which is discussed in chapter 5 of this book.

38   Roland Barthes, *Empire of Signs*, trans. Richard Howard (London: Jonathan Cape, 1982), 6.

39   *About Chinese Women*, trans. Anita Barrows (London: Marion Boyars, 1977), 7.

40   Ibid., 13.

41   Although Kristeva does not explicitly refer to the writings of Louis Althusser, there are several veiled allusions to his thought in *Revolution in Poetic Language* (e.g. 96 and 105.)

42   Shakespeare's depiction of Macbeth as a murderer-poet in acts I to III captures this violent potential in poetry.

43   *Phenomenology of Spirit*, trans. A. V. Miller (Oxford: Oxford University Press, 1977), 50.

44   Ibid., 51.

45   On Hegel's interest in the continuum from mystical German to philosophical German, see the informative essay, "Hegel and his language," in Michael Inwood, *A Hegel Dictionary* (Oxford: Blackwell, 1992), who points out that Hegel considered Jacob Böhme the first German philosopher (9). Two of the most important comprehensive studies of Hegel in English are Charles Taylor, *Hegel* (Cambridge: Cambridge University Press, 1975) and M. J. Inwood, *Hegel* (London: Routledge & Kegan Paul, 1983). Margaret Waller (252) has a useful note on the inconsistencies in rendering Hegel's *Verneinung, negativ, das Negative*, and *Negativität* into English.

46   Although Miller uses the English word "negation" here, in his index he uses "negativity" (594).

47   I have adapted here some of what Michael Inwood has written about "negation" and "negativity" in *A Hegel Dictionary*, 199–202, which is an excellent discussion that is unnecessarily complicated by not referring to any specific text by Hegel. I assume, however, that Inwood also is alluding to the passage in *Phenomenology* that I have just discussed.

48   *Phenomenology of Spirit*, 489. The emphasis is Hegel's.

49   For Hegel's discussion of force and understanding, see *Phenomenology of Spirit*, sections 132–65. Inwood has a helpful discussion of Hegel's language of force in *A Hegel Dictionary*, 105–7.

50   Surprisingly, he only once mentions Hegel by name (SE, IV:55).

51   Conventionally, of course, the colon is a sign of antithesis; but since Hegel's dialectic is here being questioned, even a dialectical marker must be read cautiously.

52   Cf. Dominique Auffret's provocative study, *Alexandre Kojève: la philosophie, l'État, la fin de l'Histoire* (Paris: Grasset, 1990). There is a neoconservative movement in the United States, derived from the teachings of Leo Strauss, that also claims the legacy of Kojève. Allan Bloom is perhaps the best known participant in this movement, which has been consistently hostile to French literary theory. Readings of Kojève's

lectures on Hegel have obviously taken different turns in France and in the United States.

53   *Phenomenology of Spirit*, 493.

54   For a recent account of Hegel's philosophy of religion, see W. Jaeschke, *Reason in Religion: The Foundations of Hegel's Philosophy of Religion* (Berkeley: University of California Press, 1990).

55   See especially *Phenomenology of Spirit*, section 94–99.

56   Although Kristeva remains aloof from this section of Hegel's text, the difficult but important discussion of the "this" in consciousness is highly relevant to her appropriation of Hegel's anticipation of the divided subject (sections 90–110).

57   Inwood has no entry for "desire" in *A Hegel Dictionary*. In his "Analysis of the Text," which accompanies A. V. Miller's translation, J. N. Findlay misleadingly equates desire with need (519). Richard Norman, in his otherwise deservedly celebrated *Hegel's Phenomenology: A Philosophical Introduction* (London: Sussex University Press, 1976), finds Hegel's discussion of desire "unrewarding" and "unintelligible" (46). Although she does not say so here, Kristeva would seem to be reading Hegel here – to great profit – by way of Lacan. See *Ecrits: A Selection*, 286, where Lacan seems to anticipate the equation of desire with need in Hegel.

58   *Phenomenology of Spirit*, 109 (translation slightly modified).

59   See *Ecrits: A Selection*, 304–24. Lacan alludes to Hegel's theory of desire throughout these pages.

60   *Phenomenology of Spirit*, 110.

61   This approximate acknowledgment appears in *Writing and Difference*, trans. Alan Bass (Chicago: University of Chicago Press, 1978), 153.

62   *Of Grammatology*, 158.

63   Ibid., 4. For a recent consideration of the question, "Does Derridean indecidability make ethical responsibility theoretically impossible?," see John Llewelyn, "Responsibility with Indecidability," in *Derrida: A Critical Reader*, 72–96. Llewelyn refers to *Grammatology* only in passing, perhaps to avoid repeating his earlier discussion of that text in *Derrida on the Threshold of Sense* (London: Macmillan, 1986).

64   In a recent interview in the Channel 4 (UK) series "Talking Liberties," Derrida gives every indication of affirming a conception of the subject that agrees with Lacan's in its principal details. Although Derrida continues to write warily of Lacan, his views have not been as radically opposed to Lacan's as the harsh comments in *Positions*, 107–13, suggest.

65   Ignoring for a moment the respective dates of the texts involved, if this passage of Kristeva's were read in light of the critique of origins in *Grammatology*, her text could not avoid being seen as a search for the ultimate origin of language and the subject in a way that exceeds even Rousseau's efforts. But Kristeva already knew about Derrida's objection to the concept of the chora in *Positions*, 75 and 106n. (239n.).

66   I assume, with some uncertainty, that Kristeva's *agressivité permanente* is
      continuous with Lacan's term "aggressivity," or willed aggression,
      without the clinical context that he provides for it.

67   *Phenomenology of Spirit*, 51.

68   There is no suggestion by Kristeva of a direct influence of Hegel on
      these poets. A good general account of the introduction of Hegelian
      thought into France, especially by way of Alexandre Kojéve's lectures
      on Hegel in 1933–9, which were especially important for Lacan, can be
      found in Vincent Descombes, *Modern French Philosophy*, trans. L. Scott-
      Fox and J. M. Harding (Cambridge: Cambridge University Press, 1980),
      27–48. In 1867 Mallarmé reflected, in a letter to Henri Cazalis, on his
      own thought processes in a way that approximates Hegel's theory of
      consciousness: "My Thought has thought itself through and reached a
      Pure Idea. What the rest of me has suffered during that long agony,
      is indescribable. But, fortunately, I am quite dead now": Stéphane
      Mallarmé, *Selected Poetry and Prose*, ed. Mary Ann Caws (New York:
      New Directions, 1982), 87. Jean Hyppolite, whose translation of *Phenom-
      enology of Spirit* Kristeva uses, is reported by Jean d'Ormesson in *Au
      revoir et merci* (Paris: Gallimard, 1976), 71 to have taught Hegel through
      such poetic texts as Mallarmé's *Un coup de dés jamais n'abolira le hasard*.
      One of the most important tributes to Hyppolite's work and influence is
      Michel Foucault's "Nietzsche, Genealogy, History," in *Language, Coun-
      ter-Memory, Practice: Selected Essays and Interviews*, ed. Donald F.
      Bouchard (Ithaca: Cornell University Press, 1977), 139–64.

69   In the final pages of section III (e.g. 188), Kristeva begins to distinguish
      more sharply between "modern" and "nineteenth-century" texts than
      she did earlier (e.g. 57). (The date of Mallarmé's *Igitur* is 1869.) Kristeva
      concludes *La Révolution du langage poétique* with a synoptic table (R, 635–
      41) that suggests relationships among the textual practices of Lautré-
      amont and Mallarmé and important social and intellectual events that
      occurred during their lives. Kristeva reads modern texts as endlessly
      self-analytical and heavily invested in the "unary subject" (188).

70   The final chapter of Kristeva's *About Chinese Women* (196–201) is a good
      example of how open Kristeva's social views were to change in 1974.
      Moi, *The Kristeva Reader*, 5–9, offers a succinct account of the evolution
      of Kristeva's politics during the following decade.

71   *Phenomenology of Spirit*, 55.

72   *Hegel's Science of Logic*, trans. W. H. Johnston and L. G. Struthers
      (London: Allen & Unwin, 1929), vol. II, 424. Here as earlier in her text
      (109), Kristeva reads *Science of Logic* through Lenin's "Conspectus of
      Hegel's Book on *The Science of Logic*."

73   *Phenomenology of Spirit*, 56.

74   Kristeva dates the writing of *Revolution in Poetic Language* as 1972–3 (R,
      620).

75 See *Selected Readings from the Works of Mao Tsetung* (Peking: Foreign Languages Press, 1971), 71.

76 Cf. Didier Eribon, *Michel Foucault*, trans. Betsy Wing (London: Faber and Faber, 1992), esp. 33–4. Eribon supports Althusser's claim that Foucault left the Communist Party in 1953 because of its condemnation of homosexuality (56). There is a good exposition of Althusser's theory of "ideological state apparatuses" in Ted Benton, *The Rise and Fall of Structural Marxism: Althusser and his Influence* (London: Macmillan, 1984), 96–107. Eribon provides a helpful context for understanding the importance of Hegel in France after World War II (15–23). Although her reading of Hegel comes much later than his, Kristeva's, like Foucault's, is more in the tradition of Jean Hyppolite than, like Lacan's, under the direct influence of Kojève. Recent assessments of Hegel's reception, especially in the United States, have slighted Hyppolite, at least in part because of Allan Bloom's promotion of Kojève: see Alexandre Kojève, *Introduction to the Reading of Hegel: Lectures on the "Phenomenology of Spirit,"* ed. Allan Bloom (Ithaca: Cornell University Press, 1969). In addition to his translation of the *Phenomenology*, Hyppolite's work on Hegel includes his monumental *Genesis and Structure of Hegel's "Phenomenology of Spirit"* (1949), (Evanston, IL: Northwestern University Press, 1974).

77 See *Of Grammatology*, 158.

78 Foreword to Karl Jaspers, *Strindberg and Van Gogh: An Attempt at a Pathogenic Analysis with Reference to Parallel Cases of Swedenborg and Hölderlin* (Tucson: University of Arizona Press, 1977), 12. Blanchot's sentence is a concise statement of the process that Jaspers refers to as the shipwreck of reason.

79 Comte de Lautréamont, *Maldoror and Poems*, trans. Paul Knight (London: Penguin, 1978), 272 and 277.

80 Ibid., 265.

81 Ibid., 265.

5

Reading Paintings

Despite Michel Foucault's provocative distinction between the textual culture of the Renaissance and the visual culture of the seventeenth century, inscribed texts are a common feature of German and Dutch painting during both periods.[1] Clearly legible texts on chalkboards, tombs, buildings, musical instruments; carefully labeled objects, such as captured ships, oversized radishes and gallstones; as well as magnificent displays of mapmaking, calligraphy, and bookmaking appear often in the works of sixteenth- and seventeenth-century artists.[2] It is not surprising that within this tradition of painting inscribed texts, portraits of subjects in the act of reading have an important place. Gerard Dou, Rembrandt's first pupil, painted nine portraits of his master's mother. In five of these she is reading. The finest of the series is the portrait usually titled simply *Rembrandt's Mother*. So carefully rendered is the printed text she holds in this picture that it can now be precisely identified as an illustrated Catholic lectionary.[3] The book is open to Luke 19.[4] The textual illustration, which is a traditional depiction of Zacchaeus, the man who climbs the sycamore tree in order to see Jesus, is not clearly visible in the painting, even though the commentary above, which identifies this as a text to be read on the day of the consecration of the Church, is entirely legible. Were this painting an allegory of reading, it might be seen to illustrate not only the difficult and uncertain relationship between the visual and the verbal, but also the impact of institutional controls on reading. Even though there is little in the way of detailed, contemporary information available on Rembrandt's life, it has been established that his father belonged to the Reformed Church, while his mother continued to practice her Roman Catholicism.[5] Dou's portrait unmistakeably captures an avid reader devouring a text, even though she is dependent for her access to the gospels on institutional mediation, which is perhaps why the one line in the Dutch text that is most easily readable by the viewer of the picture identifies the book as a lectionary.[6] When Rembrandt painted his mother reading in a picture usually titled simply *An Old Woman,* he fictionalized her as Hannah and has her reading not a scroll but a book in which at most two Hebrew letters are visible. Since Hannah's son Samuel devastatingly challenges the authority of Eli, the High Priest, Dou's and Rembrandt's paintings may be read as conflicting views of the authority of the reading subject: Dou, with greater biographical realism, shows his subject reading an institutionally mediated text, while Rembrandt, by way of a biblical fiction, proclaims that his mother (or Samuel's) reads the language of God.[7]

Lacan, Kristeva, and Derrida have each written important texts on painting that amplify their theories of the divided subject, semiotics, and deconstruction. Lacan, in *The Four Fundamental Concepts of Psychoanalysis,* gives a brief analysis of Holbein's *The Ambassadors* as an important illustrative example of his theory of "the gaze," which is one of the four fundamental concepts treated in the series of his 1964 seminars. Kristeva discusses at greater length Holbein's *The Body of the Dead Christ in the Tomb* in the context of her exposition of melancholia in *Black Sun.* And Derrida concludes his volume *The Truth in Painting* with an even more detailed meditation on Van Gogh's enigmatic picture *Old Shoes.* These are not simply occasional discussions of works of art, however illuminating they are as readings of individual pictures; rather, they serve to advance Lacan's, Kristeva's, and Derrida's theoretical projects in ways that language alone seems unable to do. Whereas Lacan openly acknowledges Bosch's *The Garden of Earthly Delights* as a visual reference point in his paper "Aggressivity in psychoanalysis," that painting serves him principally as a means of bringing together verbal images of the fragmented body that he has been discussing. As in the mirror stage, what is seen with the eye is often for Lacan a deceptive lure; thus, his theoretical work leads him usually to prefer hidden objects, such as the concealed phallus in the Villa of Mysteries. In the French text of *Revolution in Poetic Language,* Kristeva prefaces her discussion of practice with a print of Kandinsky's *Asserting,* but she does not refer to it in her text. Apparently for that reason the painting is not reproduced in the English translation. Like Lacan, Kristeva usually emphasizes poetic language, rather than painting, for its power to reveal the condition of the signifying subject. Derrida's writing in *Grammatology* is no less baroque in its imagery than Lacan's, but he, too, seems wary of the visual. At the key moment in the history or structure of thought when "the new" is born, Derrida is ready to look away from what then appears as a monstrosity because it is yet unnamed.[9] It would seem that blindness, because it invites critique, is usually more philosophically potent for him than sight. As their theories develop, however, all three find in painting a necessary complement to their earlier, productive exploitation of the verbal image. Theory appears to have presupposed vision all along.

I

Lacan and *The Ambassadors*

Lacan turns to Holbein's double portrait of Jean de Dinteville and Georges de Selve to illustrate his theory of the gaze, which he announces with disarming simplicity: "in the scopic field, the gaze is outside[;] I am looked at[;] that is to say, I am a picture."[10] As a way of thinking about objects, the gaze is no less startling than Lacan's theory of the divided subject. Rather than passively waiting to be seen by the viewer, who then mirrors or represents them, objects are to be thought of as establishing the conditions of their perception.[11] *Their* gaze controls the subject's scopic field. Holbein's *The Ambassadors* (Plate 1) would seem to be the perfect example of this reversal. Although the eyes of many of Holbein's subjects stare at the viewer in such a way as to demand submissive attention,[12] that effect is multiplied in this painting, first, by the double subject; second, by the intriguing objects on the two-leveled table; and third, by the device on Dinteville's cap, the crucifix that can just be seen behind the green curtain at his back, and the anamorphic skull that stares at the viewer even before he is aware of its presence in the painting. The size of the picture, 206 cm × 209 cm, is important in these respects because Dinteville and Selve are painted life-size, and the objects on the table are large enough for each of them to be examined separately.[13] By thus being drawn into the picture, however, the viewer cannot help but be disturbed by the one thing he cannot clearly see while being captured by the gaze of the rest of the painting. Only by disengaging himself from the gaze of Dinteville and Selve – and the composition of table, objects, cloth, jewels, and mosaic floor – will it be possible to see the skull clearly and become aware of that other gaze that has held the viewer captive all along.

Plate 1: Hans Holbein the Younger, *Double Portrait of Jean de Dinteville and Georges de Selve* (*The Ambassadors*)

In 1533 Dinteville was in England as the ambassador for Francis I, when he was visited by his friend Selve, a scholar, who was soon to be consecrated bishop of Lavaur.[14] The political purpose of their visit to England was almost certainly connected with Henry VIII's secret marriage to Anne Boleyn and the role of Dinteville's brother, the bishop of Auxerre, in arranging the marriage of the Duke of Orléans to the Pope's niece. Henry had probably been led to believe that these French negotiations would also include efforts to influence the Pope in taking a favorable view of his marriage. That the outcome of these efforts was a strong anti-reformist policy in France, rather than a discovery of common ground between the Church and the reformers, may not have been the intention of the ambassadors. Dinteville had been a patron of efforts at the Sorbonne to produce biblical translations and commentaries, and Selve's diplomatic career was consistently supportive of religious tolerance.[15] Furthermore, the way the ambassadors lean on the table and the casual scattering of the objects there imply an intimate personal connection with the instruments of liberal learning. Representations of the Quadrivium are suggested by these musical and mathematical instruments, and the books indicate the efforts of a reform movement that was being undermined even as it occurred: a German hymn book is open to Luther's translation of the "Veni Creator Spiritus" and his text of the Ten Commandments, and (on the other side of the lute) a German book of arithmetic is kept open by a square. Taken together, as Stephen Greenblatt has noted, these objects might have come out of a handbook on the art of perspective.[16] In a portrait of his friend Nicolas Kratzer, an astronomer, mathematician, and instrument designer, Holbein depicts the construction of similar objects. That both Holbein and Kratzer were part of the circle of ecumenical reformers under the protection of Anne Boleyn at the time *The Ambassadors* was painted also opens the possibility that Holbein may have hoped for more from the ambassadors than they were prepared to deliver.

The emphasis on perspective, both in the depiction of the instruments by which it is achieved and in Holbein's display of his mastery of its art, is highly ironic, however. In Sonnet 24 Shakespeare describes the eye as glazing the object it gazes upon as part of the poem's elaborate argument that "perspective . . . is best painter's art." This is the Neoplatonic tradition of perspective that offers men a god-like power to measure, map, mirror, represent – and by these means, to re-create – the world. The power of perspective, in this sense, enables the human mind to be the unifying force and the measurer of all things.[17] Holbein manifests this Neoplatonic art in his entire composition, from the geometric pattern in the *cosmati* pavement of Westminster Abbey to the representation of the globes and sundial and lute, to the uncertain angle of the ambassadors' stare. They seem as much to look *through* as *at* the viewer. Most of all, of course, it is the anamorphic painting of the skull that displays Holbein's greatest achievement in the art of perspective, and the purposeful undermining of it as well. Lacan warns that to restore "the function of the existence of others as looking at me" (84) is not to sacrifice the subject but rather to sustain the subject "in a function of desire" (85).

At the moment the viewer moves to the extreme right of the painting away from the ambassadors' gaze and allows the skull to come into view, there is another, more powerful gaze that holds the viewer with its empty sockets. "All this shows," Lacan writes,

> that at the very heart of the period in which the subject emerged and geometrical optics was an object of research, Holbein makes visible for us here something that is simply the subject as annihilated – annihilated in the form that is, strictly speaking, the imaged embodiment of the minus-phi $[(-\phi)]$ of castration, which for us, centres the whole organization of the desires through the framework of the fundamental drives. But it is further still that we must seek the function of vision. We shall then see emerging on the basis of vision, not the phallic symbol, the anamorphic ghost, but the gaze as such, in its pulsatile, dazzling and spread out function, as it is in this picture. This picture is simply what any picture is, a trap for the gaze. In any picture, it is precisely in seeking the gaze in each of its points that you will see it disappear. (88–9)

Barely visible on Dinteville's cap is a piece of jewelry engraved with a silver skull. Although he does not mention it, this might be for Lacan what is other than the gaze. Even if this were the historical Dinteville's own device or badge, it is, like the Neoplatonists' claims of mastery over the measured world, an arrogant reduction by which the other, the gaze, art, and death all become trinkets. Had the viewer carefully examined the beautiful lute, he would have seen a broken string, a warning, perhaps, that a facile perception of harmony and unity is the trap of the art of perspective. It may be that Lacan goes too far in saying that this is "any picture . . . a trap for the gaze." But it is certainly a picture that gazes at Lacan, trapping him as it does any careful viewer; it is as though the artist knows too well the discordant death's head, which his art first conceals in order more suddenly to capture the viewer in its gaze.

II

Kristeva and *The Body of the Dead Christ in the Tomb*

Kristeva begins her book *Black Sun* by announcing an insurmountable problem in writing about melancholia. To write about it meaningfully

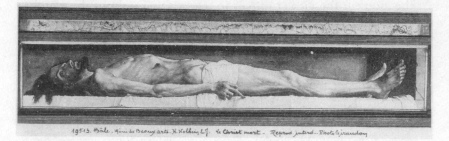

19513. Bâle. Musée des Beaux arts. H. Holbein l.J. Le Christ mort. Repros interd. Photo Giraudon

Plate 2: Hans Holbein the Younger, *The Body of the Dead Christ in the Tomb*

requires that the writing spring out of melancholia itself. But melancholia is "a noncommunicable grief" that persists by laying such claims on the subject who suffers from it that "all interest in words, actions, and even life itself" is swallowed in despair.[18] To suffer melancholia is to "live a living death," even though in this state of alienation from others' meaning there is a sense of "metaphysical lucidity," an "arrogant" sense of access to the "meaninglessness of Being." Melancholia is the "hidden side" or "mute sister" of philosophy (4). Holbein's *The Body of the Dead Christ in the Tomb* (Plate 2) eloquently expresses this devastating muteness of the black sun. Like *The Ambassadors*, this painting achieves much of its powerful effect from its proportions and unsparing detail. The dimensions are 30.5 × 200 cm, which gives the sense that by some means the viewer has been allowed visual entrance to Christ's coffin. The body is seen slightly from below, accentuating by this means the claustrophobic sensation of its confinement. Even the ornamentation on the frame of the picture with angels, instruments of the Passion, and the still mocking title *IESUS NAZARENUS REX IUDAEORUM*, which runs the entire length of the painting, intensifies the sense of devastating despair. It is the stunning finality of death rather than any anticipation of its transcendence that the painting seems to insist upon: "this corpse shall never rise again" (110). Indeed, the coffin lid seems to press down upon the place of the corpse and to define sharply the range of the viewer's attention.

The representation of the body itself is unsparing in its anatomically precise depiction of suffering and decay. The limbs are stiff, the flesh is green and swollen around the wounds, and the stigmata of the crucifixion have stiffened the now rigid middle finger. The unseeing eyes and mouth remain open as though to express the hopelessness of

Psalm 22: "My God, my God, why hast thou forsaken me?" By way of contrast, Kristeva recalls that Italian iconography typically surrounds the suffering Christ with figures who grieve, while embellishing and ennobling his appearance during the Passion. Holbein instead isolates Christ in death and transfers the despair to him. But this isolation of Christ also creates an ambiguity and debilitating uncertainty in the viewing of the painting. Christ's hair, elbow, loincloth, and – most prominently – his hand all edge out of the space of the tomb and toward the viewer. Thus, Kristeva comments,

> This enclosed recess, this well-isolated coffin simultaneously rejects us and invites us. Indeed, the corpse fills the entire field of the painting, without any labored reference to the Passion. Our gaze follows the slightest physical detail, it is, as it were, nailed, crucified, and is reveted to the hand placed at the center of the composition. Should it attempt to flee it quickly stops, locked in at the distressed face or the feet propped against the black stone. (114)

Kristeva's emphasis on the gaze of the viewer, in contrast to Lacan's gaze of the painting, implies that the viewer has replaced the traditional mourners and is made to share Christ's hiatus or caesura, the moment of his despair in the face of death (132). The fundamental ambiguity of the painting for Kristeva is then whether or not that moment is an instance of negativity, an incorporated but ultimately transcended part of Christ as the "absolute subject" of Christianity.

Kristeva's reading of the painting is thoroughly Hegelian in the form of its presentation and in its return to the concept of negativity, which was of critical importance in *Revolution in Poetic Language*. For this reason it is fitting that she begins her reading with a long quotation from Dostoevsky's *The Idiot* in which Ippolit gives an eloquent account of the painting after Prince Myshkin has been unable to speak of it except to say, "Why, some people may *lose their faith* by looking at that picture!" (107). Although Ippolit is thoroughly knowledgeable about the Church's interpretations of the Passion, he reads the painting as shattering all hope and all belief:

> I know that the Christian Church laid it down in the first few centuries of its existence that Christ really did suffer and that the Passion was not symbolical. His body on the cross was therefore fully and entirely subject to the laws of nature. In the picture the face is terribly smashed with blows, tumefied, covered with terrible, swollen, and bloodstained

bruises, the eyes open and squinting; the large, open whites of the eyes have a sort of dead and glassy glint. But, strange to say, as one looks at the dead body of this tortured man, one cannot help asking oneself the peculiar, arresting question: if such a corpse (and it must have been just like that) was seen by all His disciples, by His future chief apostles, by the women who followed Him and stood by the cross, by all who believed in Him and worshipped Him, then how could they possibly have believed, confronted with such a sight, that this martyr would rise again? (108)

Kristeva begins Ippolit's reading of the painting in order to arrive dialectically at Hegel's idea of the duality of death in Christianity: the natural death of the body, which is so clearly manifest in Holbein's painting, and death as the highest form of renunciation of the self for the Other and thus the highest form of love. Kristeva finds at the heart of Christian thought – and in Christ, its "absolute subject" – the transforming effects of reconciliation and forgiveness that are such as to endow the processes of psychic initiation and incorporated negativity with "an aura of glory and unwavering hope for those who believe" (134). Kristeva argues that it is because Christianity sets the splitting or negativity of the subject at the center of its faith, representing it in the Passion, that it brings "to consciousness the essential dramas that are internal to the becoming of each and every subject" (132). By this means Christianity is endowed with great cathartic power, which Holbein captures in the relationship between Christ in the tomb and the viewer of the painting. He first leads his viewer to "the ultimate edge of belief" and then by the form of his art restores, in Kristeva's view, the serenity of forgiveness and the salvation of love.

III

Derrida and *Old Shoes*

In his text on Van Gogh's *Old Shoes*, (Plate 3) Derrida would seem to set out to settle a debt he owes to Heidegger.[19] In *Positions* he says, "What I have attempted to do would not have been possible without the opening of Heidegger's questions"; and in a later interview,

Plate 3: Vincent Van Gogh, *Oude Schoenen (Old Shoes)*

published in the same volume, "Heidegger's text is extremely important to me . . . it constitutes a novel, irreversible advance all of whose
critical resources we are far from having exploited." Indeed, Derrida
claims that all of the essays he published up to 1971 constitute "a
departure from Heideggerian problematic"; they display a kind of
fanaticism" in their calling into question "the *thought of presence*" in
Heidegger.[20] Heidegger's concepts of origin, fall, propriety, proper
meaning, proximity to the self, body, consciousness, language –
especially etymologism in philosophy and rhetoric – Derrida puts into
question. Yet he is careful to distance himself from those who have
reduced Heidegger to German ideology between the wars or to anti-
Semitism. During the last fifteen years, Heidegger's importance for
Derrida has in no way subsided. Unlike Derrida's readings of Plato,
Rousseau, Poe, Mallarmé, Freud, Saussure, Genet, Artaud, Lévi-
Strauss, however, his readings of Heidegger have been more thematic
than textual, focusing more on single words or concepts than on

their full textual embodiment.[21] The notable exception to this procedure is the long final section of *The Truth in Painting*, entitled "Restitutions of the truth in pointing." Here Derrida offers a meticulous reading of Heidegger's *The Origin of the Work of Art*, his most sustained meditation on a Heideggerian text, and through that reading, a commentary on Van Gogh's *Old Shoes*.

"Restitutions" is one of Derrida's most complex texts. It takes the form of a polylogue for an indeterminable – *n* + 1 – number of voices. Although Derrida's headnote identifies the voices as female, one is explicitly revealed to be the author of *Margins of Philosophy*.[22] Quotations or allusions to *Glas* and *The Post Card*, the closest textual relatives to "Restitutions," also disrupt the dramatic frame. One speaker has a fixation on the question, "What is a pair?," insisting, "I came here [as a woman] to ask this question" (325). Yet another voice speaks, often eloquently, at great length and by doing so invites the others' skeptical questions. At least one of the speakers arrives later than the others and, thus, works at an ironic disadvantage (291). Two-thirds of the way through the dialogue one of the voices speaks directly about the form of the text in the self-reflexive manner of a character out of Shakespeare or Beckett who has known all along that she or he is a dramatic fiction; but by revealing that he knows that she is a fiction, he steps out of the frame that can no longer contain him/her. This voice says,

> It remains that the figure of this interlaced correspondence (for a long time we have no longer known who is talking in it and if there is talk) does not come under any established rhetoric. Because it is not simply a discourse, of course, but also because even if transported, by rhetoric, outside of discursive rhetoric, tropes and figures would not work here. This interlacing correspondence, for example the interminable overflowing of the whole by the part which explodes the frame or makes us jump over it ... is not produced inside a framing or framed element, like the figures of rhetoric in language or discourse, like the figures of "pictorial" "rhetoric" in the system of painting. (344)

Much later in the dialogue this textual self-reflection gives way to dramatic despair: "We no longer know," says one of the voices, "whose turn it is to speak and how far we've got" (358).

The form of this text, then, enacts a number of Derridean grammatological themes: texts are always multi-voiced; they constitute structures that already include the deconstructive resources for their

own critiques; what is inside the text and what is outside it – as well
as what is in the margin and what at the center – refuse to remain in
their proper places; each text is a link in a chain of texts that refuses
to yield its first or original link; texts seem uncannily aware that they
are being read and take evasive action accordingly. Even more importantly than the reiteration of these grammatological themes, the
dialogue form dramatizes the conceptual metaphor of *interlacing* that
recurs throughout this reading of Heidegger. True to its dramatic
genre, "Restitutions" both presents and disrupts a narrative, which is
here interlaced by and with the voices. At one point (371) the narrative is assigned the figure of a square with the corners presumably
named Van Gogh, Heidegger, Kurt Goldstein, and Meyer Schapiro.
The story might then be laced together as follows.

From 1881, the year Van Gogh decided to become an artist,
through 1888, two years before his death, he completed eight paintings of shoes. In his letters to his brother, Van Gogh distinguishes
two phases in his career. From 1881 to 1885 his work concentrated
on peasant life. "My intention was," he writes, "that it should make
people think of a way of life different from that of our refined society." Thus, *The Potato Eaters*, for example, tries, as he puts it, "to
instil . . . the idea that the people it depicts at their meal have dug the
earth with the hands they are dipping into the dish." In 1886 Van
Gogh left Antwerp for Paris. Of the pictures painted in this second
period, epitomized, perhaps, by *Night Café*, he writes, "Instead of
trying to reproduce exactly what was before my eyes, I use colour
more arbitrarily so as to express myself more forcefully."[23] The
paintings of the first period, this interpretation suggests, emphasize
otherness – the minute physical details of peasant life – while the
paintings of the second period are forceful expressions of Van Gogh
himself. The eight paintings of shoes are not confined to either
period. Although Derrida mentions none of these details, which form
a parergon of sorts (an outside that refuses to remain neatly outside
the text), he does allude to Van Gogh's letters and to his "peasant
ideology" (273, 368).

In 1935–6 Heidegger delivered a series of lectures that were soon
published as *The Origin of the Work of Art*. In his text Heidegger
refers to "a well-known painting by Van Gogh" as a pictorial example of "a common sort of equipment – a pair of peasant shoes."
He says they are the shoes of a peasant woman. It is "only in the
picture," Heidegger insists, that certain things about the shoes are
noticeable:

From the dark opening of the worn insides of the shoes the toilsome tread of the worker stares forth. In the stiffly rugged heaviness of the shoes there is the accumulated tenacity of her slow trudge through the far-spreading and ever-uniform furrows of the field swept by a raw wind. On the leather lie the dampness and richness of the soil. Under the soles slides the loneliness of the field-path as evening falls. In the shoes vibrates the silent call of the earth, its quiet gift of the ripening grain and its unexplained self-refusal in the fallow desolation of the wintry field. This equipment is pervaded by uncomplaining anxiety as to the certainty of bread, the wordless joy of having once more withstood want, the trembling before the impending childbed and shivering at the surrounding menace of death. This equipment belongs to the *earth*, and it is protected in the *world* of the peasant woman. From out of this protected belonging the equipment itself rises to its resting-within-itself.[24]

This passage becomes the focal point of Derrida's dialogue.

Two years before Heidegger delivered his lecture course, the Jewish psychologist Kurt Goldstein fled from Nazi Germany by way, significantly, of Amsterdam. Goldstein later took up a position at Columbia University and did extensive work on the psychopathology of war victims. Goldstein drew the attention of the art historian Meyer Schapiro, a colleague of his on the Columbia faculty, to *The Origin of the Work of Art*. Soon after Goldstein's death Schapiro wrote a brief paper entitled "The Still Life as Personal Object: A Note on Heidegger and Van Gogh," which he contributed to a volume published in Goldstein's memory in 1968.[25] In preparation for writing his paper, Schapiro wrote to Heidegger asking him to identify which of the eight paintings of shoes by Van Gogh he had referred to in his text. In a personal letter to Schapiro, Heidegger identified the painting in question as number 255, usually given the title *Old Shoes*. In his paper, Schapiro claims that Heidegger is in error when he assigns the shoes to a peasant woman. The shoes are Van Gogh's, Schapiro claims. In 1977 at Columbia Derrida "acted out or narrated" (272) part of the text of "Restitutions" with Schapiro taking part in the debate that followed. Schapiro's original paper was subsequently translated into French and published with Derrida's polylogue in the journal *Macula*.

One way of thinking of the shoes, in terms of this narrative, is to see them moving from one point to another on the square: from Van Gogh to Heidegger to Schapiro (by way of Goldstein) and then back to Van Gogh. Another way of thinking about them is to see them taken from Heidegger by Schapiro to be given as a memorial offering to his friend Goldstein. In Derrida's dialogue, however, the lines of argument run between Derrida and Heidegger and Schapiro; and restitution is no longer as much a matter of restoring the shoes to their rightful owner as it is a matter of truth in painting and in the texts of Schapiro and Heidegger.

The text of "Restitutions" exploits the tension between the forward narrative drive – the "ghost story" (257), as it is called – and the dramatic or dialogic interplay among the speaking voices, which both disrupt the narrative drive and constitute the only source of the story. The questions asked by the voices generate both the narrative and its interruptions; these include but are not limited to the following problems:

Whose are the shoes? What are they made of? (257) Why always say of a painting that it renders, that it restitutes? (258) Are the shoes a pair? What is a pair? (259) What is one doing when one attributes a painting? (266) Could it be that, like a glove turned inside out, the shoe sometimes has the convex "form" of the foot (penis), and sometimes the concave form enveloping the foot (vagina)? (267) Who is going to believe that this episode [between Schapiro and Heidegger] is merely a theoretical or philosophical dispute for the interpretation of a work or The Work of art? (272) Which picture exactly [was Heidegger] referring to? (276) How do we explain Heidegger's naïve, impulsive, precritical attribution of the shoes in a painting to such a determined "subject" . . . the peasant woman? (286–7) Is it a matter of rendering justice to Heidegger, of restituting what is his due, his truth? (301) Is Schapiro right? (308) What is reference in painting? (322) Are we reading? Are we looking? (326) [Is the point] to make ghosts come back? Or on the contrary to stop them from coming back? (339)

In the interest of considering at least some of these questions, let us now unlace Derrida's dialogue, trying to forget for a moment that the entire text is mediated by an indeterminate number of female voices, in an attempt to listen to Schapiro and Heidegger on these questions. "Schapiro" and "Heidegger" are here not only names for dramatic speakers presented to the reader of Derrida's text by the female voices. They are also writers not framed by the text any more than the text frames itself. Indeed, "Restitutions" so aggressively insists on its own intertextual dependencies that on two occasions (294, 345) Derrida prints three rows of dots in place of key quotations in three languages from Schapiro and Heidegger. Reading "Restitutions" returns the reader to the Schapiro and Heidegger texts as much as to the Van Gogh painting. What is outside and what inside – where the truth of the text or painting lies – is as much a textual problem as a topic discussed "in" the text. Pointing [*pointure*] becomes Derrida's principal metaphor in the dialogue for this piercing of the text or canvas with an invisible lace that stitches it "onto its internal and external worlds" (304).

First, then, in this unlacing of the text, we hear from Schapiro: Heidegger's interpretation of the painting by Van Gogh, Schapiro argues, illustrates "the nature of art as a disclosure of truth." Heidegger turns to the picture when he is distinguishing between three modes of being: "useful artifacts," "natural things," and "works of art." Without recourse to any philosophical theory, he proceeds to describe "a familiar sort of equipment – a pair of peasant shoes"; and he chooses "a well-known painting by Van Gogh" in the interest of facilitating "the visual realization" of the shoes. He further argues that to grasp the "equipmental being of equipment," one must know "how shoes actually serve." They serve the peasant woman who stands and walks in them without her thinking about them or looking at them. For her, their being is their use. For the one who looks at Van Gogh's painting, however, the equipmental being of the shoes is undiscoverable. By looking at the picture of the "empty" shoes, however, the life of the peasant woman, her labor, the earth with which she toils, her anxieties and joys, her world can be seen to rise "to its resting-in-itself."[26]

Heidegger knew Van Gogh painted such shoes many times, but he does not specify the picture he has in mind, apparently thinking they all present "the same truth." In response to Schapiro's question, Heidegger identifies the picture as number 255, which he saw in Amsterdam in March 1930. Nevertheless, Schapiro suggests, he may have conflated number 255 with number 250 in which the sole of a shoe is exposed, since he refers to the sole in his account. "But from neither of these pictures, nor from any of the others," Schapiro insists, "could one properly say that a painting of shoes by Van Gogh expresses the being or essence of a peasant woman's shoes and her relation to nature and work."[27] These are the shoes not of a peasant woman but of the artist, he concludes, "a man of the town and city." In misattributing the shoes, Heidegger has "deceived himself." The sets of associations with peasants "are not sustained by the picture itself but are grounded rather in his own social outlook with its heavy pathos of the primordial and earthy." Heidegger's "error" is not only the result of projection, "which replaces a close and true attention to the work of art"; it also lies in his concept of "the metaphysical power of art," which "remains here a theoretical idea." The position of the shoes, "isolated on the floor . . . facing us," gives them the appearance of "veridical portraits of aging shoes." Van Gogh's "feeling for these shoes" is close to Knut Hamsun's description of his own shoes in his novel *Hunger*, and the identification of them as the artist's own shoes is supported by Gauguin's reminiscences of Van Gogh. Nevertheless, it is not clear which of the paintings of shoes Gauguin had seen. "It does not matter . . . Gauguin's story confirms the essential fact that for Van Gogh the shoes were a piece of his own life."[28]

Now Heidegger: what we notice about the shoes we notice *in* the picture. It would be the "worst self-deception" to suggest that the description offered is "a subjective action" or a projection "into the painting". Van Gogh's painting discloses what the pair of peasant shoes "*is* in truth". "If there occurs in the work a disclosure of a particular being, disclosing what and how it is, then there is here an occurring, a happening of truth at work". A work of art "sets up a world" that is never itself an object but rather "the ever-nonobjective to which we are subject". The material of a work of art (stone, paint, metal, wood, words) does not disappear but rather comes into the open when a work is made. The earth comes forth in the work of art, the earth upon which "historical man grounds his dwelling in the world". "The establishing of truth in the work" is to bring forth a unique being that was not previously present and will never be again. "Truth establishes itself as a strife within a being that is to be brought forth only in such a way that the conflict opens up in this being".[29]

Derrida's dialogue in its dramatic form and in its strategy of pointing to Heidegger's text by piercing through Schapiro's becomes heavily invested in this conception of truth as a strife that opens up. For Schapiro truth in art is correspondence between visual image and written text – thus the attempt to make the Gauguin reminiscences relevant – this view he develops in his monograph, *Words and Pictures*.[30] Heidegger, however, insists that the opening up is into metaphysics, into the essence of being. Derrida, on the other hand, argues that it is an exploitation of the self-critical resources within one structure of thought that opens that structure up from the inside to what is beyond it. I take it that this is the critical point of departure: Heidegger into metaphysics by way of strife, Derrida out of metaphysics by way of the self-critical resources of metaphysical

texts. The argument at this point returns to Derrida's earlier critique of Heidegger's *An Introduction to Metaphysics* in *Grammatology*.
That Heideggerian text, like *The Origin of the Work of Art*, comes
from Freiburg in 1935; there, too, reference is made, however
briefly, to "a painting by Van Gogh" and to "a pair of rough peasant
shoes."[31]

"Restitutions" has its own network of metaphors. Four of these –
pointure, lace, trap, and ghost – are elaborately developed in the course
of the dialogue and shape much of its thought. *Pointure* has the advantage for Derrida of being a term from printing and shoemaking: a
"small iron blade with a point, used to fix the page to be printed on
to the tympan," "the hole which it makes in the paper," and a "term
from shoemaking" referring to the "number of stitches in a shoe or
glove" (256). In the title of the dialogue pointing [*pointure*] replaces
the word *painting* in the phrase "truth in painting," which allows
simultaneously the sense that the painting in question is an exercise
in the art of *pointure* and that its truth is not simply framed by the picture – truth, then, is not simply contained in painting – rather it pricks,
punctures, penetrates the canvas when the picture is bombarded
with interpretative questions. Here is a critical difference between
Cézanne and Van Gogh, both of whom Derrida quotes on his title
page. Cézanne writes, "I owe you the truth in painting, and I will tell
it to you" (256). He promises pictocentric truth, truth present in
painting, though he is still compelled to speak it. The consequence of
this view – that the truth of painting cannot be rendered in paint but
only in words – Heidegger thought through and affirmed: "art is in
essence poetry," he writes in *The Origin of the Work of Art*. Despite
their disagreement on the attribution of the shoes, Schapiro and
Heidegger agree on the relation of language to painting, except that
Heidegger argues that the visual arts are on the way to language
as they break "open an open place in whose openness everything is
other than usual".[32] Schapiro, on the other hand, thinks of painting as
emerging from language; the word is the origin of the picture. The
art critic, in his view, performs an act of restitution when he restores
the truth of the shoes by matching them, for example, to the text of
Gauguin's reminiscences. Van Gogh, on the other hand, writes, "But
truth is so dear to me, and so is the *seeking to make true* [Derrida's
italics], that indeed I believe . . . I would still rather be a cobbler than a
musician with colors" (256). Despite Heidegger's privileged place for
poetry, it is Van Gogh who maintains the metaphor; "a cobbler . . .
with colors" sustains and develops the ambiguity of *pointure*.

Now to betray that metaphor for a moment, let us say what we can about the image of truth it offers us in the dialogue. Truth is not formalistically contained by the painting any more than the signified can be found within the signifier. In his catalogue for the exhibition he mounted at the Louvre in the fall of 1990 on the theme of blindness, Derrida further develops this Saussurean parallel: "There is an abyss of heterogeneity between the thing drawn and the drawing line, even between a thing represented and its representation, the model and the image."[33] Language in its search for truth punctures the painting, not as one might take a knife to a canvas but as one might lace a shoe. Writing about art has the effect of lacing one canvas to another. This pictural intertextuality points not only to the inter-relations among paintings but also to the relationships of painting to the world and to language. Derrida's insistence here on the metaphor – the link between two distinct things in such a way as to bring into the open a point of otherwise hidden similarity – restitutes the distinctness of the individual paintings, as well as the distinctiveness of painting, language, painter, and critic. Derrida would have us see the frame of the picture, like the margins of the printed page, as that which "cuts out but also sews back together . . . by an invisible lace which pierces the canvas", just as the *pointure* pierces the paper, passes into it in order to sew it back into its milieu, into its "internal and external worlds" (304).

The metaphor of the lace is already active in the shoemaking aspect of *pointure*, but the painting in question provides considerable specificity and a pictorial ground for this metaphor. The lace of one shoe curls in the lower right corner of the picture as though to encircle the name of the artist. But there is no name. The absence of "Vincent" from its usual place, a place here seemingly marked by the ○ of the lace, is convenient for Derrida's calling into question Schapiro's assertion that still life is a "personal object" and Heidegger's logocentrism of truth's presence in the word to which painting aspires. Already, however, I have said more than the voices do about the circle of lace and have fallen into its trap. The voices say, "the loop is *open*;" it is "as *though* . . . it stood in place of the signature" (277, my italics). The temptation to fill in the strange loop is to succumb to another meaning of the French word for lace [*le lacet*], which is "trap" or "snare." The loop of lace is a metonymy for the empty shoes, a trap that Van Gogh tempts us to fill in.

Pointure, lace, and trap are also related to ghosts. A voice calls the dialogue a ghost story (258); the shoes are "hallucinogenic" (273); for

Schapiro they seem to face the viewer and are a kind of spectral
portrait of the artist; for Heidegger, too, they are a portrait, and as he
looks into their "dark opening" he sees staring at him the toilsome
life of the peasant woman. The shoes do not quite seem to touch the
ground or the floor; there is an underneath beneath their underneath.
As Heidegger's visual example of "thing" and "work," they are meta-
physically haunted by "the fundamental Greek experience of the
Being of beings in general" (287). In his conflation of the several
paintings of shoes, Heidegger allows the paintings themselves to take
on a ghostly quality, as though they were visible yet transparent.
Then there is the matter of the disembodied voices in the dialogue
who invite the reader to doubt that what is at stake between Schapiro
and Heidegger is simply the interpretation of the pictures. "There are
other, more urgent things at stake" (329), one voice says. Then this:

> But an army of ghosts are demanding their shoes. Ghosts up in arms,
> an immense tide of deportees searching for their names. If you want to
> go to this theatre, here's the road of affect: the bottomless memory of
> a dispossession, an expropriation, a despoilment. And there are tons of
> shoes piled up there, pairs mixed up and lost. (330–1)

These words recall the unbearable photographs of the Holocaust with
the nightmarish visual metonymy of piles of personal property recalling the millions who died. On February 6, 1943, Himmler received
an inventory that lists "22,000 pairs of children's shoes" collected
from Birkenau. An eyewitness at Dachau recalls, "We were shaken to
the depths of our soul when the first transports of children's shoes
arrived from Auschwitz."[34] Photographic essays of life in the Warsaw
ghetto have also stressed the ragged shoes of Jews, deported, dis-
possessed, expropriated, despoiled, and nameless.[35] The voices suggest the painting is haunted by such ghosts of a later time.

In repaying his debt to Heidegger, Derrida has not avoided
Heidegger's writings of the thirties but rather given that work his
most sustained critical attention. In doing so, he has not been an
apologist for Heidegger's Nazism; instead, especially in "Restitutions," he has relentlessly exceeded Heidegger's example in giving
careful attention to the textuality of philosophy, here applying deconstructive critical procedures, as in so much of his earlier writing, to
Heidegger's own texts. Even when he has available to him Schapiro's
note, which manifests a generous, personal motive and a political
or textual unconscious to which he would, doubtless, otherwise have

been more than sympathetic, Derrida refuses to allow the issue of truth to be sacrificed. "The task of a destruction of the history of ontology," as Heidegger calls it,[36] continues to be Derrida's principal project, nonetheless when it exposes the terrible fallibility of Heidegger himself.

NOTES

1 This distinction figures importantly in the argument of *The Order of Things* (New York: Vintage Books, 1973). The *ouverture* to the book is a brilliant reading of Velàzquez's painting, *Las Meninas*.
2 Svetlana Alpers has done an informative study of Dutch paintings with inscribed texts: see *The Art of Describing: Dutch Art in the Seventeenth Century* (London: Penguin, 1989), esp. xvii–xxvii and 169–221.
3 H. M. Rotermund, "Rembrandt's Bibel," *Nederlands Kunsthistorisch Jaarboek*, 8 (1971), 134.
4 C. Hofstede de Groot, *A Catalogue Raisonné of the Works of the Most Eminent Dutch Painters of the Seventeenth Century*, trans. Edward G. Hawke (London: Macmillan, 1907), vol. I, 454, incorrectly identifies the book as a Bible and misreads the chapter number.
5 Christopher White, *Rembrandt* (London: Thames and Hudson, 1984), 10.
6 It reads, "op den dach der kerk wijden zij."
7 See Alpers's comparison of the two paintings, which concludes with this observation: "To generalize the differences: while other Dutch artists offer us visible texts, Rembrandt insists that it is the Word within and not the surface of the texts that must be valued" (188–9). Rembrandt rarely paints inscribed texts that are visible. An important exception, as Alpers notes, is his *Moses*, where God's words written on his tablets in Hebrew can be read.
8 *Écrits: A Selection*, 11, 288.
9 "Structure, Sign and Play in the Discourse of the Human Sciences," in *Writing and Difference*, trans. Alan Bass (Chicago: University of Chicago Press, 1978), 293.
10 *The Four Fundamental Concepts of Psycho-analysis*, trans. Alan Sheridan (London: Penguin, 1977), 106. Further references are given in parentheses.
11 There is a good discussion of the gaze as a critique of philosophical idealism in Jonathan Scott Lee, *Jacques Lacan* (Amherst: University of Massachusetts Press, 1990), 154–61.
12 See, for example, the portraits of John Godsalve and Charles de Solier.
13 Unfortunately, the painting as it is now exhibited at the National Gallery in London is almost impossible to view properly. Because it is hanging about eighteen inches too high, it is only by standing on the

bench in front of it that it can be seen in perspective by anyone under seven feet tall. It would also seem that the picture should be displayed with a door immediately to the viewer's right to allow the skull to come into focus as one passes through the door. The photograph of *The Ambassadors* in John Rowlands's otherwise excellent *Holbein: The Paintings of Hans Holbein the Younger* (Oxford: Phaidon, 1985), 99, trims off the crucifix, which should be just visible beyond the green curtain in the upper left-hand corner – and also cuts off part of the lower right jawbone of the skull, its shadow, and the border of floor design.

14 See Mary F. S. Hervey, *Holbein's "Ambassadors," the Picture and the Men. An Historical Study* (London, 1900), and the excellent commentary by Stephen Greenblatt, *Renaissance Self-Fashioning: From More to Shakespeare* (Chicago: University of Chicago Press, 1980), 17–24, which is the best study of the painting in English since Miss Hervey's book.

15 Rowlands, *Holbein*, 86.

16 Greenblatt, *Renaissance Self-Fashioning*, 17.

17 Ibid., 18.

18 *Black Sun*, trans. Leon S. Roudiez (New York, Columbia University Press, 1989), 3. Further citations are given in parentheses.

19 I have discussed Derrida's reading of this picture more fully in "Derrida, Heidegger, and Van Gogh's 'Old Shoes,'" *Textual Practice*, (Spring, 1992), 87–100.

20 Jacques Derrida, *Positions*, trans. Alan Bass (London: Athlone Press, 1987), 9, 54–5.

21 See, for example, the six papers on Heidegger in *Psyché: inventions de l'autre* (Paris: Galilée, 1987) and *De l'esprit. Heidegger et la question* (Paris: Galilée, 1987).

22 *The Truth in Painting*, trans. Geoff Bennington and Ian McLeod (Chicago: University of Chicago Press, 1987), 264. Further citations from this text are noted in parentheses.

23 Quoted in Harold Osborne, ed., *The Oxford Companion to Art* (Oxford: Oxford University Press, 1970), 486–7.

24 *Poetry, Language, Thought*, trans. Albert Hofstadter (New York: Harper & Row, 1971), 32–4.

25 *The Reach of Mind: Essays in Memory of Kurt Goldstein*, ed. Marianne L. Simmel (New York: Springer, 1968).

26 Ibid., 203–4.

27 Ibid., 205.

28 Ibid., 205–8.

29 Heidegger, *Poetry, Language, Thought*, 34, 35–6, 44, 46, 62–3.

30 (The Hague: Mouton, 1973).

31 *An Introduction to Metaphysics*, trans. Ralph Manheim (New Haven: Yale University Press, 1959 (1935), 35.

32 Heidegger, *Poetry, Language, Thought*, 73, 72.

33 "The Blindness of Beginning', trans. Geoffrey Bennington, *The Guardian* (November 2, 1990), 25.

34 Martin Gilbert, *The Holocaust: The Jewish Tragedy* (Glasgow: William Collins, 1987), 539–41.

35 See, for example, Ulrich Keller, *The Warsaw Ghetto in Photographs* (Magnolia, MA: Peter Smith, 1941). In his recent book, *Cinders*, trans. Ned Lukacher (Lincoln: University of Nebraska Press, 1991), Derrida returns to the subject of the Holocaust by way of the form of polylogue.

36 *Being and Time*, trans. John MacQuarrie and Edward Robinson (New York: Harper & Row, 1962 (1927), 86.

Appendix I:
Lacan's Use of Freud's German Terms

The following chart is based on the glossary in *Ecrits: A Selection*, p. 336. I have corrected misprints and supplied a list of translations as they appear in Strachey's Standard Edition of Freud and in Sheridan's translation of Lacan (the latter appear in brackets in column two). When a term is discussed in detail in J. Laplanche and J.-B. Pontalis, *The Language of Psychoanalysis*, I have supplied the relevant page numbers in brackets in column three. Otherwise page numbers refer to Sheridan's text.

Asymptotisch	[asymptote]	212
Aufgehoben	[raised]	288
Aufhebt	[annul]	286
Aufhebung	[sublation]	288, 294
Begehren	[desire]	286
Bejahung	[affirmation]	200–1
Bildung	[formation]	139
Darstellbarkeit (Rücksicht auf-)	representability (considerations of)	160 [389]
Durcharbeiten (-ung)	working-through	41, 265 [488]
Endliche (Analyse)	[finite analysis]	278, 281
Entstellung	distortion	160, 264 [124]
Erniedrigung	[depreciation]	245, 290
Es (das)	id	128–9, 171 [197]
Fixierung	fixation	270 [162]
Fort! Da!	[child's game: "Gone! There!"]	103–4, 215, 234
Grundsprache	[basic language]	184
Ich (das)	ego	128–9 [130]
Ideal ich	ideal ego	2 [201]

Kern unseres Wesen	[the nucleus of our being]	166, 173, 228
Mensch	man	281
Nachträglich	deferred	48 [111]
Prägung	[instinctual imprint]	141
Schauplatz (ein andere)	[another scene]	193, 264, 285
Spaltung	splitting	269, 277, 285, 287, 288, 313 [427, 430]
Tagtraum	[daydreams]	161
Traumarbeit	dream work	160 [485]
Traumdeutung	interpretation of dreams	160, 259
Traumgedanke	unconscious mental processes	161
Trieb	instinct (drive)	236, 301 [214]
Übertragung	transference	170 [455]
Unbehagen in der Kultur	[the suffering of civilized man]	69
Unendliche (Analyse)	[unending analysis]	278
Urbild	[original, archetypal]	21, 138
Urverdrängt/ Urverdrängung	primal repression	286, 314 [333]
Verdichtung	condensation	160 [82]
Verdrängt/ Verdrängung	repression	200 [398] 288, 290, 291 [390]
Verneinung	negation	6, 15, 201, 235 [261]
Verschiebung	displacement	160 [121]
Versöhnung	reintegration, reconciliation	171
Verwerfung	[foreclosure]	201, 217, 220, 221 [166]
Wiederholungszwang	compulsion to repeat	200 [78]
Witz	joke	170, 177
Wo Es war, soll Ich werden	[where id was, there ego shall be]	128–9, 136, 171, 279, 299

Wunsch	wish [desire]	256 [481]
Wunscherfüllung	wish-fulfillment	161, 264 [483]
Zeichen	signal [sign]	201
Zwangsbefürchtung	[apprehension]	111
Zwangsneurose	obsessional neurosis	69 [281]

Appendix II:
Abbreviations used in *Of Grammatology*

Crit I   *Critique*, 223 (December, 1965). Derrida's review article containing much of what appears in *Of Grammatology*, part I.

Crit II   *Critique*, 224 (January, 1966). Continuation of Derrida's review article.

DE   *Le Débat sur les écritures et l'hieroglyphe aux XVIIe et XVIIIe siècles* by Madeleine V.-David (1965).

Dis   *La Dissémination* by Derrida (1972).

Ec   *Écrits* by Jacques Lacan (1966).

ED   *L'Écriture et la différence* by Derrida (1967).

EM   "The Ends of Man" by Derrida (1969).

EP   *L'Écriture et la psychologie des peuples* (1963). Proceedings of a colloquium.

FF   *French Freud, Yale French Studies*, 48 (1972).

FV   "Le facteur de la verité" by Derrida (1975).

GM   "Zur Genealogie der Moral" ("The Genealogy of Morals") by Friedrich Nietzsche (1969 edn).

GP   *Le Geste et la parole* by André Leroi-Gourhan (1965).

GS   *The Gay Science* by Friedrich Nietzsche (1974 edn).

GW   *Gesammelte Werke* by Sigmund Freud (1940 edn).

HN   *Nietzsche* by Martin Heidegger (1961).

KPM E   *Kant and the Problem of Metaphysics* by Martin Heidegger (1962 edn).

KPM G   *Kant und das Problem der Metaphysik* by Martin Heidegger (1951).

MP   *Marges de la philosophie* by Derrida (1972).

Pos E I   First portion of the English translation of *Positions* (interviews with Derrida), *Diacritics*, 2, iv (Winter, 1972), 6–14.

Pos E II   Second portion of the English translation of *Positions*, *Diacritics*, 3, i (Spring, 1973), 33–46.

Pos F   *Positions* by Derrida (1972).

QB   *The Question of Being* by Martin Heidegger (1958 edn).

QS   "La question du style" in *Nietzsche aujourd-hui?* by Derrida (1973).

Sc   *Scilicet* I by Jacques Lacan (1968).

SC   *The Languages of Criticism and the Sciences of Man: The Structuralist Controversy*, ed. Richard Macksey and Eugenio Donato (1970).

SE   *The Standard Edition of the Complete Psychological Works of Sigmund Freud*, trans. James Strachey (1959).

SP   *Speech and Phenomena* by Derrida (1967).

TF   "On Truth and Falsity in their Ultramoral Sense" by Friedrich Nietzsche (1964 edn).

UA   "Vom Nutzen und Nachtheil der Historie für das Leben" ("The Use and Abuse of History") by Friedrich Nietzsche (1964 edn).

VP   *La Voix et le phénomène: introduction au problème du signe dans la phénoménologie de Husserl* (*Speech and Phenomena*) by Derrida (1967).

WM 1   "Der Wille zur Macht," books 1 and 2, by Friedrich Nietzsche (1911 edn).

WM 2   "Der Wille zur Macht," books 3 and 4, by Friedrich Nietzsche (1911 edn).

WP   *Will to Power* by Friedrich Nietzsche (1968 edn).

Appendix III:
Some Kristevan Terms

Kristeva's theoretical language is no less mercurial than Lacan's or Derrida's. The following brief lexicon simply collects some rather explicit definitions of terms that Kristeva uses in distinct and recurring ways, without suggesting that these are static concepts in her text. The definitions are in language that is as close as possible to that of the translated text. The first page numbers refer to the English translation and the second to the French text.

chora (25–8; R, 22–6) (via Plato's *Timaeus*): a nourishing and maternal, pre-verbal semiotic space or state in which the linguistic sign has not yet been articulated as the absence of an object; the space or state in which the speaking subject is formed.

contemplation (95–9; R, 91–4) (via Pythagoras's "theoria": a signifying system – including such "genres" as religion, philosophy, deconstruction, law – composed of instinctual, interpenetrating but non-synthetic dyads; a critically important, but also limited, means of access to the processes of signifiance.

fetishism (64–5) (via Freud): the substitution of the book or the work – but not the text – for the thetic phase; art being the fetish *par excellence*, as are poets "as individuals," the poetic function converges with fetishism, while not being identical to it.

genotext (86–8; R, 83–6): a process that forms articulate structures out of instinctual dyads, family structure, psychic structures, and related forms; the underlying foundation of language.

heterogeneity (177–80; R, 41–3): rejection acting through negativity, which precipitates the heterogeneity of the subject that cannot be grasped, contained, or synthesized by linguistic or ideological structures.

ideology (250–1; R, 79, n. 117): a cognitive synthesis that underlies every act of enunciation (such designations as "good" or "bad" ideology are simply dependent on socioeconomic position).

intertextuality (59–60): semiotic polyvalence; the transposition of one or more sign system(s) into another. Kristeva favors the term "transposition" in *Revolution in Poetic Language*, although in *Séméiotiké* she defines "intertextuality" as signifying the mosaic of quotations of which any text is constructed, bringing the term closer to Bakhtin's "dialogism."

mimesis (57; R, 57): the construction of an object according to verisimilitude, rather than truth; a violation of the thetic.

negativity (184; R, 165) (via Hegel): a previously conceived limit of consciousness that is exceeded but incorporated as consciousness develops.

phenotext (86–8; R, 83–5): a structure of language – in contrast to the *process* of the genotext – serving to communicate and presupposing a speaker and an addressee.

poetic language (188, 211–23; R, 168, 186–95): neither confined to poetry as a genre nor inclusive of all poetry, poetic language inscribes the signifying process and manifests the negativity, rejection, and heterogeneity of the subject; its potential is most readily available (or most fully realized) in the nineteenth-century texts discussed, especially those by Mallarmé and Lautréamont, which expose repressed philosophical material without any adherence to a unary subject.

practice (17; R, 14–15): a transformation of biological urges and social resistances that have entered the code of linguistic and social communication.

rejection (147–8; R, 50–1): the key moment that shatters unity and constitutes the real object as lost or absent, thus giving rise to the symbolic function.

semanalysis ("The System and the Speaking Subject," 28): conception of meaning as a signifying process, rather than a sign-system.

the semiotic (40–1; R, 39): a fundamental stage in the process of the subject, which is hidden by the symbolic; it is a heterogeneous, psychosomatic functioning – biological and social – or modality of the signifying process; the semiotic is thus a "precursory sign" (25; R, 22).

subject (22, 58; R, 19, 58): the subject is in process/on trial [*en procès*] by virtue of its position of enunciation (i.e. absent from the signifier) and by its relation to poetic language (i.e. the infinite possibilities of the semiotic); also, the continuing effects of negativity and rejection keep the subject from becoming unary.

the symbolic (49; R, 46): any process of contractural joining of the split parts of an "object;" the bringing together of the two edges of a fissure.

text (99–106; R, 94–100): the process or place in which opposing terms alternate in endless rhythm, supported by the chora; as instinctual rhythms pass through specific theses, meaning is constituted and is exceeded by what is outside meaning (materiality, for example); the text is produced by these psycho-social-biological processes.

the thetic (43–5; R, 41–3) (or Husserl's *thesis*): the condition of all enunciation, which requires separation (of subject from his image and from objects) so that they may be identified, redistributed, and combined; the thetic phase is the "deepest structure" of signification in that it contains the object, the proposition, and the complicity between them; all signs are thetic.

Index

This index includes names, concepts, and terms that appear in the main text and in the discursive footnotes. French, German, and Greek terms are listed only when they are discussed; otherwise, see Appendix I.

Abhinavagupta, 56–7, 58
absence, 52, 90, 91, 110, 149
Actaeon and Diana, 64–7, 74, 79, 105n
aggression, 34–5
aggressivity, 34–42
aha experience, 27–8
aletheia, 6, 7n
alienation, 41, 47–8, 51, 101n
allusion, 50, 65, 111
Alpers, Svetlana, 231n
Althusser, Louis, 200, 208n
"always already," 13, 120, 121
amour-propre, 39, 73
anagogic monad, 92
analogy, 50
anamnesis, 48–9, 51
aphasia, 81
aporia, 34–5, 37, 45, 54, 95
appurtenance, 122
Aquinas, Thomas, 94, 108n
arche-writing, 138
Aristotle, 64, 120, 142; *Historia Animalium*, 167; *De interpretatione*, 122, 123, 131; *Nichomachean Ethics*, 34–5
Artaud, Antonin, 136, 164, 165, 178, 197
Aufhebung, 130, 172, 188
Augustine, ix, 39
Aulus Gellius, 43, 56, 101n

Bakhtin, Mikhail, 157n, 163
Bally, Charles, 133
Barromean knot, 93
Barthes, Roland, 135, 162, 163, 178, 205n; *Empire of Signs*, 178–9
Bataille, Georges, 136, 183
Baudelaire, Charles Pierre, 7, 9
Beckett, Samuel, 222
Bedeutung, 175–6
Begierde, 40, 186, 188–9, 209n
Bellini, Giovanni, 168
Benveniste, Emile, 166, 167
Bible, 97; 2 Corinthians, 46; Ecclesiastes, 141; Exodus, 46; John, 51, 121, 123; Luke, 212; Proverbs, 64; Psalms, 114, 219
biology, 30–2, 35, 41–2, 43, 44, 50, 59, 196
Blake, William, 18, 111, 137
Blanchot, Maurice, 136, 202, 211n
Bloom, Allan, 208n, 211n
Bloom, Harold, 84, 107n
Boileau-Despréaux, Nicolas, 43
Boleyn, Anne, 215–16
book, 116–31
Bosch, Hieronymus, 32–3, 36–7, 100n; *The Garden of Earthly Delights*, 36–7, 213; *The Last Judgment*, 36–7
Bowie, Malcolm, 99n, 101n, 102n, 104n, 105n, 107n

Browning, Robert, 45
Brueghel, Pieter, 60
Bruno, Giordano, 67; *De gli eroici furiori*, 67
Buffon, Georges Louis Leclerc de, 47
Bühler, Charlotte, 39
Byron, George Gordon, 202

Cage, John, 111
Caillois, Roger, 30, 100n
canny/uncanny, 8
Cartesian linguistics, 20, 22
castration complex, 86–91, 93–4, 174–5
Celan, Paul, 136
center, 12–13, 15, 22, 23, 61
Césaire, Aimé, 106n
Cézanne, Paul, 228
Chinese prejudice *see* European hallucination
Chomsky, Noam, 25n, 106n, 107n, 162, 165; *Syntactic Structures*, 75
chora, 167–70, 175, 176, 177–8, 180–1, 182, 189, 194, 200, 206n, 209n, 239
chorion, 167–9, 178, 206n
chosisme, 62–74
Claudel, Paul Louis Charles, 100n
Cleopatra, 64, 105n
closure, 110, 115
commentary, 131–2, 201
condensation, 20, 50, 60, 81, 92, 141, 167, 177
de Condillac, Etienne Bonnot, 131, 147, 153–5, 157n, 161n; *An Essay on the Origin of Human Knowledge*, 139, 151, 153–5
contemplation *see* theory
Copernicus, Nicolaus, 61
Copleston, Frederick, 112
corps morcelé, 32, 36
Coulmas, Florian, 158n, 159n
counter-transference, 10, 45, 69
Cousin, Victor, 40
Cramer, Gabriel, 154

Culler, Jonathan, 103n
culture, 16, 33, 54, 77, 143, 146

Dali, Salvador, 28–9, 33, 80, 100n; "The Rotten Monkey," 28–9
Dante Alighieri, ix
Darwin, Charles, 35, 41–2, 47, 53; *The Origin of Species*, 119
Dasein, 137
David, Madeleine V., 110, 131, 139
death instinct, 35, 36, 42, 45, 59, 60
deconstruction, vii, 13–15, 104n, 110, 113, 116, 121–4, 126, 127, 130, 132, 135, 136, 138, 142, 148, 154–5, 157n, 191, 201, 204, 213, 222; as birth, 17–18, 22; as process, 14, 21
dehiscence, 31, 37
Derrida, Jacques, vii–ix, 1–2, 12, 20, 21–3, 64, 104n, 110–61, 163, 166, 168, 170, 177, 179, 188, 189, 190–2, 196, 200, 207n; *The Archeology of the Frivolous: Reading Condillac*, 154–5; *Cinders*, 111, 233n; *Glas*, 111, 222; *Of Grammatology*, 2, 11, 13, 18, 80, 103n, 104n, 105n, 110–61, 162, 163, 213; *Margins of Philosophy*, 222; *Positions*, 110, 220–1; *The Post Card: From Socrates to Freud and Beyond*, 103n, 118, 121, 123, 222; "Restitutions of the truth in pointing," 220–31; *Speech and Phenomena*, 2; *Of Spirit: Heidegger and the Question*, 126, 128; "Structure, Sign, and Play," 2, 11–18, 20, 103n, 170; *The Truth in Painting*, 213, 220–31; *Writing and Difference*, 2, 111, 189
Derrida, Marguerite, 141
Descartes, René, 75, 94, 139, 142, 166
desire, 19, 33, 40, 41, 51, 54, 73, 76, 83–4, 85, 91–9, 110, 150–1, 186, 195, 209n, 216
dhvani, 56–7, 58, 59
dialectic, 95, 97–8

différance, 18, 104n, 129, 146, 149–50, 186, 189, 190, 192

difference, 13, 14, 18, 61, 68, 82, 189

de Dinteville, Jean, 214–16, 217

Dionysus and Ariadne, 89–90

displacement, 4–5, 6, 14, 20, 50, 51, 65, 81, 141, 167, 177

Dostoevsky, Fyodor: *The Idiot*, 219–20

Dou, Gerard: *Rembrandt's Mother*, 212–13

dreams, 51, 52, 64, 65, 80, 104n

dream-work, 81–2

Ducasse, Isidore *see* Lautréamont

durcharbeiten, 47

l'écriture, 114, 117–18, 121

ego, 20, 22, 29–32, 37–42, 48, 54, 58–9, 62, 68–9, 70–3, 83–4, 93, 95, 106n, 166–7, 171, 173, 174, 185

eidos, 137, 174

Einfühlung, 40

Eliot, T. S., 59, 60; "Tradition and the Individual Talent," 56–7; *The Waste Land*, 43, 54–5

Ellis, John, 157n–158n, 159n

emblems, 63–4, 67, 92, 105n

Entfremdung, 41

Entstellung, 80

epistémé, 20

epistomophilia, 66, 83–4, 87–91, 98, 105n

Erasmus, Desiderius, 71, 105n; *The Praise of Folly*, 63–4

erasure [*sous rature*], 138

Erfahrung, 199, 200

ethnocentrism, 15, 114, 130, 146

ethnology, 15

European hallucination, 139–42

exergue, 113–14

fetishism, 181–2, 239

Feuerbach, Ludwig, 186

Flaubert, Gustave, 136

foreclosure, 5

Fort! Da!, 52–3, 55, 56

Foucault, Michel, 48, 102n, 200, 211n, 212; *The Order of Things*, 43, 231n

fragmented body, 32, 36, 213

Francis I, 215

Frank, Manfred, 104n

Frege, Gottlob, 170, 175–8, 180, 186, 188, 207n; *Logical Investigations*, 185

Freud, Sigmund, vii, 7, 9, 11, 14, 15, 17, 20, 21, 29, 34, 37, 40, 41–2, 43, 44, 45, 46, 49, 50, 51, 52, 56, 57, 59, 62, 63, 65, 66, 68, 74, 75, 79, 81–5, 86, 88, 90–1, 94, 95, 97, 99, 100n, 110, 111, 113, 162, 164, 166, 167, 171, 173, 174, 177, 181, 183, 185, 186, 188, 192, 194; "The Acquisition of Fire," 44; "The Aetiology of Hysteria," 48; *Analysis Terminable and Interminable*, 90; *An Autobiographical Study*, 35; *Beyond the Pleasure Principle*, 2, 3–4, 7, 9, 10, 18, 35, 52–3, 54, 55, 194; *Civilization and Its Discontents*, 38–9, 42, 44, 90, 122; *Delusions and Dreams in Jensen's Gradiva*, 90; "The Dynamics of Transference," 28; "The Economic Problem of Masochism," 28; *The Ego and the Id*, 31, 38–9, 69; *Five Lectures on Psycho-analysis*, 42, 61; *The Future of an Illusion*, 70; "The Future Prospects of Psycho-analytic Theory," 10; *Interpretation of Dreams*, 51, 53, 75, 80; *Introductory Lectures on Psycho-analysis*, 81; *Jokes and Their Relation to the Unconscious*, 50; *Moses and Monotheism*, 167, 182; "Negation," 185–7; *New Introductory Lectures in Psycho-analysis*, 68–9, 72, 90–1; "On the Universal Tendency to Debasement in the Sphere of Love," 28; *An Outline of Psycho-analysis*, 38; *Project for a Scientific Psychology*, 30, 35, 50; *The Psychopathology of Everyday Life*, 61; *The Question of Lay Analysis*, 76; "Remembering,

Repeating and Working-Through,"
47; *The Sexual Theories of Children,*
86–8, 90; *Three Essays on the Theory
of Sexuality,* 30, 66, 83, 182; "The
Uncanny," 7–8

Gasché, Rodolfe, 158n
Gauguin, Paul, 227
gaze, 213–17
genotext, 239
Gide, André, 84
Girard, René, 12; *Violence and the
Sacred,* 182
glossematics, 134–6, 173, 176
glosseme, 137
Goethe, Johann Wolfgang von, 2–3,
35, 202
Goldstein, Kurt, 223, 224 5
grammatology, 110–61, 189–91
grapheme, 137
Greenblatt, Stephen, 216

Halle, Morris *see* Jakobson, Roman
Hamsun, Knut: *Hunger,* 227
Hegel, G. W. F., 21–2, 41–2, 43, 46,
47, 56, 57, 64, 94, 97, 98, 108n, 113,
114, 120, 122, 123, 130–1, 142, 149,
162, 186, 201, 202, 208n, 209n,
210n, 219, 220; *Phenomenology of
Spirit,* 40–1, 94, 95, 183–94, 197–8,
199; *The Philosophy of Fine Art,* 122;
Philosophy of History, 98; *Science of
Logic,* 199–201
Heidegger, Martin, 6, 13, 14, 15, 24n,
31, 43, 59, 70, 104n, 110, 112, 113,
114, 120, 122, 123, 126–7, 128–30,
132, 137, 155, 155n, 156n, 166, 186,
192, 220–1; *Being and Time,* 49, 130;
An Introduction to Metaphysics,
124–6, 128–30, 228; "Letter on
Humanism," 83; "Logos," 75–6;
Nietzsche, 126; *The Origin of the
Work of Art,* 222–31; *The Question
of Being,* 138; "The Thing," 62–3;
What Is Called Thinking?, 124; *What

Is Philosophy?,* 124; *What Is a Thing?,*
124
heimlich/unheimlich, 8
Heraclitus, 31, 39, 125
heterogeneity, 20–2, 194–8, 239
hieroglyphics, 80, 152–3
Himmler, Heinrich, 230
historiography, 113
Hitler, Adolf, 112
Hjelmslev, Louis, 135–6, 162, 170,
173–4, 176, 178
Holbein, Hans, vii; *The Ambassadors,*
213–17; *The Body of the Dead Christ
in the Tomb,* 213, 217–20
Hölderlin, Friedrich, 83
Homer, 49, 164
Husserl, Edmund, 162, 166, 170–8,
180, 185, 191, 192, 205n–206n,
207n; *Formal and Transcendental
Logic,* 171; *Ideas,* 171–2
hyletic data, 171
Hyman, Stanley Edgar, 102n
Hyppolite, Jean, 210n, 211n
hysteria, 48

identification, 28
ideology, 19, 139, 142, 177, 197, 200,
201, 239
imaginary, 4, 45
imagination, 150–1
imago, 28–30, 36
incest prohibition, 16, 54, 86
Innenwelt/Umwelt, 32, 39
l'instance, 74–5
Instanz, 74–5
interpretant, 135
intertextuality, 23, 157n, 177, 178,
205n, 229, 240
irony, 46–7, 59, 64, 71

Jakobson, Roman, 50, 56, 80, 81–2;
Fundamentals of Language, 75–8
Janet, Pierre, 39
Jesus, 51, 117, 139, 212, 218–20
le jeu, 12, 18

Johnson, Samuel, viii
Jones, Ernest, 86, 108n
jouissance, 92–4, 99, 190
Joyce, James, 136, 164, 165, 178, 180, 183
Jung, Carl Gustav, 61, 194

kakon, 39
Kandinsky, Wassily: *Asserting*, 213
Kant, Immanuel, 112
Kermode, Frank, 97–8
al-Khwarizmi, 83
Kierkegaard, Søren, 46, 57, 186, 191
Klein, Melanie, 39, 101n, 159n, 164; *The Psycho-analysis of Children*, 167; "The Role of the School in the Libidinal Development of the Child," 141
Köhler, Elsa, 39
Kojève, Alexandre, 40–1, 47, 95, 101n, 186, 208n, 210n, 211n
Kratzer, Nicolas, 216
Kris, Ernst, 58
Kristeva, Julia, 157n; *Black Sun*, 106n, 213, 217–20; *Language the Unknown*, 174; "Motherhood According to Giovanni Bellini," 168; *Revolution in Poetic Language*, 2, 23, 162–211, 213, 219; "The System and the Speaking Subject," 19–22; "Women's Time," 170

Lacan, Jacques, vii–ix, 1–11, 12, 20, 21, 22–3, 26–109, 110, 127, 140, 156n, 163, 164, 168, 170, 172, 173, 174, 176, 177, 178, 186, 189, 191, 192, 194, 196, 207n, 209n, 210n; "The Agency of the letter," 56, 74–85, 91; "Aggressivity in psychoanalysis," 34–42, 43, 47, 53, 213; *De la psychose paranoïaque dans ses rapports avec la personnalité*, 26, 29; *Écrits*, 1–2, 11, 26–109, 162; "La Famille," 26; *Four Fundamental Concepts of Psychoanalysis*, 105n, 213,

214–17; "The Freudian thing," 54, 60–74; "The Function and field of speech" (the "Rome Discourse"), 42–60, 163; "The Mirror stage," 4, 26–34, 35, 53, 72, 92; "Seminar on 'The Purloined Letter,'" 1–11, 18, 31, 35; "The Signification of the phallus," 85–91, 174–5; "The Subversion of the subject," 91–9, 189
Laing, R. D., 102n
language, 19, 20, 35, 42–60, 68, 69, 72, 74–85, 95, 131–8, 162–211; as game, 135–6
Laplanche, J. and J. B. Pontalis, 50
La Rochefoucauld, François de, 39, 101n
Lautréamont, 162, 163, 164, 176, 178, 183, 193–4, 197, 201; *Chant de Maldoror*, 202–3; *Poésies*, 202–4
law, 9, 54, 73, 149
Lehman, David, 160n
Leibniz, Gottfried Wilhelm, 139, 140, 142
Lenin, Nikolai, 185, 198, 199–200
Leonardo da Vinci, 32, 74
Leroi-Gourhan, André, 110, 140
Lévi-Strauss, Claude, 15, 17, 43, 53, 110, 112, 113, 116, 159n–160n; *The Elementary Structures of Kinship*, 16, 54; *The Raw and the Cooked*, 16; *Tristes Tropiques*, 119, 131, 142–6; *La Vie familiale et sociale des Indiens Nambikwara*, 143
Lewis, Philip E., 205n, 206n
linguistics, 19, 52, 54, 56, 59, 68, 75–7, 127, 129, 131–8, 162, 164, 167, 174, 196
literature, viii, 76, 113, 123, 136, 142, 154, 158n, 162, 165, 169, 196
logocentrism, 67, 114, 117, 119, 120, 122, 125, 126, 127, 130, 134, 140, 142, 229
logos, 76, 103n, 115, 121, 122, 125, 126, 128, 131, 134, 137

Longus: *Daphnis and Chloe*, 88–9
Lucretius, 64–5
Luther, Martin, 216

Macey, David, 99n, 100n, 107n
Malinowski, B. K., 43
Mallarmé, Stéphane, 21, 24n, 43, 48, 136, 142, 162, 163, 164, 169, 176, 178, 180, 183, 193–4, 197, 200, 201, 202, 210n; *Un coup de dés*, 203–4; *Igitur*, 203–4; "The Mystery of Literature," 169–70, 182
de Man, Paul, 97–8, 137, 160n; "The Resistance to Theory," 69
Manheim, Ralph, 125
Mao Tse-tung, 198; "On Practice," 200
Marx, Karl, 21, 41, 47, 68, 162, 186, 191, 198, 199–200
Marxism, 145, 200
mathematical models, 79, 82–3, 92
méconnaissances, 34, 38, 40, 45, 88–9, 91, 97–8
melancholia, 213, 217–18
metalanguage, 20, 92
metaphor(s), 12, 20, 22, 30–1, 35, 38–9, 40, 41, 48, 49–51, 59, 66, 77, 80–2, 84, 94, 110, 111, 120, 123, 125, 134, 136–7, 138, 149, 153–4, 168, 178, 195, 223, 228–30
metaphysics, 12–13, 14, 15, 114, 117, 124, 126, 133, 134, 136, 141, 142, 148, 166, 227–8
metonymy, 12, 20, 22, 68, 77, 80–3, 84, 107n, 114, 120, 123, 153–4, 195
Miller, J. Hillis, 106n
Miller, Jacques-Alain, 99n
Milton, John, ix
mimesis, 176–7, 240
modernism, 164–5, 205n
Moebius strip, 93, 172
Moi, Toril, 105n, 205n
Molière, 43
Monakow, Constantin von, 194
monstrosity, 18, 25n

Moses, 16, 46, 152, 199
Mourgue, Raoul, 194
music, 79
mystery, 90
myth, 17, 19

name of the father, 54
nature, 16, 54
Needham, Joseph: *Science and Civilization in China*, 179
negation, 185–7
negativity, 95, 169, 183–94, 195, 197, 219, 240
Nietzsche, Friedrich, 14, 15, 18, 22, 63, 112, 113, 118, 126–7, 142; "Aus dem Gedankenkreise der Geburt der Tragödie," 117; *Daybreak*, 115
noetic, 171

other, 51, 54, 58, 73, 92, 95–6, 99
Ovid, 65

Pandey, Kanti Chandra, 56–7
paranoia, 29
paranoic-criticism, 29
paranoic knowledge, 29–30, 80
Parmenides, 125
Pascal, Blaise, 43, 105n
Paul, 46
Peirce, Charles Sanders, 19, 134–5
penis envy, 86, 88
Petronius: *Satyricon*, 55
phallocentrism, 86, 90, 91, 108n, 120
phallus, 85–91
phenomenology, 158n, 171, 173, 176
phenotext, 240
philology, 43–4, 69, 111
philosophy, 17, 43, 64, 92, 95, 113, 124, 126, 142, 147, 154, 162, 167, 174, 196, 202–4
phoneme, 135, 137
physis, 31, 124–5
Pindar, 164
pity, 149–51

Plato, 14, 15, 43, 46, 57, 99, 118, 142, 221; *Meno*, 49; *Phaedrus*, 131, 134; *Symposium*, 92, 95, 98–9, 101n, 109n; *Theaetetus*, 54, 103n; *Timaeus*, 167–70
play, 12, 15, 18, 19, 20, 110, 136
pleasure principle, 3–5, 10, 17, 45
plurivocity, 117, 120–1, 177
Poe, Edgar Allan, 221; "The Purloined Letter," 1–11
poetic language, 21, 56–7, 59–60, 78, 82, 152–4, 165, 175, 176–7, 180, 181–3, 193–4, 196, 197, 202–4, 240; *see also* metaphor(s) and metonymy
points de capiton, 79, 93
pointure, 207n, 226–30
Pompeii, 89–90
Pontalis, J. B. *see* Laplanche, J.
poststructuralism, 14, 17, 123
Pound, Ezra, 142
practice, 19–20, 165, 196, 198–204, 240
presence, 12–13, 14, 15, 18, 22, 52, 58, 90, 91, 123, 125, 137, 138, 140, 141, 142, 148, 221, 229
prosopopoeia, 70, 72, 106n
psychoanalysis, 34–6, 42–3, 44, 45, 46, 55, 56, 59, 61–2, 63, 67, 68, 69, 73, 74, 76, 82, 85, 89, 94, 162, 164, 167, 174, 191, 196; aim of, 3, 40, 42, 60; as law, 10, 24n; as talking cure, 42–60
psychology, 22, 46, 52, 68, 79

Quintilian, 46; *Institutionis Oratoriae*, 46, 80–1

Rabelais, François, 54
Randall, John Herman, 112
reading, 79, 82, 110, 112–13, 115, 127–32, 142, 200, 201, 204; importance of, ix; Lacan's method of reading Freud, 11, 62–3; as ravishing, 9

reason, 85, 95, 150
reflection: in Rousseau, 147–8
rejection, 185, 186–95, 196, 240
Rembrandt, Harmenszoon van Rijn, 212; *An Old Woman*, 213
representamen, 135, 195
repression, 4, 187, 195
Rieff, Philip, 63, 105n
Rimbaud, Arthur, 43
Rome, 42–3
Roudinesco, Elisabeth, 17, 40, 61, 99n, 100n, 102n, 103n, 104n, 106n
Rousseau, Jean-Jacques, 18, 103n, 111–15, 117, 120, 123, 132, 134, 136, 137, 139, 141–2, 143, 144, 146–51; *The Confessions*, 148; *Dialogues*, 151; *Discourse on the Origin of Inequality*, 146, 149; *Émile*, 146, 149; *Essay on the Origin of Languages*, 110, 112, 113, 114, 119, 131, 146–51
rupture, 12, 13, 15, 18
Russell, Bertrand, 112

Said, Edward, 159n
Sartre, Jean-Paul, 27, 33–4, 100n, 106n
de Saussure, Ferdinand, 19, 51–2, 53–4, 56, 62, 67–8, 69, 76–9, 80, 103n, 112, 113, 127, 145, 153, 165; *Course in General Linguistics*, 52, 58, 77, 119, 131–5, 157n
Schapiro, Meyer, 223; "The Still Life as Personal Object: A Note on Heidegger and Van Gogh," 224–7, 230–1; *Words and Pictures*, 227
Schiller, J. C. F. von: *Die Freundschart*, 187–8
Schorske, Carl E., 104n
science and writing, 114
Sechehaye, Albert, 133
Selbstbewusstsein, 41, 94
self-consciousness, 41, 94, 95
de Selve, Georges, 214–16
semanalysis, vii, 20–1, 240
semantics, 20

seme, 135, 137
semiotic, 167, 175, 177–8, 179, 182, 240
semiotics, vii, 19–21, 52, 132, 134–5, 213
semiology *see* semiotics
Shakespeare, William, 208n, 216, 222
Sheridan, Alan, 26, 74, 100n
Sidney, Philip, 203
sign, 14, 18, 19, 23, 43, 51–2, 56, 77–8, 115, 123, 133, 135, 137, 154, 169, 176, 195
signifiance, 165, 194
signified/signifier, 5, 6, 10, 13, 54, 57–8, 68, 77–8, 79–83, 85–91, 119, 122, 125, 126, 128, 133–4, 135, 167
signifying chain, 78–9, 80, 83
silence, 47, 51
Smith, Joseph H., 102n, 106n
Socrates, 39, 42, 46–7, 48, 57, 59, 98–9, 101n, 117–18
Sollers, Philippe, 204
Sophocles, 65, 66; *Antigone*, 125; *Oedipus at Colonus*, 65; *Oedipus Tyrannos*, 65
speech, 22, 42–60, 65, 67, 73, 75, 77, 84, 93, 112, 134, 137, 138, 149, 152
Spenser, Edmund, 33
spirit, 126
Spivak, Gayatri Chakravorty, 110, 156n
Sprott, W. J. H., 69
Starobinski, Jean, 79, 107n, 112, 131, 146, 147–8, 149–51, 156n, 160n
Sterne, Laurence, 111
Strachey, James, 35, 68
Strauss, Johann, 60, 62
structuralism, 12, 20, 123
structure, 11–19, 22, 75; as metaphor, 12–13
style, 17, 50, 64, 181
subject, 7, 20–2, 27, 29, 30, 35, 40, 47–8, 49, 54, 57–8, 68, 69, 73, 84, 86, 91–9, 140, 162–7, 170, 175,

177–8, 180, 190, 194–5, 198, 199–200, 204, 213, 216, 240
supplement, 110, 119, 122, 132, 150–1
symbolic, 4–5, 19, 34, 45, 167, 175, 177–8, 182, 240
Szondi, Lipot, 194

Terence, ix
tessera, 48
text, 132, 142, 165, 175, 178–81, 197, 198, 200, 201, 204, 222–3, 240
Theocritus: *First Idyll*, 89
theology and writing, 116–31, 139, 177
theory, 97, 172, 178, 181, 214, 239; construction in children, 86–91; hostility to, 1, 23n; resistance to, 69; truth and, 63
thetic, 171, 173, 175, 177–8, 182, 240
thing *see chosisme*
Todestrieb, 35
Todorov, Tzvétan, 163
torus, 93
trace, 110, 136–7, 167, 189
transference, 9–10, 11, 21, 52, 73, 201
Traumdeutung, 51
Triebe, 171
truth, 22, 63–7, 114, 121, 122, 125, 127, 204, 205n, 227–31
Turkle, Sherry, 106n

unconscious, 22, 27, 39, 44, 49, 50, 51, 52, 60, 67, 71, 72, 73, 74–85, 91–9, 122, 173, 186, 196
Unwelt see Innenwelt
Upanishads, 55–6, 59, 104n

Valéry, Paul, 43, 79, 107n
Van Gogh, Vincent: *Night Café*, 223; *Old Shoes*, 213, 220–31; *The Potato Eaters*, 223
Verdichtung see condensation
Verneinung see negation
Verschiebung see displacement

Vico, Giambattista, 131; *The New Science*, 151–3
Vienna, 60–1, 65
Villa of Mysteries, 89–90, 213
Vlastos, Gregory, 46

Waller, Margaret, 163
Wallon, Henri, 27–30, 39, 53
Warburton, William, 131, 139; *The Divine Legation of Moses Demonstrated*, 139, 151–3

Wheatley, Phillis, ix
Wiederholungszwang, 3
Wilden, Anthony, 102n
Windelband, Wilhelm, 112
"Wo Es war, soll Ich werden," 68–9, 84
Woolf, Virginia, 43
working through, 47
writing, 22, 51, 75, 77, 84, 110–61, 189

Yates, Frances, 105n